SOTHEBY'S GUIDE TO
Buying and Selling at Auction

SOTHEBY'S GUIDE TO

Buying and Selling at Auction

C. HUGH HILDESLEY

A Giniger Book

published in association with

W · W · NORTON & COMPANY

NEW YORK · LONDON

THE TEXT OF THIS BOOK *is composed in Baskerville with display type set in Garamond Oldstyle. Composition and manufacturing are by The Maple-Vail Book Manufacturing Group. Book design by Marjorie J. Flock.*

FIRST EDITION

Library of Congress Cataloging in Publication Data
Hildesley, C. Hugh.
  Sotheby's guide to buying and selling at auction.

  "A Giniger book"
  1. Auctions. I. Sotheby & Co. (London, England)
II. Title. III. Title: Guide to buying and selling
at auction.
HF5476.H49 1983   658.8′4   83-13138

ISBN 0-393-01782-6

W. W. Norton & Company, Inc.,
500 Fifth Avenue, New York, N.Y. 10110
W. W. Norton & Company Ltd.,
37 Great Russell Street, London WC1B 3NU

1 2 3 4 5 6 7 8 9 0

CONTENTS

CHAPTER FIVE

Further Services of the Auction House   112

CHAPTER SIX

The Role of the Auction House in the Art Market   170

APPENDIX A

Useful Facts and Documents   173

APPENDIX B
London Facts and Documents   195

INTRODUCTION

SALE BY AUCTION, achieving greater popularity each day, can by no means be described as a new phenomenon. Herodotus called this method of sale ideally suited for the exchange of marriageable females, one of the few categories of art no longer sold at auction in these more enlightened times. One suspects indeed that sale by competitive bidding, which is after all the basis of the auction process, has probably been in place as long as commerce itself. Auctioneers have not always maintained the highest standards of business ethics and certainly the travelling merchants of the eighteenth century probably had much in common with the boardwalk practitioners of today in Atlantic City, a mecca for the gullible who may enjoy rigged auctions. Such was the reputation of the foreign auctioneers who invaded America in the early eighteenth century that, in Florida, a law was passed in which these merchants were restricted to conducting sales "by public outcry" below the high water line on the beaches. Their contemporary counterparts tend to conduct carpet sales in motels near major airports. Healthy cynicism about such manifestations of the auction medium should be encouraged.

Fine art auctions as they have developed today originated in the seventeenth century in Europe and the eighteenth century in England. Students of seventeenth century Dutch art will probably recall the auction of Rembrandt's collection in December, 1657, which took place as an attempt to raise cash to meet his overwhelming debts.

This auction of the contents of Rembrandt's house lasted three weeks and was conducted by the municipal auctioneer of Amsterdam, thus indicating that in the seventeenth century, as nowadays, the auction process is on occasion used in cases of financial distress. It is interesting to note that, in February of 1658, Rembrandt's house was itself sold at auction, although the painter did not move out until almost two years later. While the sale of houses at auction has become the norm in England, the perception of its connection with unfortunate personal circumstances has continued to render it an unpopular mode of selling real estate in America. The function of the municipal auctioneer is performed periodically by judges in some courts of the United States, one of the few opportunities remaining in which to secure a bargain at auction, since these sales lack the expertise, marketing ability and publicity functions of the professional auctioneer.

Less well-known, perhaps, is the auction which took place in Amsterdam on the sixteenth of May in 1697, at which twenty-one works by Jan Vermeer of Delft were sold. For an artist who produced less than forty known works, this was a truly remarkable auction. Museums and collectors of today can indeed be envious of one Jacob Abrahamsz Dissius of Delft, who owned nineteen of this artist's works in the late seventeenth century.

The eighteenth century in England witnessed the establishment of both Sotheby's in 1744 and Christies in 1766, the former restricting its sales more specifically to books and literary material. There are grounds for believing that Sotheby's actually began operating as early as 1733, but the world will survive a small degree of uncertainty on this issue. Auctions were sufficiently popular in the eighteenth century in England that the acute observer Thomas Rowlandson took the opportunity to depict the denizens of both major rooms.

It is not the purpose of this book to relate the history of the auction process as it developed, but rather to study it in its present form, which to the neophyte may appear convoluted, mysterious and therefore suspect. By following the process step by step, it is intended to demonstrate that the auction process is logical and that it is available to all, at many levels of activity. With the attention paid to record prices and the small top layer of extraordinary works of art, the myth of exclusivity arises. Auction houses today survive on their ability to process a vast quantity of inexpensive works of art efficiently. In the current vernacular this book might have been entitled: "Everything you wanted to know about auctions, but were afraid to ask."

In seeking to answer a wide variety of questions, this author has chosen to follow the various processes through as logically as possible. This approach will inevitably lead to repetition and duplication. While there may be those sufficiently intrigued to read through this guide systematically from cover to cover, it is constructed in a way that makes it possible to proceed directly to the desired section, by use of the explicit table of contents.

Modes of operation, legal and tax requirements differ from city to city and from country to country. Examples of the more standard documents from New York and London have been provided in the appendices. A word of warning however is in order. These documents are subject to frequent changes, as are the conditions which created them. The reader is thus advised to treat them as a general guide, but to refer to specific auction rooms for current documents relating to a particular need.

Thus, whether the reader intends to sell, buy or just browse, this work is offered as a practical guide for the uninitiated who, it is hoped, will as a result become acquainted with the fascination and pleasure derived from participation in this marketplace.

N.B. It should be noted that all prices quoted are given in both U.S. dollars and British sterling at the rate of conversion prevalent at the time of sale. Any opinion as to current value, not based on sale prices, reflect the author's opinion as of the time of writing (1982–83). In addition, to calculate the price actually paid by the buyer at Sotheby's for all items sold after September of 1975 in London and January 1979 in New York a ten percent buyer's premium should be added.

SOTHEBY'S GUIDE TO

Buying and Selling at Auction

CHAPTER ONE
Anatomy of an Auction House

SOLICITATION OF MATERIAL AND SOURCES
How an Auction House Finds Its Material

THE AUCTION HOUSE functions at the center of the art marketplace. Acting as an agent, it is the auction house which brings together the seller, the object to be sold and the buyer. In the auction sale itself, the fall of the hammer denotes the moment at which a contract is created between the seller and the buyer. The process of offering a particular item in a sale usually takes less than one minute. The process of creating that brief moment takes at least six months and, on occasion, longer. One of the principal functions of the auction house is to bring material to the market. What, then, are the sources and how are they tapped?

Collectors of art fall into many different categories. Many collectors are wholly unconscious of the fact that they are collectors or own a collection. These might be described more accurately as accumulators, who have, over the passage of time, acquired, either by gift or by purchase, a variety of objects which are of interest to the art market. These "hidden assets" tend to be decorative or functional and can loosely be described as house furnishings, which have both an aesthetic and a utilitarian function. Often their value has appreciated considerably over the years, elevating the objects from the role of fixtures and fittings to that of works of art. Examples of this type of material would include historical silver, antique furniture, Tiffany art glass and even veteran and vintage automobiles. This unconscious collector does not normally enjoy the fruits of recognition as a collector in his or her own lifetime, but usually becomes the source of considerable concern for the professional executor and any beneficiaries, who have to process an unprepared estate containing valuable tangible assets.

Even the private collectors who are fully aware of the nature and value of their holdings in art may be of a sufficiently possessive nature so that they cannot bear to part with a single item before their demise. While there is convincing evidence that you cannot take these possessions with you, a large portion of the art collecting world compromise by holding on as long as humanly possible. Thus, a large proportion of items appearing at auction come from estates. The art market indeed owes much of its livelihood to the fact that works of art tend to recirculate once each collecting generation. If you assume that most collectors become active at the peak of their careers, it is logical that an average holding period would be about thirty-five years.

Human nature being what it is, most generations differ in their tastes. It is therefore atypical for a collection to pass intact from one generation to another. At best, a collection my be divided among heirs, who, in many cases, will turn around and convert a portion of their inheritance to cash, once the period of sentimental attachment has decreased with the passage of time. The substantial demands made by tax authorities on an estate also tend to place collections on the market on a regular basis.

The auction house maintains its contact with potential estate material in a variety of ways. The specialist experts naturally create relationships with collectors in their particular fields during the normal course of business. The art world is sufficiently small that those involved in a market would naturally be aware of the existence and activity of like-minded individuals. The auction house makes sure that the institutional executor remains aware of the many services available to an estate and major auction rooms have departments which specialize in the procuring and processing of estate business. Close relationships with lawyers, either individually or corporately, are encouraged and trust and estate divisions of banks are constantly reminded of the superior services offered by a particular auction house to estate managers. It is indeed in the acquisition of major estate business that the major auction houses show their most competitive natures, a factor which should be borne in mind by any executor faced with the task of bringing a collection to the marketplace.

Returning to the living collector, the auction room, as part of the whole art market, provides an outlet for the disposition of items which either no longer fit the developing taste of the collector or which, through their sale, will enable the collector to upgrade in quality. Both private and institutional collectors thus have a ready market place for duplicates, which may well form the basis of another's incipient collection. While, in some cases, an owner may prefer the immediate cash benefit of a private sale, many recognize that the competition engendered in the auction room will reward them with a fair current price. The dealers' perfectly understandable tendency to attempt to purchase material as cheaply as possible often leaves the sellers in doubt as to whether they received a fair price for an object, particularly in a market which has enjoyed rapid upward price movement. Prices realized at auction can at least claim to be current. The competition between the many different buying constituencies brings reassuring results to the seller.

Museums are frequent sources of material for auction houses. The economic demands made on these important educational and cultural institutions are such that they are increasingly forced to look to their own holdings as a source of income. This is not an unhealthy tendency from the standpoint of either the museum or of the art-collecting public. The museum occupies a significant role in the operation of the art market. Not only does it supply a constant source of scholastic and academic research in all areas of the fine arts; it also in effect maintains a qualitative standard by continually withdrawing from the market items of the highest quality and greatest rarity and historical significance. Because most museum acquisitions are made with no thought of resale, the well-endowed museum will be prepared to spend considerable funds in acquiring the very best so as to attract more visitors, thereby encouraging increased funding. As with the private collector, however, there are occasions upon which the museum will intelligently sell. Duplicates have been mentioned already. There is little point in a museum hoarding vast quantities of respectable works of art which will not grace its public exhibition space in the foreseeable future, as a result of changes in taste, limitations in space or the acquisition of better examples in the same field by gift or purchase. While the factor of taste is a dangerous motive for disposal, in certain cases it is possible to conclude that there is little chance of a particular fashion returning. Minor British portrait painters of the late eighteenth and early nineteenth centuries, for example, are not likely to reacquire the popularity they achieved in the first quarter of the twentieth century. While the quality of Gainsborough's *Blue Boy* is undeniable, it is safe to assume that minor representations of anonymous deceased English ancestors are no longer of any interest to the sophisticated collector. There is good reason to suggest that the wholesale traffic in this commodity fifty years ago was in part made possible by the realization on the part of many English families that they were not losing much in disposing of these heirlooms.

By making duplicates available, the museum stimulates continuing interest in a particular field, keeps it alive and in fact encourages collection in whichever category is involved. If the supply of works of art in a specialized area dwindles significantly or dries up completely, collection in that area becomes impossible and the field becomes neglected. Collectors turn to new areas to satisfy their urge, not in itself a bad reaction, though hazardous if the collector becomes a victim of one of the many unscrupulous operators in the field of new collectibles. Thus, in this writer's opinion, responsible deaccession policies in museums are beneficial to all concerned. That an institution should turn to the auction rooms to process this activity makes sense in that the museum has thus fulfilled its fiduciary responsibility in ensuring that any item sold has realized its best possible price on the open market.

Not to be neglected in the consideration of sources of supply is the individual with a small number of works of art who may need money or who wishes to take advantage of what are high current prices.

The initial contact with an auction house may take one of many forms. A telephone enquiry to determine who is the most qualified recipient of a photograph of each item in question will often save considerable delay in processing this initial contact. If an auction house is close, there is no substitute for taking a work of art to be examined physically by the relevant expert. This has to happen eventually, so that early and accurate identification can be most useful in reaching the decision to consign or not to consign. If a large group of objects is involved, either a series of photographs, showing the character of the group, or an informal listing of the property should be submitted so that the organization can arrange for a representative to make an initial inspection. Most major auction rooms have a series of branch representatives; these can greatly facilitate your contact with the major organizations and have been created with the idea of making the consignment process easier. Auction houses also frequently arrange visits by groups of experts to particular cities. These "sweeps," as they are realistically called, are advertised in local newspapers and are offered free of charge. Another opportunity for expert identification is the "Heirloom Discovery Day," a process by which a team of experts will examine a limited number of items for a small fee, which is normally donated to the cultural institution which hosts the event. This does not produce a written figure, but gives an owner a reasonable idea of what a particular item may be worth. There is no obligation to consign and the institution benefits from the exercise. This process has gained a wide variety of names, because each auction house has its own variation on the basic theme. In looking for advertisements for such events, however, certain key words tend to reoccur, denoting hidden treasure, discovery, surprise and excitement. It should be borne in mind that, on the majority of occasions, family tradition will have tended to exaggerate the potential value of objects submitted to this process. Be prepared to be disappointed, but take comfort from the fact that most experts are surprisingly human and have gained considerable experience in conveying bad news in a delicate and sensitive manner.

The initial photograph need not be a major work of art in itself. Most experts are used to forming a provisional judgement on the basis of a Polaroid snapshot; the invention of self-focusing has done much to improve the quality of these photographs.

In addressing photographs of your works of art to a major auction house, remember that you are one of thousands making such contact. Write your name and address on the reverse of the photograph. Include the measurements and the existence of any signature, date or other identifying marks. The more information you give the expert, the more likely it is that the initial identification and sale estimate will be accurate. Bear in mind that, if a group of photographs has been submitted, it is highly possible that the photographs will be distributed among several experts. Some auction houses have coordinators who will gather all the experts' responses together and respond in a single letter, but it is just as likely that you will receive a stream of individualized answers over a span of time created by the availability and working habits of particular experts. A delay of two weeks in this process should not cause undue alarm. If an answer has not been received in the period of a month, a written reminder may produce the desired effect. Because auction houses make money by selling works of art, the potential consignor should not hesitate in making contact. This is the stuff of business.

It should also be remembered that fine art auction is a two-tiered business. While the newspapers cover the dramatic, million-dollar sales, even the most prestigious auction rooms survive and make a profit by selling vast quantities of less valuable items. They do much to dispel the myth of unapproachability and the owner of any work of art should feel free to call on their services.

IDENTIFICATION
The Expert Eye

Through its expert staffing, a major auction house attempts to have on hand experienced cataloguers able to identify correctly any work of art brought to it for inspection. Correct presentation of an item at sale is dependent upon the accuracy of the auction catalogue and thus the reputation of a major house relies on both the depth and breadth of its collective knowledge in the fields of the arts which it sells.

Whatever the purpose of the first contact with the auction house—curiosity, the need for an insurance evaluation, potential sale, estate tax appraisal or authentication—the initial reaction of the expert when confronted with a work of art must be to ask what might appear to be superfluous questions. However, the answers to these questions prepare the ground for correct identification.

What is it? Where was it done? When? How? Who did it?

Not only must all of these questions be answered, but the answers must be consistent in order for identification to be satisfactory. Let us take the example of old master paintings, an area in which this writer has some familiarity, and ask these questions again.

What is it? A painting—or so it appears to be at first sight. But it may also be a reproduction, a painted-over photograph mounted on canvas or panel, a heavily varnished print or machine-printed canvas, or any one of a dozen techniques created to deceive.

Where was it done? In narrowing down the geographical limits within which a work of art has been produced, one begins to close the identification gap. If this hypothetical Rembrandt was painted on a panel, what type of wood is involved? Should the painting be on cypress, a problem arises, because not many have experienced the pleasure of strolling through a cypress grove in the Netherlands. The guilds in the Netherlands preferred the immediate availability of oak for their prepared panels and often stamped the reverse of the panels with the guild mark. The bevelling on the panel should clearly in this case be the product of hand-planing and finishing. Evidence of the even cut of a modern machine tool should at least arouse healthy suspicion in the viewer!

Without laboring the point, both visual inspection and technical testing must be rigorously undertaken to determine that all elements of a particular work of art could have been available at the time and in the area of its purported source. One must nevertheless be alert to the possibility that, during the course of its existence, a particular work of art may have been modified or supplemented. It is possible that the Rembrandt painting was transferred from its original oak panel to a masonite backing in 1948. No one would expect to find masonite in Holland in the seventeenth century, yet the work remains intact thus newly mounted. However, the desirability of totally original condition should not be forgotten.

When? Having established geographical source, the determination of exact dating brings the expert much closer to positive identification. Once again, close visual inspection, on occasion, coupled with accurate technical analysis remains a *sine qua non*. Different fields require different technical tests and it is beyond the scope of this writer and this work to describe these in any detail. Suffice it to say that carbon 14 testing, X-ray, ultraviolet light, radiation dating and chemical analysis are frequently employed to determine the age of a particular work of art. Individual experts acquire an extraordinary ability to recognize the normal signs of aging within their particular fields of endeavor. The ability to read craquelure, the small age cracks that appear, for instance, in both paintings and porcelain, does much to intensify the accuracy of dating in these two fields, though it needs to be said immediately that these conditions can be falsely induced.

The problem with many technical tests arises in their lack of availability or mobility. The expert from an auction house, making an initial inspection visit cannot drive up to a private house with a mobile laboratory in one van and a complete art reference library in another. In most cases the expert will have to rely initially upon educated visual inspection. In attempting to date a work of art visually, the expert must draw upon an extensive knowledge of what might be called domestic history. Hollywood has, since its early days, relied upon a department known as "continuity." It is the task of the continuity experts to make sure that Julius Caesar does not appear wearing a wrist watch; that a helicopter is not seen hovering over the field of Agincourt; that Napoleon does not pass a hamburger stand on his retreat from Moscow. These exaggerated examples point to what must become an exact science in the dating of works of art. A seventeenth century painting must be examined with care to ensure that no single element in its composition is not contemporary with the period of the painting. Furniture design, costume, botany, architecture, literary references and many other disciplines can come to the aid of the artistic detective in the pursuit of an accurate determination.

How? The actual techniques employed in creating a work of art are immensely useful in narrowing down several elements in the identification process. To take the example of furniture: craftsmen from differing periods and locations will use entirely different methods to join the various pieces of wood used in the construction of their products and these methods will tend to be consistent. The comparison between English and American chairs of the last quarter of the eighteenth century, while they may display startling similarities of design, will show that the actual manner of construction was different in many aspects, not to mention the fundamental distinction in the materials used.

In every field of art, one who would come even close to the skills required for correct identification should, at the very least, familiarize himself with the basic techniques involved. How were tapestries woven? How was glass blown? How were bronzes cast? What tools did the cabinetmaker, silversmith, engraver use? How was Limoges enamel created? Not only is this exercise essential to correct identification, but it becomes a fascinating and rewarding study in and of itself.

Who did it? The label on the frame says Rembrandt van Rijn. The hand-written label on the reverse of the stretcher says, in elaborate nineteenth century script: "I bequeath this portrait by Rembrandt to my niece, Jane Doe. Signed this first day of April, 1832. Algernon Doe." An ancient inventory and appraisal of 1922 lists the painting as Rembrandt van Rijn and values it at $8,000, mentioning its appearance in the *catalogue raisonné* of C. Hofstede de Groot. The portrait is signed and dated 1637 in what appears to be the hand of the artist.

And yet, none of the above qualifies as conclusive evidence that one is indeed in the presence of a masterpiece by the great seventeenth century master. For, at best, one can only reach a consensus as to the authorship of a particular work. Further questioning assures one of greater accuracy in an exercise of educated guesswork, but attribution will never be a totally exact science.

The final answer to this vexing question of who did it will depend, in the last analysis, on the completeness of the expert's grasp of his or her field. For, if an expert is fully familiar with a particular area, the artists or craftsmen are sufficiently well-known to the expert that their products become recognizable at first sight. It is instructive to make the comparison between the painter and the writer. Every literate human being has a form of handwriting that is unique. None of us writes in an identical manner, though our writing techniques may be similar. Over a period of time, a person's handwriting becomes sufficiently familiar so that a quick glance at an envelope will indicate the source of a particular communication. The better we know an individual, be it a member of the family or a business colleague, the more accurate our identification of handwriting becomes. We do not need to see the signature on the letter to determine its authorship. Not only will the handwriting become familiar, but the style of writing, the form of composition and even the vocabulary will become easily recognizable.

The analogy with the work of a painter or any other craftsman in the fine arts becomes obvious. The painter's brushwork becomes his handwriting; the elements in his subjects are his vocabulary; his painterly style in composition acquires a consistency. The expert recognizes these traits as in a member of the family or a close friend. Thus the expert achieves an ability to produce an immediate identification based on intimate familiarity with the creator.

The questions addressed above will be answered almost subconsciously and the expert may finally have to rely on his years of experience to exclaim quite validly that a particular work is not by a certain artist or craftsman because it neither looks nor feels right.

EVALUATION

Creating a Pre-Sale Estimate

Because the auction process exists to provide a service to both sellers and buyers and is essentially a market place, evaluation remains a key issue in all transactions. The potential consignor will decide to sell principally on the basis of the initial evaluation made by the representative of the auction house. While such questions as date, style and authorship are intriguing, the one fixed area of concern in every transaction remains: What is it worth?

Whether the expert from the auction house is visiting a client in a house or examining an object brought to the business premises, the initial estimates are usually given as a range and will tend to be of wider range than the eventual official estimate placed in the actual catalogue. An estimate of eight to twelve hundred for instance allows for a wide margin of difference, in this case a margin of fifty percent between the "low" and the "high." Nevertheless, if a client is considering selling an item, it is useful to know that the least he is likely to receive is eight hundred and that he is doing extremely well if the item exceeds twelve hundred. Assuming reasonable accuracy on the part of the expert, decisions can be made on the basis of this original estimate. The acknowledged expert will form an opinion on this estimate within seconds of seeing a particular item. New clients are often amazed at the speed with which an expert will form this initial judgment. Through training and experience, the expert is in fact making an immediate comparison with other similar items that have passed through the auction rooms and judging the quality of the particular item in front of him. The quality of an art object depends on many criteria, all of them to some degree subjective. The elements of value will be discussed in greater detail in the section of this book devoted to appraisal. Amongst other criteria subconsciously affecting the expert's immediate evaluation will be condition, attractiveness of composition or subject, color, rarity, historical importance, extremes of size, provenance, and current trends in a particular market, including recent high and low prices. The list could continue indefinitely, but overriding all other considerations is the personal reaction of the expert to the object in question. If he is properly trained, this personal reaction is a valid part of the evaluation process because the expert earns his living by reacting correctly to the objects he evaluates. In a phrase, he knows his business instinctively. Further research will serve to refine this opinion, but initial reactions tend to be remarkably accurate.

In offering an initial estimate, the responsible expert will be careful to strike a balance between the desire to encourage the potential consignor to sell and the danger of overestimation which leads to false hopes and subsequent disappointment, one of the classic methods of losing clients over the long term. Not only does the habit of estimating too highly lose clients, it places the expert in a predicament when attempting to fix a reserve price on an item prior to sale, of which more will be said later. It is a fact of auction life that, regardless of any number of protestations as to the provisional and preliminary nature of this first evaluaton, it is the one figure the client never forgets. What is more, when faced with subsequent adjustment of the estimate in a downward direction, the client tends to engage in what might be described as selective amnesia. He forgets the low estimate and concentrates on the high. Using the previously cited example, the family heirloom is already considered to be worth at least twelve hundred dollars "because your expert said so." A further law of auction nature provides that the higher the estimate the greater the expertise. Thus an assistant cataloguer, fresh out of college with six months experience in evaluation, may look at a painting and suggest that it is a fine example of Rembrandt's work and worth two million dollars. Should the head of the old master painting department, twenty years older, with fifteen years more experience in evaluation, then suggest that the subject work is in fact a work by Rembrandt's pupil Willem de Poorter from the 1630s, in questionable condition and portraying a dead ox, the least attractive of subject matters, and thus only worth about two to three thousand, the client may well choose to suggest that the novice was, of course, correct in the initial identification and evaluation. Being human, many clients hear what they prefer to hear. Owners tend to adopt an optimistic view both as to authenticity, authorship and evaluation—and hope springs eternal. Family tradition and deathbed statements as to value tend to enhance existing inflated values and often quoted is the following statement: "If ever you are in need, this work of art will see you through."

The prudent and responsible expert, in the face of these and other dangers, will tend to be conservative in this process of first evaluation. A few properties may be lost to the competitor who promises the moon but, in the long run, reputation will depend on close observation at the center of the market on a daily basis. The major auction houses provide this accuracy by the very nature of their operations.

DESCRIPTION AND DEFINITION
Preparation of a Reliable Catalogue Entry

In seeking to describe and define a particular work of art, the expert in the auction house is in fact beginning the process which will be complete when the auction catalogue is printed. As in the matter of initial identification, the ultimate goal in description of an item is total accuracy. In years now happily past, the expertise of a cataloguer was measured by the elaborateness of his description and the number of superlatives and adjectives to the square inch of print. Nowhere was this tendency more visible than in the furniture descriptions in the great household dispersals in the first half of this century. Words like "magnificent," "highly important" and "outstanding" seemed to arouse the possessive urge and place an almost sacred awe around the act of sale. The auctioneer, the great high priest of the sale, would employ every possible dramatic skill to further this atmosphere, lecturing his flock in soothing tones of bombastic pomposity. The language of the ringmaster and the toastmaster convey the formality of this performance. The auctioneer of today sacrifices dramatic opportunity in the interest of speed and efficiency. His audience is better qualified to judge the quality of the offerings and would be insulted by the condescension of the past. A good definition contains a clear statement of all the relevant facts regarding a particular item. The elements will vary according to the field involved, but superfluous embellishments are eliminated in the interest of clarity. Omission of vital facts is a serious fault in the other direction. By means of illustration, the following descriptions are given from a diverse group of areas:

■ **216 DIAMOND AND SAPPHIRE BRACELET**
Platinum mount with pierced decoration, set with 183 old-mine and rose-cut diamonds weighing approximately 10 carats, 1 oval-shaped and 11 old-mine diamonds weighing approximately 5.50 carats and 7 old-mine diamonds weighing approximately 3.50 carats, centering 1 cushion-shaped synthetic sapphire and 1 cushion-shaped natural sapphire.

signed CARTIER

■ **208 DIAMOND AND EMERALD PENDANT
WITH WHITE GOLD CHAIN**
The platinum pendant mount set with an emerald-cut emerald weighing approximately 2.75 carats, an emerald-cut diamond weighing approximately 5.75 carats, 6 round diamonds weighing approximately 12 carats and 56 round diamonds weighing approximately 7 carats.

Property of a Descendant of the Original Owner

■ **188 FINE AND VERY RARE AMERICAN SILVER
TWO-HANDLED BOWL, Benjamin Wynkoop, New York,
circa 1707,** of shaped circular form with applied conforming foot,

curved sides divided into six panels by deep chased lines, in each panel
an escutcheon formed by a deep chased line and the center chased
with a flower, engraved below the rim with contemporary initials, the
base chased underneath with a stylized flowerhead, cast foliate scroll
handles, the foot flat-chased with a band of conjoining diamond
motif, *marked twice below the rim* "W + K" over "·B·" *in an outlined
heart*, 15 ozs. 12 dwts. *Diameter 8 inches (20.3 cm.), Length over handles
11 inches (27.9 cm.)*

> The initials are those of Nicholas Roosevelt (1658-1742) and his wife Hillitje
> who were married in December 26, 1682. It is quite possible that this bowl is
> a twenty-fifth wedding anniversary present dating from 1707. Nicholas
> Roosevelt is listed in 1690 as having the occupation of a "Bolter" and in
> 1698 was made a "freeman". "He was an Alderman of the Leislerian party in
> 1700 and 1709, and although a Burgher of the 'major right', he espoused the
> popular side of the contest of the colonies with the mother country".
> (American Biographical Dictionary, Archives, New York City). He was
> Alderman from 1698-1701 and also Alderman for the West Ward in 1715.
> His son was Nicholas Roosevelt, the silversmith.

> Fewer than twenty bowls of this type, made in New York State between
> 1680 and 1730, are known to exist today. The shape and decoration of this
> bowl are similar to Dutch silverwork of the period and reflect the continued
> Dutch influence in the former New Netherlands. A very similar bowl by
> Benjamin Wynkoop is in the New York Historical Society given by the de
> Peyster family in 1911.

Exhibitions

> Smithsonian Institution, Hall of Everyday Life in the American Past,
>   1961-1971.
> Smithsonian Institution, "Nation of Nations", Bicentennial Exhibit,
>   1976-1980.

Literature

> Antiques Magazine, October 1961, p. 341.
> Martha Gandy Fales, *Early American Silver*, p. 134, pl. 132.

■ 185   AMERICAN SILVER TODDY LADLE, John Blowers,
Boston, circa 1730-40, the bowl of bulbous circular form, engraved
with a crest, silver and wood-turned handle, (repair to bowl), *marked on
base* Blowers *in italics in a rectangle, rubbed. Length 14 inches (35.5
cm.)*

> The crest is that of Byfield probably for Nathaniel Byfield (1653-1733).
> Richard, his father, was one of the Westminister assembly divines, his
> mother was sister of Bishop Juxon. He arrived in Boston in 1664, became a
> merchant, and soon after King Philip's war one of the four proprietors and
> the principal settler of Bristol, R.I. He returned to Boston in 1724. He was at
> one time speaker of the house of representatives, was for thirty-eight years
> judge of the court of common pleas in Bristol, and for two years in Suffolk
> co., for many years a member of the council, and judge of the
> vice-admiralty in 1704-15 and 1729. (Appleton's *Cyclopedia of American
> Biography*)

■ 1681   IMPORTANT AND FINE PAIR OF GEORGE II
CARVED MAHOGANY HALL BENCHES, By James Moore
the younger to designs by William Kent, 1731, for Sherbourne
House, Gloucestershire, each with a rectangular top, fluted frieze,
scrolling leaf-carved apron centering a shell and bell-flower pendant,
leaf-carved corbelled legs. *Height 18 inches (46 cm.); width 36¹/₂ inches
(93 cm.); depth 21 inches (54 cm.)*

Originally a set of four from a suite also including a pair of settees and six
hall chairs, made by James Moore the younger to a design by William Kent,
for Sherbourne House in 1731. The existing invoice records the purchase
price at £20 for the four. In 1940 this group of furniture was sold by Lord
Sherbourne to Leonard Knight, Ltd. who subsequently sold the two settees
to Temple Newsam, Leeds, and the four benches and six hall chairs to Lord
Wilton for Ditchley Park, Oxfordshire. Lord Wilton upon selling Ditchley
in the 1950's again sold the group of furniture. The above lot constitutes
one pair of benches, a pair of hall chairs are at present in the Collection of
Mr. Peter Palumbo. The other pieces have not been traced.

Literature

Fitzgerald, Desmond, *Apollo*, March 1967, A New Yorker's
Unusual Collection, p. 164, fig. 7.

Gilbert, Christopher, *James Moore the Younger and William Kent at
Sherbourne House*, Burlington, March 1969, pp. 148–150, fig. 52;
illustrated p. 149.

REMBRANDT HARMENSZ VAN RIJN   DUTCH: 1606-1669
7. *ARISTOTLE CONTEMPLATING THE BUST OF HOMER.* The
philosopher, wearing a broad-brimmed black hat, and with a golden yellow mantle
draped over his dark robes, stands at three-quarter-length gazing down to left at a
sculptured marble bust of the blind poet, which rests on a table before him. He wears
a golden chain with a pendant portrait medallion of Alexander the Great, his most
famous pupil. Behind the group hangs a drapery partly concealing a pile of books.
Signed on the base of the bust REMBRANDT *f.*, and dated 1653.   56½ x 53¾ *inches*

Note: The genesis of this picture forms part of one of the most curious events
of Rembrandt's life. In the 'fifties, his popularity as a painter had declined sharply in
Holland, and he was entering on a period of financial straits which culminated in
the cession of his possessions to his creditors in July 1656, and the forced sale of his
collection of paintings, including a number of his own works. Nevertheless, his fame
had spread widely through Europe; and in 1652, Don Antonio Ruffo, a Sicilian
nobleman of Messina, wrote to the painter and commissioned from him the present
painting, which was completed in 1653, and delivered in the following year. It may
be noted that the bust of Homer shown in the picture is mentioned in Rembrandt's
own inventory; it was probably a cast of the original, which is in the Naples Museum.

In the *Bolletino d'Arte* of 1916, appeared an extended study written by the
Marquis Vincenzo Ruffo of the history of the vast collection of paintings once owned
by his family; and from the surviving documents he published, among other historical
material of the time, the full story of his ancestor's transactions with Rembrandt,
from which we extract the data which follow.

As indicated above, the painting ordered from Rembrandt was delivered in
1654; the Marquis was so pleased with this work, which was christened *Aristotle*, that
he decided to have two companion pieces executed by the Italian painters Guercino
and Preti; and the former went so far as to paint for him *a Cosmographer*, in which

the subject is shown contemplating a globe, this being Guercino's concept of a suit-able companion to the *Aristotle,* which he took to represent a 'physiognomist.'

The Marquis then changed his mind and decided to order the two additional paintings from Rembrandt himself; and the painter sent him in 1661 an *Alexander the Great,* and in 1662 a *Homer,* the latter of which was returned to be changed at the owner's request. The two last pictures dropped from sight during the ultimate dis-persal of the Ruffo collections, and present authorities can only speculate on their identity with various known works (e.g. Dr. Bredius' *Homer* at The Hague, which is actually dated 1663, and is published by him as being the Ruffo picture). The last known appearance of the *Alexander* occurred when the collection as a whole passed in 1743 to a cadet branch of the family, owing to the death of the older members from the plague; this picture became alienated from the estate and was sold at auc-tion in Amsterdam on June 5, 1765.

Further details of interest concerning the *Aristotle* include the fact that the intermediary by which it was delivered was a certain Cornelius Eysbert van Goor of Amsterdam; the cost of the painting was five hundred florins, and of the packing, weighing, transportation, etc., fl. 15.85. The correspondence also indicates the manner in which the payments could be remitted, as prescribed by the agent van Goor. The painting was carried from Texel to Naples in the ship *Bartholomeus,* and then transported from Naples to Messina.

The *Aristotle* seems to have left the Ruffo collection during the lordship of Don Giovanni, who became the head of the family about 1760; and it was already in the well-known collection of Sir Abraham Hume at the beginning of the nineteenth century. At this time, the history and title had become obscured, and it was known throughout the century under different names (*vide infra*); as late as 1910, the sub-ject was variously styled in the considerable Rembrandt literature.

Painted for the Marquis Antonio Ruffo in 1652-53 (*vide supra*)

Collection of the Ruffo family of Messina, Sicily

Collection of Don Giovanni Ruffo e la Rocca, Messina, *c.* 1760

Collection of Sir Abraham Hume, Bart., Ashridge Park, Herts., before 1815

Collection of Earl Brownlow, Ashridge Park, Herts., his son-in-law

Collection of Rodolphe Kann, Paris, cat. no. 65 (*as* Portrait of a Savant)

From Duveen Bros., Inc., New York

Collection of Mrs Collis P. Huntington, New York

From Duveen Bros., Inc., New York, 1928

Exhibited at the British Institution, London, 1815, no. 39 (*as* Portrait of Pieter Cor-nelius van Hooft)

Royal Academy Winter Exhibition, London, 1893, no. 125 (*as* Portrait of a Man)

Dutch Masters Exhibition, Hudson-Fulton Celebration, Metropolitan Museum of Art, New York, 1909, no. 97, illus. in the catalogue (*as* The Savant)

Rembrandt Exhibition, Detroit Institute of Arts, Detroit, Mich., 1930, no. 51, illus. in the catalogue

Art Treasures Exhibition, London, 1932, no. 1355, illus. in the catalogue

Tercentennial Exhibition of the University of Amsterdam, Rijksmuseum, Amster-dam, 1932, no. 26, illus. in the catalogue

Century of Progress Exhibition, Art Institute of Chicago, Chicago, Ill., 1933, no. 73, illus. in the catalogue, pl. XXXIII

Exhibition, Allied Art for Allied Aid, Knoedler Galleries, New York, 1940, no. 5, illus. in the catalogue

Loan Exhibition in Honor of Royal Cortissoz, Knoedler Galleries, New York, 1941, no. 16, illus. in the catalogue

Recorded in C. Vosmaer, *Rembrandt, Sa Vie et Ses Oeuvres,* 1877, p. 551

Recorded in Dutuit, *L'Oeuvre Complet de Rembrandt,* 1881-85, vol. III, p 43

Recorded in Emile Michel, *Rembrandt*, 1893, p. 555

Recorded and illustrated in W. von Bode and C. Hofstede de Groot, *The Complete Works of Rembrandt*, 1901, vol. V, no. 385, pl. opp. p. 184

Recorded and illustrated in W. Valentiner, *Rembrandt, Des Meisters Gemälde (Klassiker der Kunst)*, 1908, no. 426 (*as* Virgil)

Recorded in C. Hofstede de Groot, *Catalogue Raisonné*, 1916, vol. VI, no. 413 (*as* A Bearded Man Before a Bust of Homer)

Described by Vincenzo Ruffo, *La Galleria Ruffo ... Secolo XVII*, in *Bolletino d'Arte*, 1916

Described and illustrated in Corrado Ricci, *Rembrandt in Italia*, 1918, p. 8ff.

Described and illustrated in W. R. Valentiner, *Rembrandt Paintings in America*, 1931, no. 115

Illustrated in *The Art Digest*, May 1933

Illustrated in *Art News*, May 1933

Recorded and illustrated in A. Bredius, *The Paintings of Rembrandt* (Phaidon ed.) [1942], no. 478

Recorded and illustrated in Jakob Rosenberg, *Rembrandt*, 1948, pp. 165-68, 198, fig. 242

Described in Seymour Slive, *Rembrandt and His Critics*, 1953, pp. 59-62

Mentioned in Otto Benesch, *Rembrandt* (Skira 'Taste of Our Time' series), 1957, pp. 91, 93, 96

Described and illustrated in *Rembrandt* (Phaidon ed.), 1960, no. 77

Within each description, the form has achieved a measure of formality, so that all those involved in the market are speaking the same language and can in effect read the description as if it were in technical shorthand. This standardization is beneficial to all parties though care must be exercised to avoid negligence when using a standard operating procedure. The author recalls from his early days of employment a particular incident in which a cataloguer was waging the familiar battle with a catalogue deadline and, to expedite the process, was dictating his descriptions directly to a secretary who was typing them immediately onto the printer's copy sheet. The luxury of proofing was not available on this occasion and the midnight oil was burning. The sale consisted of minor nineteenth century English landscapes and the monotony of the subject matter was beginning to prey on the patience of the beleaguered expert. When the catalogue finally appeared in print, it contained the following description:

English School, 19th Century
Another bloody river landscape with a brace of cows mooching around in the foreground.

This description did little to enhance the beauty of this painting, thus denying the consignor due attention, so the description was blacked out and the painting offered in a subsequent sale.

Editorial comment should not constitute any part of a proper description. Accurate facts stand on their own.

RESEARCH
Checking Facts and Establishing Authenticity

Once the expert at the auction house has reached his initial conclusion with regard to the attribution and authenticity of the items under consideration, further research is then undertaken to support this opinion as strongly as possible.

This research can take diverse forms. In many areas, much of the documentation is contained in the extensive libraries, archives, and records maintained by auction rooms. Experts also naturally develop close working realtionships with academic scholars and museum curators in their fields of interest. Particularly in the areas of Impressionist and modern paintings, the leading expert on a particular artist will be consulted, because a successful sale will often depend upon a vote of confidence from this prime source. Authenticity must, at best, be the consensus of the leading experts on a period. Many artists and craftsmen are the subject of *catalogues raisonnés* of their entire output. In cases where such a catalogue exists, the failure of a particular item to appear can have a severe if not disastrous effect on a potential sale.

An example of this which will be familiar to many is the considerable difficulty of selling a work of Corot, should it not be listed in the standard reference work on this artist, the *catalogue raisonné* of his work by Alfred Robaut, which continues to be revised by the current leading scholar on Corot, Pierre Dieterle.

Research will often take the form of sending accurate transparencies of the work to several experts, comparing them with other known works by this particular hand, technological tests, such as the thermoluminescence test used on terra cotta to measure age. A further important area of research involves the documentation of the work's history, referred to as provenance, and literature on the item in question, as well as references to any appearances in previous sales or exhibitions.

Once again, the more complete the history, ideally tracing an item back to the moment of its creation, the more widespread the serious documentation in accepted monographs, the more frequent the appearances in major specialized exhibitions, the stronger the chance of success at the moment of sale.

Much of this research will involve testing the veracity of representations made by a consignor whose interests may not be entirely unbiased. The bed in which George Washington slept has no value unless the occasion can be fully documented. Family hearsay and wishful thinking are notoriously inaccurate, leading one to question if this historic American ever spent any of his time awake, so widespread are the claims of his propensity for sleeping in strange beds.

Even the collector of contemporary art should be aware of the importance of record-keeping, since the contemporary work of today will become the old master of tomorrow. Those who will inevitably and eventually acquire these works by gift or purchase have every right to satisfactory documentation. One missing link in a chain of provenance can destroy the credibility of a description.

A notable feature of the auction process, when compared to, say, the work of a museum curator, is the ever-present time pressure exerted upon the auction cataloguer. The museum curator may spend years researching one individual item. The auction cataloguer is working against a constant deadline, with literally hundreds of items to be researched within a matter of weeks. In this context, it is clear that a compromise has to be reached in the interest of satisfactorily servicing the consignor's need to sell the item and to receive payment within a period of approximately six months.

This compromise, on occasion, gives rise to surprising results. For, when a potential buyer has possession of information that has not come to the attention of the cataloguer, the eventual identification of the item may alter radically. Where only one potential buyer has this additional information, the possibility exists of a major item changing hands at less than fair market value, to be the subject of subsequent private resale at a far higher price. These incidents, referred to in the trade as "sleepers," do not occur with great frequency in the major auction houses, but occur sufficiently often to keep the bargain-hunter coming back. Where more than one potential buyer has identified an instance of under-cataloguing, the sleeper may well achieve an extraordinarily high price, rendering the cataloguers official pre-sale estimate significantly out of range. This phenomenon, providing that it does not become standard operating procedure, adds to the excitement of the auction market. In lesser rooms, where the knowledge of the buyer more frequently exceeds the knowledge of the cataloguer, such occasions become sufficiently commonplace that reputation is sacrificed. Reasonable research is thus seen to be a cornerstone of reputable performance in the cataloguing function.

THE EXPERT

The Auction House's Most Valuable Asset

The expert, or cataloguer, remains the key to the auction business. The very use of the word expert has been challenged, but remains defensible.

What makes an expert and at which point can one working in a particular field claim such a title? Here a problem of definition arises, for there is no formal qualifying process in the art auction business. A master's degree from an accredited institute of fine art history may indeed equip a would-be cataloguer with an ability to differentiate between Rubens' Italian and Antwerp periods, but in no way guarantees that a scholar can differentiate between a painting and a reproduction nor whether the subject painting is worth fifty thousand or two million dollars.

While both of the major auction houses offer training courses of one kind or another, these must be treated as broad introductory views of the business and in no way can the graduate claim to be ready to take responsibility for an accurate catalogue as a result of this preliminary training. Serious training in the auction business has traditionally taken place experientially.

There is no substitute for daily contact with items in a chosen field. The "expert-in-training" should gain experience with all levels of quality within a subject. He must learn to differentiate between good and bad, authentic and fake, original condition and extensive restoration. This knowledge is acquired by handling as many examples as possible. The trainee must be given the opportunity to examine the important valuable items alongside the insignificant. As judgment as to quality is acquired, the incipient cataloguer must learn to place a value on each item, based on observed comparables in the salesroom. Coupled with this on-the-job training must be extensive reading on and around the subject. Historical background must be learned together with a knowledge of the standard visual tests to be performed. The standard writings on a subject must be committed to memory and the would-be expert must acquire a mental file of past prices recorded. The development of a photographic memory for both objects and prices is invaluable, for, when working in the field, the expert will need the ability to recall instantly as many sales of similar pieces as possible.

The latent expert must accept a fact of life taken for granted by the acknowledged professional that the learning process is never over. Every opportunity to visit a museum or a commercial gallery is grasped in order to broaden and deepen knowledge of a subject. Aggressive browsing and the habit of continually questioning one's judgment further serve to sharpen the skills. The writer remembers visiting the Frick Museum on his first trip to New York and committing the sacrilegious act of walking around that remarkable collection performing a mental fair market value appraisal. Study of the finest examples known creates a standard by which to judge lesser examples. The author also recalls being forbidden to give estimates on consigned property for at least a week after returning from studying the paintings in Venice, because his superior quite correctly assumed that his judgment would have been heavily impaired by exposure to such a large quantity of major art.

The offerings which daily poured into Sotheby's in London did indeed pale in comparison for a while. It goes almost without saying that constant monitoring of activity "in the trade," in the commercial galleries, is essential to a grasp of the market. The reputable dealer, often trained purely experientially, nevertheless possesses the greatest practical expertise. To succeed, the dealer's judgment has to be right as often as possible. The acid test of the dealer's ability comes very directly. What figure is he prepared to write on that check? The museum curator, the art history professor and the auction house cataloguer are not spending their own money. Their economic survival is not immediately dependent upon the accuracy of their determinations. The knowledge of the dealer thus deserves great respect. A reputable dealer will always be prepared to educate his clients for, in this way, he develops a client who, if satisfied, will continue to return to make purchases. On the other hand, a dealer who is unwilling to answer pertinent questions presumably has something to hide.

An understanding of the interdependency of the dealers and the major auction houses helps to convey the nature of the market and its fluctuations. This will be considered during a description of the buying and selling components of the auction market later in this book.

However, the impression should not be gained that an academic approach to training is irrelevant. The principal fine art institutions are significant contributors to the expertise in the auction houses. The Institute of Fine Arts of New York University, the postgraduate course of study at the Fogg Museum at Harvard, the art history departments in such universities as Yale, Princeton, Smith and Oberlin, to name a few, make invaluable contributions both in research and in personnel to the major auction rooms. In England, the Courtauld Institute and the Warburg Institute offer advanced training; Cambridge University provides a degree in the history of art and the Victoria and Albert and British Museums, along with the National Gallery, have continued to supply the auction houses with world-renowned experts. While the flow of personnel tends to be from the museums towards the auction field for reasons which may stem from a desire for increased remuneration, over the years a number of auction house experts have been elevated to the museum curatorial function, an acknowledgment of the value of the training received in the market itself.

Perhaps the single most significant development in the principal auction rooms in the last thirty years has been the development of highly specialized departmentalization. Sales devoted to a narrow field have

generally replaced the mixed sale of contents approach to sales, with the
notable exception of on-premises house sales. The reason for this is not
difficult to determine. The concentration of the expert upon a particular
area can only improve the quality of the expertise. Also, in its role as an
agent between seller and buyer, the auction house must do its utmost to
satisfy both constituencies. To achieve the highest possible price for the
consignor and offer the specialized collector the broadest possible range
of items within a field, the grouping of similar material in a single catalogue will clearly arouse the greatest interest. For example, a London
dealer in Dutch seventeenth century paintings will probably not risk
travelling to a general sale in Chicago on the chance of acquiring a single
lot in that sale described as: "A landscape by Van Goyen. Signed and
dated: 1635." If, on the other hand, he sees a catalogue of old master
paintings from a New York room, in which are illustrated at least a
hundred Dutch landscapes, all reasonably accurately catalogued, nothing will prevent him from crossing the Atlantic and attending the auction sale. The testing of his expertise against that of the preparer of the
catalogue provides part of the incentive to travel.

FACILITIES
A Museum Whose Exhibitions Change Every Day

The public, in visiting an auction room, will be confined to a limited
area. Typically, this area will include the exhibition rooms, the salesroom
itself, a counter attached to the accounting department and the reception areas in which clients can consult with experts, especially when
bringing items in for inspection. Primarily for reasons of security, the
public will be prevented from visiting behind the scenes, although most
auction rooms arrange tours for small groups upon request. In a large
auction house, the public area is likely to account for approximately one
quarter of the total space. What the client sees is the tip of the iceberg.
The quality of the service provided is dependent upon the efficiency of
the hidden three-quarters.

In continually moving property through the selling operation, storage space, sophisticated handling and inventory control remain vital
considerations. For the saleroom which handles literally hundreds of
thousands of objects each year, the number of movements required by
each item must be kept to a minimum, thereby ensuring accurate tracking of progress within the system and a minimum exposure to risk of
damage. With the vast increase in business during the 1970s, the major
houses are confronted with the need for modernization in all the technical aspects of their business. Space planning, linked with streamlined
accounting functions, serve to increase the chance of processing sales

within a reasonable time. The introduction of big business methods to the hitherto gentlemanly pace of the art world has led to an inevitable compromise in the style of transactions. These sacrifices become apparent when the client receives a computerized receipt, coded by category and item number, keyed to the eventual settlement check. The quill pen has been thrown out of the window and the computer screen has replaced the manually maintained ledger. It is sometimes hard for the owner of the individual family heirloom to grasp the enormity of the task the auction room faces in merely keeping track of an object's progress through the necessary processes. In the broadest terms, each item must at the very least be received and unpacked, receipted, moved to an expert storage area, inspected by an expert, catalogued, photographed, numbered, prepared for exhibition, moved to an exhibition area, displayed during the auction sale itself, moved to a shipping / collection point, be packed and finally be signed out—at least fourteen physical actions, without accounting for further inspections by potential buyers and visiting experts, both during and before the public exhibition. Warehousing and storage space must be adapted to suit the needs of each category. Paintings are stored in bins and separated individually to avoid abrasions; jewelry requires secure storage safes; furniture acres of open storage space; porcelain appropriate shelving. Once the exhibition stage is reached, every effort is made to display every item to the best possible advantage. The exhibition rooms must present the items in a way that makes it possible for the potential buyer to examine the lots as closely as desired. Space and lighting become prime considerations. Unlike the museum, much of which is given over to permanent installations, the auction room may be displaying as many as six different sales simultaneously, "breaking down" one exhibition and replacing it with another virtually every day of the week.

Adaptability becomes an essential ingredient. The difficulty of reconciling availability with reasonable security leads to the need for highly developed control functions. An idea of this formidable task is to imagine the chaos engendered should the Metropolitan or the British Museum one day decide that the public had the right to touch and physically inspect every object on its premises, including the contents of vast storage areas!

The shape and design of the auction room itself is determined by its function. Once again, the items for sale must literally be displayed in the best possible light. Sotheby's, in New York, have developed a revolving stage technique so that, as one item is being sold, the next one is being set up. The auctioneer's rostrum, by definition, must be near the stage so that the auctioneer can be certain that he is selling the right item, but must also be positioned so that he can see and be seen by the entire audience of potential bidders, who should be comfortable, but not too comfortable. It is an observable fact that, if the seats are too soft or the auction room too warm, the bidders will become lethargic in the course of a session of selling. Such considerations cannot be ignored in the design of this essential function. With the growth in the international nature of the market, a recent innovation in the auction room has been the introduction of digital currency converter displays, enabling the foreign buyer to determine immediately the amount being bid in his native currency.

Visibility and audibility become primary concerns in the auction room. The *bête noir* of the architect in this connection is the standard pillar, often an inevitable feature of large buildings converted to use as auction rooms. The need for eye contact between auctioneer and bidder renders extremes of length or breadth in a saleroom undesirable, because either extreme leads to the necessity of using assisting "bid-callers" which breaks the rhythm of the sale and extends the risk of confusion between auctioneer and bidder. To cite one example of the difficulties the design of the auction space can create, the writer recalls selling a section of an on-premises sale in a tent in a thunderstorm. The mixture of insufficient light and the sound of torrential rain on the canvas six inches above the rostrum made identification of a bidder in the back of the tent all but impossible. The normally adequate paddle-numbers could not be read accurately and no amplification could compete with the natural orchestration outside the tent.

The major sale events produce a whole new series of demands upon the auction facilities. Secondary salerooms, with either closed-circuit television or slide viewing facilities, administered by auxiliary auctioneers who are linked to the main auction room sound system, enable large numbers to participate actively in these dramatic sales. A crowd of two thousand is not considered unusual for a major Impressionist sale in New York, each one of those two thousand demanding a front row seat in the main auction room and stoutly claiming a determination to acquire the major item in the sale. For lack of a better system, seating is awarded on the basis of past purchasing performance. As a result of this it is not uncommon to hear the auctioneer tell a successful bidder in a subsidiary auction room: "You'll get a seat in the main room next time!" Some professional clients prefer the anonymity of the subsidiary rooms, a subject which will be covered in greater depth when the sale process itself is described.

Each item only spends approximately one minute in the saleroom itself. The majority of its sojourn in the auction facility is spent in storage as close to the expert as possible. The expert areas are designed to give the expert the optimum conditions for research and cataloguing and at the same time making the expert available to the client, without whom there would be nothing to catalogue. Typically the expert will have an office halfway between a public reception area and his departmental working area, for the expert's time is divided between client contact, both with potential sellers and potential buyers, and cataloguing functions, which have already been described. The serious collector will not only invest valuable time in forming a close relationship with the experts in a particular field, he will learn to avail himself of the opportunity to learn with the experts as they inspect and catalogue property so, that by the time the public exhibition takes place, he already knows which items are of interest and has a real idea of their potential sale price. The expert areas are designed to make these relationships possible without allowing them to make the expert's ongoing responsibilities impossible. The major auction rooms have to some extent engendered the false impression that they wish to keep the clients away from the experts. Most experts realize that it is through personal contact that the neophyte of today becomes the dedicated major collector of tomorrow. The experts' sound counsel is available; they enjoy sharing their knowledge with the serious and offer it free of charge, until it is written down!

ACCOUNTS AND FINANCE

The Demands That Auction Imposes
in the Financial Area

The financial organization of a major auction house is necessarily complicated and it can be assumed that no two companies are organized in precisely the same fashion. An additional complication arises in that the great growth of business in this field over the last ten years leaves the major rooms in a period of transition from the familiar manual operations of the small concern to the automated computerized systems of big business.

The financial division of an auction house will be concerned with four principal functions: collection of money from the buyer; payment of money to the seller; handling of cash balances; and internal accounting and control systems. While both payment by the purchaser and settlement to the seller will be discussed in the appropriate sections later on, the scope of the internal fiscal operations can be grasped by a brief outline of the main functions performed.

In Sotheby's in New York, of the four hundred and fifty employees, sixty are involved in finance. The proportion in London is similar. Management information systems involve not only the basic financial record-keeping functions necessary to any business, but also a sophisticated inventory control system which must track works of art that move at least fifteen times in their time at the auction house. Much of the contractual and sale settlement processing is computerized and the day is not far off when all record-keeping will be fully automated. Meanwhile, employees have to be paid, general and administrative expenses have to be met and the myriad outside contractors, from printers to advertising agents, from suppliers of stationery to expert consultants, have to receive their due. In a business which involves constant travel, keeping track of employee expenditure alone can be something of a nightmare. Add to these functions the need to create regular reports for the group financial director in the company headquarters and it can be seen that the lot of the senior financial officer in an auction room is not always a happy one.

For the client who seeks assistance in reaching the correct financial office within an auction house the best advice is to envision a three-part organization, services to the seller, services to the buyer, and all systems. Reference to a customer service agent may be the best alternative to self-help in this area.

PHOTOGRAPHIC PRESENTATION OF SALE ITEMS
Illustrations and Advertising

The visual presentation of a work of art makes a tremendous difference to the eventual sales result. As the auction houses broaden their buying constituency, the need for accurate photography increases. While the golden rule remains that no one should contemplate buying a work of art without inspecting the item itself, or at least having an agent carry out this inspection on his behalf, the quality of the photography throughout the auction process may well determine whether or not a potential bidder's interest is aroused.

Taking the process chronologically, photographs may be taken at the first instance as an aid to research. International experts are consulted on the basis of eight by ten inch black and white prints or color transparencies. Already accuracy in photography may influence the ability of a recognized expert to make a positive identification.

Long before the catalogue goes to press, the auction house has to consider its advertising strategy for a given sale. Once again, the quality of the illustrations will influence the thousands of potential bidders who are reached through the media. Each category of art requires its own photographic skills. For example, silver has to be sprayed to eliminate reflections; jewelry has to be set against a background that will set off its true color as accurately as possible. Imagine the complications of shooting a carpet forty by sixty feet in size!

The next demand on the photographic department concerns the illustrations in the catalogue. As the auction business increases more and more buyers depend on fully illustrated catalogues to determine their initial interest in a sale. Details of a work of art must be clear from the illustration. The angle chosen by the photographer can aid the collector considerably in determining the quality of an object. In the paintings field, an illustration should be sufficiently clear that a signature can be observed easily. With major paintings, where color work is involved, it is standard procedure to shoot at least five transparencies and then to reject a whole series of color separations. Even with every professional precaution observed, it is possible for the final run of the catalogue to appear with one or two color illustrations seriously inaccurate. Hence the galleries offer potential buyers the ability to consult by telephone as to the comparison between the illustration and the actual work. The warning is obvious: never buy a major painting or any work of art, for that matter, on the basis of a color illustration in a sales catalogue or art magazine. Color photography remains far from an exact science. Recognize also that this photography is carried out under optimum lighting conditions, which also prevail during the exhibition and sale. Under normal circumstances, the lighting arrangements in the collector's home will be less dramatic. Bear this in mind both when viewing a work that seems alarmingly bright; it will tone down under normal lighting. When having difficulty picking out detail in a dark-toned painting on exhibition, remember it will all but disappear when placed in residential surroundings!

The demand for photographic accuracy is not yet over. Once the advertising is processed and the catalogue is printed, potential bidders will frequently request photographs of items or details of particular items. The appetites of known collectors are whetted by experts who know what their collection lacks. One of the principal duties of the auction room expert is to know the likes and dislikes of his particular regular clients. The writer knows of a collector, for instance, who collects Dutch seventeenth century paintings with special reference to subjects involving chemistry and Old Testament themes. Because neither of these themes can be described as popular, this collector is quickly made aware of any painting which appears in his chosen fields.

In many cases, an auction will either be conducted entirely from slides, jewelry being a prime example, or slides will be used in a subsidiary salesroom, as already discussed in the case of major Impressionist sales. Bids will clearly be affected by the quality of these slides.

The sale over, the demand for photographic work continues. Archives are maintained so that a complete record of past sales is available. A year book is prepared illustrating the major items sold in the past season and both the media and the academic community demand photographs of items previously sold.

It will therefore come as no surprise that the major auction houses maintain extensive photographic departments and that they do as much of the processing as they technically can. Such are the pressures imposed upon them.

As a footnote on the matter of photography, a word to the amateur photographer. The extensive steps taken to ensure accuracy of photography at every stage of the auction process indicate the importance attached to this technical function. In making an initial approach to an auction house with regard to any work of art, it should by now be apparent that the quality of the photograph submitted will have a significant effect of the ability of an expert to judge the identity, quality and value of an item. If a would-be consignor suspects an item may have considerable value, he would be well advised to have a professional photographer take these initial photographs. If such service is not readily available, the following hints are offered to the gifted amateur photographer. Daylight works better than flash. Take the heirloom out into the garden or onto the street and shoot it against a contrasting background. If forced to use flash indoors, do not shoot from directly in front of a painting or other work of art; the reflection of the flash will dominate the photograph. Either note the size of the item on the photograph itself or put an indicator of size next to the object, (a foot ruler will do well). If you are photographing a three-dimensionsal object, take it from several different angles, thus giving the expert a better chance at exact identification. Take detailed close-up shots of any and all hallmarks, seals, labels, signatures and other identifying insignia. They are vital clues in the identification process. Remember that black and white can be more accurate for detail than color, although color is immensely useful in identification in most fields. Do not expect identification from photographs to be one hundred percent accurate; you will be acquiring an initial impression which will normally have to be adjusted when the expert is confronted by the object itself.

CATALOGUE PRODUCTION
Creating a New Publication each Working Day

As has already been suggested, the quality and the accuracy of the auction catalogue play a vital role in the maintenance of an auction house's reputation. The catalogue is the organization's principal marketing tool. Given the pressure under which they work, the catalogue production staff in the major rooms daily perform minor miracles. The writer, having spent fifteen years in New York, is more familiar with the mode of operation in America and will therefore give a broad description of the function of catalogue production in New York, in order to acquaint the reader with some idea of the time involved. Consignors are sometimes surprised that their art object, once delivered to an auction room, does not appear fully illustrated and described in a catalogue the following week. A survey of the stages of catalogue production alone will serve to illustrate the impossibility of such a notion.

At Sotheby's in New York, in the 1980–1981 season, two hundred and fifty eight catalogues were published. This is the equivalent of producing one new catalogue each working day. Working with at least seven printers, each member of the production staff will be supervising the creation of between six and twelve catalogues at a given time. A catalogue run will vary from three to ten thousand, depending on the importance of the sale and the popularity of the art category involved. The closeness of the timing is extraordinary since the success of an auction operation is dependent upon moving property through the process as quickly as possible, while reaching the maximum number of potential bidders with the maximum amount of accuracy in the catalogue descriptions. The primary objective is to have the catalogue ready to send to subscribers and to sell individually at least one month prior to the sale date. The whole schedule is structured to achieve this end.

The master production schedule for a catalogue is created three months before the auction itself. The typed manuscript is due from the catalogue department ten weeks prior to the sale. This allows a period of approximately five weeks for actual catalogue production. The catalogue production staff, in consultation with the expert departments, the legal department, the marketing and other design consultants are responsible for a final product that conforms to the corporate style and design, is consistent with corporate policies and conditions of sale and contains all such legal matter as is required by the auction process in the location in which the sale is to be held. The requirements for an auction of wine in Chicago will differ from the sale of live Arabian horses in Phoenix and neither will have much in common with the sale of Impressionist paintings in New York. The catalogue must reflect these differing circumstances.

During the five weeks of production, the catalogue passes through thirteen principal stages. These do not include color work and cover design which take place simultaneously with the production of the catalogue copy. Indeed, color-proofing continues right up until the moment that the mechanicals are returned to the printer for final processing.

The production proceeds in the following manner:

The typed manuscript is received by the production department,

who, once assured that it is complete and in order, deliver it to whichever printer is favoured for the type of sale in question. Galleys are
returned by the printer to the production department. One set goes to
the production department proofreader, skilled in detecting technical
and typographical errors. Two sets of galleys are delivered to the expert
department, one of which is read for errors and author's alterations, the
second of which is used to prepare a paste-up "dummy," together with
photographs. It is important to recognize that the cataloguing experts
play an essential role in the design of both the order and the look of
their sale catalogues.

The paste-up completed, it is returned to the production coordinator, who will have been selected on the basis of the particular printer
being employed. Since various departments will tend to use specific
printers, a team will usually develop which can automatically adhere to
set principles within a given catalogue, increasing the speed and efficiency of the process. The production coordinator will check the galley
for design accuracy and sizing.

At the next stage, pagination will be created and color impositioning
will be established. By now color choices have been sized and separated,
a cover design has been selected from two or three mockups, and these,
together with galleys and photographs, are returned to the appropriate
printer.

The printer then delivers the material for reproduction back to
catalogue production, who are responsible for initiating the "mechanical" stage, either with the printer or with an outside subcontractor specializing in "mechanical" processing. In simple terms, the mechanical
stage pulls together the catalogue dummy, the photoprints, the color
proofs, the type and the pagination. It should, however, be borne in
mind that color-proofing may continue past this stage, if it is deemed
necessary.

As further evidence of the expert's continuing role in controlling
the quality of his catalogue, the expert will then see the mechanical for
final corrections, though this is not viewed by the production staff as an
appropriate moment for highly expensive last minute author's alterations.

Mechanicals, color separations, and cover film now go to the printer
and, in a final quality control procedure, the final blue line is shown to
the expert to ensure that all the required corrections have been made
satisfactorily.

There then follows a seven to ten day hiatus, in which the catalogue
is printed, bound and packed for shipment and delivery. At the end of
this period, the "book" arrives, not always perfect, but given the pressure
under which it was conceived and created, a remarkable testament to the

skill and professionalism of the catalogue production staff and the "author," the expert in charge of the catalogue, who is already worrying about his consignors, his potential buyers and what he can possibly find for his next sale, whose ten-week deadline is fast approaching.

MARKETING AND PROMOTION
The Auction House Reaches Its Public

As can be seen, the quality of the sale catalogue will distinguish the major auction house from the secondary organization. Reputations are gained or lost on the basis of the expertise shown in the principal communication between the auctioneer as agent and the buying public. However, the sale of a work of art does not come about through the distribution of the catalogue alone. The contact between the expert and the individual collector has been mentioned as an essential ingredient. The success of an auction room will also depend heavily on the efficiency of its marketing program. Gone are the days when marketing was left to the cataloguer himself. Professional marketing services have become part of the auction function.

Typically, the marketing of an auction room's functions will fall into five categories: business development, corporate sales, promotion, advertising and press relations. A brief review of these components will serve to demonstrate that the expansion of the auction market during the last ten years is no accident, but the result of conscious strategic planning.

The business development function encompasses both strategic planning and coordination. Who are the customers? Where are they located? How can they be reached? How can one service their needs? What are those needs? From such questions will come initiatives as the appointment of regional representatives, the opening of branch offices and the creation of regional auction centers. Through selective planning, certain areas will receive increased attention. The presence of many new Latin American buyers in the market will lead to a strengthening of the staffing in that area and the opening of a representative office in Mexico City. Business development, if it is to make any sense, must respond to perceived and tested needs and opportunities. With the acute rise in operational costs, the auction rooms have to take this fundamental element of marketing seriously.

Auction rooms have traditionally sold to individual collectors, dealers and educational institutions, such as museums and libraries. The increased interest of corporations in the acquisition of art, with which to improve the quality of corporate surroundings and to protect the corporate assets at the same time, leads the major auction house in the direction of providing a liaison with this new constituency. The major auction houses continually seek to broaden their markets and their share thereof through dialogue with banks, investment houses, pension fund managers, corporate designers and others who are concerned with corporate participation in the art market.

Promotion of the many and varied services offered through the auction house facilities takes many forms. Experts and executives in a major house will find their time increasingly occupied in lecturing to selected audiences, participating in seminars, conducting tours and even writing articles and books on their chosen fields! Much of the best promotion occurs through personal contact and social interaction. Every cocktail or dinner party, every long distance flight or vacation produces opportunities for new business. Most people are intrigued when they begin to learn more about this art business and, make no mistake about it, it is becoming a very big business.

Advertising is, without a doubt, one of the leading expenditures for the auction house, an expenditure which it is customary for the consignor to share. While institutional advertising remains vital in this competitive marketplace, it is the highly selective advertising of the individual works of art which contributes notably to their successful eventual sale. The international scope of the buying public makes it necessary that each major work of art has reached the broadest possible group of potential buyers. This could lead to such diverse results in advertising that, in the same Impressionist and modern painting sale, a Picasso oil might be advertised in a Tokyo newspaper, a Kandinsky water color in Weltkunst in Germany, a Henry Moore bronze in the Burlington Magazine in London and a Munnings equestrian portrait in Town and Country. With a Turner oil of *Juliet and her nurse* selling for $6.4 million to a private collector from Latin America, it is apparent that advertising strategy must remain imaginative and far-reaching, within the restraints of economic common sense.

One of the great advantages of the art auction world is that it creates good press by its very nature. Behind every successful sale lies a human interest story. Each "discovery" of a hitherto lost or unidentified valuable object is natural copy for the media. Besides this, by their essentially artistic composition, works illustrate well in the newspapers or on television. The auction process itself is extremely rewarding theatre, to the point where "audiences" applaud record prices without having to be prompted. The press relations function of the auction room consists primarily of keeping the media informed of the ongoing opportunities to observe and comment on this continuous show.

For all of the above reasons, the auction world probably achieves an inordinate share of media coverage compared with the total size of the art market. Paintings are more attractive than stock certificates. Discovering a lost Titian is more interesting, though not necessarily more profitable, than discovering oil and the whole cultural aspect of art collection renders it a natural subject for extensive media coverage.

Because interest tends to center around high prices and world records, this coverage tends to promote misconceptions which need to be exploded. The illusion that major auction rooms sell only million dollar items to millionaires should be corrected. *The New York Times,* for obvious reasons, does not place on their front page an illustration of a candlestick that is sold for five hundred dollars. The media tend to concentrate on the elevated top of the market. The survival of the auction house depends upon its satisfactory servicing of the vast but less spectacular lower tier. Marketing makes this possible by making auctions popular. This is achieved by continually inviting the public in.

SHIPPING
Moving Works of Art Safely

In a business whose principal purpose is the transfer of ownership of fine art property from seller to buyer, the importance of effective shipping capability need hardly be stressed. Works of art, by their very nature, require careful and specialized handling. In the interest of providing clients with professional assistance in the shipping area, the major rooms can provide extensive help to their clients in all facets of art transportation.

Thus, the client has at his disposal a worldwide import-export shipping operation offering many distinct advantages. Sotheby's in New York offer complete customs clearance, obtaining any necessary licenses or documents. They have their own bonded outside examining rooms, achieving greater security than at the airport cargo areas. In domestic shipping, advantageous rates can be obtained by allowing the auction house to negotiate with familiar and experienced packers. The auction house will negotiate also with the appropriate customs broker, once again saving the customer from overcharging which can arise from lack of familiarity with the process.

Skilled knowledge of import-export procedures is required to avoid unnecessary duties. Many items under one hundred years of age are dutiable unless the proper procedures are followed. A Gallé vase will be charged as a glass kitchen utensil if not properly documented. Rugs, handmade in wool, are dutiable, unless a hundred years old. Can this age be documented? Some categories of goods are subject to seizure. Eagle's feathers cannot be sold under federal law. Ivory requires a license based on its origin; is it whale, walrus or elephant? Antique guns come under the provisions of certain firearms legislation. The sale of certain species of tortoise shell is prohibited in the United States. It is at customs that many of these problems can arise.

Each category of fine art creates its own shipping needs and the auction house personnel can immediately identify appropriate solutions. Consignors are offered the advantage that payment for shipping services can be deducted from the proceeds of sale. Buyers can have their purchases shipped on a cash on delivery basis. For valuable jewelry being shipped internationally, courier services can be arranged; in the internal shipment of medium value jewelry, it may surprise the uninitiated to learn that the most effective mode of shipment is insured, registered mail.

With the vast increase in air freight capacity and efficiency, the client involved in international shipment of fine arts will be advised to use air rather than sea shipment, except where the size or the weight of the property renders air transport impractical, as with massive pieces of furniture or extremely heavy sculpture. The length of time involved in sea shipment alone increases the risk of loss or damage far beyond any advantage gained in cost-saving.

A few commonsense basic rules apply both in internal and international shipping.

First, it is strongly recommended that expert advice be sought. The procedures are complicated and tiresome. Give art transport departments at least two weeks notice of an intended shipment; better yet, allow them to help you make proper arrangements.

Second, supply the auction house or the shipper with as much relevant information as possible. Customs, for instance, require the following information for a commercial invoice:

1) The consignor's name and address.

2) The name of the agent of the auction house receiving the property.

3) The title and description of each item, including a statement of the materials used in its creation.

4) The age or approximate date of the item.

5) The artist's or craftsman's name.

6) The size and weight of each item.

7) A breakdown of value of each item.

Certain categories of art require further information. Works of art on paper must be accompanied by an indication of whether or not they are framed. If they are framed, the frame must have a declared value. In the case of statues and sculpture, a cast number must be supplied or else a statement must be made that the item is unique, original and one of a kind.

Antiques must be accompanied by a declaration of antiquity stating them to be over one hundred years old at the time of importation. False statements in this context can lead to a penalty.

Packing lists are essential to effective shipment. Contents of crates have to be specifically enumerated and valued. Failure to comply with these requirements can lead to significant hardships in the event of loss or damage.

Each procedure takes time when correctly followed. Failure to follow the regulations can lead to delays of up to six months or more. In no other area of the art and antiques business does petty bureaucracy thrive as it does in international art transport. Professional assistance becomes a *sine qua non*.

The temptation afforded the individual to hand carry major art works through customs should be resisted in the majority of cases. The possible saving in brokers fees in no way justifies the agony involved in attempting to fill out the various forms that are encountered in seeking to register the entry of art works, dutiable or otherwise. The forms appear to have been devised in such a way that no normal human can understand the questions, let alone supply the answers. He who does will be informed that the customs agent is not permitted to assist in filling out the form, let alone give hints or clues as to potentially satisfactory answers.

The brief survey above will have suggested that the matters of packing, shipment and the accompanying insurance are best referred to qualified individuals at the earliest opportunity. The experience and organization of the major auction house together with its ability to assess competitive charges make it a natural direction to turn in any matter concerning the shipment of works of art. This is an area in which "do-it-yourself" is tantamount to a prescription for disaster.

CHAPTER TWO
The Role of the Consignor

INITIAL CONTACT
A Guide to Reaching the Right Person

IT MIGHT BE SAID that the auction house does not mind how it is contacted provided it *is* contacted. The larger the operation, the more concerned the management must become over what can be broadly described as its customer relationships, nowhere more vital than in the area of consignment. Whether the potential consignment is a single unique object or a vast varied collection the consignor is primarily interested in finding out what the property is worth, a matter that has already been treated under solicitation of material, and, having received an estimate, the consignor's next concern has to be selling the property as successfully as possible. This success will consist of a top price in the shortest possible time within the constraints of the auction process.

There can be little doubt that the consignor will be vastly aided in knowing whom to contact initially within a particular auction house. While no two are the same, certain general principles apply. Some examples should clarify. If the consignor has a single work or a group of objects all in the same particular category, the best route is a direct call to the head of a cataloguing department. That individual will not only be the most knowledgeable in the subject, but will be most interested in giving the potential consignor the information required. These experts are often remarkably well protected from the public by a battery of assistants, secretaries and junior colleagues. It is therefore advisable to acquire any sale catalogue from the auction house and to look up the department head's name in the relevant listing. A reasonably confident demand to speak to Mr. Smith in person should circumvent any delaying tactics forced upon some departments by the mere volume of business transacted.

This first example presupposes an initial telephone call. If geographical location permits a personal meeting with the expert or experts involved, this is strongly recommended. While auction houses publicly suggest that they are happy to see clients between ten and five on weekdays, it is strongly suggested that an appointment be arranged in advance, once again with the specialist in the area of concern. Because the department heads are responsible for selecting material and making appraisals throughout the continent in which they are based, there can be no guarantee that they are sitting in their offices patiently awaiting an unheralded visit. Failure to make an appointment may thus lead to handling by a junior expert or assistant, who will probably be friendly and helpful, but who will obviously have to defer to the later judgment of the returning head of the department. Should the would-be consignor find himself in this situation, despair is not indicated. Reputable firms will give a receipt for objects or photographs of objects left for inspection and do not indulge in wanton damage or casual loss. Their reputations dependent upon continuing reliable service and the ability to process consignments under a variety of circumstances, they will get back to the consignor within a reasonable period with the required information. Because experts do travel extensively, the consignor should not be alarmed if the initial estimating process takes up to two weeks.

Assuming contact has been made with the head of the department and an appointment has been set, either at the auction house, or, better yet, where practicable, at the consignor's residence, it should be remembered that both the estimate of sale value and the negotiation of sale terms can only take place once the property has been physically examined by the expert. If the consignment consists of a few easily portable objects and there is a representative office of the auction house of your choice relatively near, the items should be brought in. In the auction centers, the experts may be consulted directly; in a representative office, a visit can be arranged to coincide with the regular solicitation journeys made by senior experts. Neither final estimates nor sale terms can be given on the basis of telephone conversations or even professional photographs. These useful initial contacts can only produce provisional statements as to value and adjustable statements as to selling terms.

All this presupposes that the consignor is alive, knows the nature of the art object or objects under discussion and has a relatively clear idea of how to proceed in an initial contact with the auction house. Needless to say, the reality often falls short of this ideal. Other avenues have been devised to aid the novice consignor, who should not become anxious about his lack of experience.

Should the potential consignment contain works from a variety of categories, two options of approach exist. The consignor should either contact the department head in which the preponderance of both quantity or value probably exist, should that judgment be possible, or, for lack of ability to determine this, most large auction rooms have a client service department specifically designated to serve "mixed consignments." This department will not only coordinate the function of garnering estimates from a whole series of departments, but will continue to hold a particular client's hand throughout the consignment, sale and final settlement processes. The staff is typically selected on the basis of friendliness and efficiency and can provide an invaluable key to easy understanding of what can by its very nature be a complicated transaction.

With the expansion of the auction business, various segments of the consignment market have been perceived to require more specific treatment. Their needs are significantly different from those of the living private consignor, who accounts for most of the business. These special consignors, of whom more will be said at a later stage, include estates, museums and educational institutions, corporate sales and off-premises or "house" sales. In each case, the major rooms have departments designed to coordinate the process, so that the person from the estate or institution involved can liaise with one "account executive," who will provide a buffer between the consignor and the large number of staff necessary to completing the process in the auction house. These coordinators are specialists in the form of consignment under their supervision and should be used whenever relevant because they ease the process immeasurably.

NEGOTIATION OF TERMS
Commissions, Charges, and Strategies

The consignor should remember that the auction house survives on the basis of selling a vast quantity of property. The auction house cannot thus afford to sell this bulk at commission rates which fail to cover the costs involved. The cost of selling a fifty thousand dollar item is not much greater than the cost of selling a five thousand dollar item. Their treatment will be similar both in terms of time spent and logistical progress. The nature of the property consigned and the expenses it generates will have a significant effect upon the commission structure and the terms that the auction house will offer. The consignor should also bear in mind that the commission charged on a sale makes up only a part of the whole structure of charges and that a percentage gain in commission may be lost in additional charges.

The terms of sale vary with each auction house. However, two factors should not be overlooked. If a consignment is highly attractive to an auction house and any property over a quarter of a million dollars would fit this definition, the terms are likely to be negotiable. Secondly, many auction rooms are prepared to make cash offers for property. While the top auction rooms do not engage in this practice, with lesser property it is a satisfactory way to eliminate an indefinite waiting period and to receive instant cash.

The standard commission charged by the major international auction rooms is ten percent to the seller on items sold for more than $3,000 and fifteen percent on items sold for $3,000 or less, and ten percent to the buyer. The buyer's commission is not negotiable; the seller's commission is negotiable, where considerable value is involved. Dealers typically receive a partially reduced seller's commission. In seeking to negotiate on the seller's commission, it must be realized that value alone may not be a criterion for reduction. A property worth two hundred and fifty thousand dollars may consist of five hundred items worth on average five hundred dollars each, of which half are large items of furniture. It is virtually impossible for the auction house to make a profit on such a consignment. If, on the other hand, the quarter million dollar value resides in one watercolor by Winslow Homer, enthusiastic negotiation is indicated. The auctioneer does not wish any competitor to take it away. Most major auctioneers levy an additional percentage selling commission on items which realize less than a stated price level. The consignor should expect to pay up to fifteen percent on these low level items because they are expensive to handle and the margins are nominal.

In negotiation with an auction house, it should be recognized that successful reduction is more likely in the area of additional charges. These charges include packing, shipping, insurance, photography and illustration, advertisement, framing, restoration, special exhibition and buy-in charges should the item fail to reach its reserve price. Providing the auction house has confidence in its pre-sale estimate and providing the consignor has not insisted on an unrealistically high reserve, the last charge, the buy-in commission, which can be as much as five percent of the reserve price, is one of the first charges the auction house will be prepared to waive. They make money, after all, on successful sales, not on failures. Illustration and advertising and promotional charges are likely to be the next best areas of negotiation. If the auctioneers really want to sell the items at the highest possible price, thus earning the most commission possible for themselves, they are likely to undertake a full program of illustration, advertising and publicity to achieve this aim, regardless of whether or not the consignor is prepared to share in this role. The consignor should nevertheless realize that negotiation on these charges is only worthwhile with important property which will enhance the auction room's reputation as it increases its profitability. Where it is suggested that framing, or re-framing, or cleaning and restoration may be necessary, it is unlikely that the auction room will assume these charges. They are only suggested where it is considered absolutely necessary and the cost will very easily be absorbed by the resulting enhancement of the sale price. It is always advisable to heed these practical suggestions. The experts in the auction houses learn early the importance of correct presentation of an item for exhibition and sale. If it is suggested that the frame constructed by a gifted amateur carpenter who happened to be a grandparent does less than justice to that Copley portrait, the intelligent consignor will bury family pride and agree to the replacement.

The risk of loss charge, one of the major charges which is added to the consignor's account, plays a significant role in a consignment negotiation. At a cost of ten dollars per thousand, insurance can become a considerable factor when dealing with highly valued properties. It represents a substantial cost to the auctioneer, so it is likely to remain the last ditch in the negotiating strategy. The consignor will need to be in an incredibly strong position to effect a reduction or waiver of this charge. Artists like Rembrandt or Vermeer, craftsmen like Carlin or Kaendler, in their best manifestations, need to be involved before the prudent auction house negotiator gives away the insurance charge. Consignors can provide their own insurance coverage provided they make appropriate arrangements in accordance with the consignment agreement.

Packing and shipping are customarily paid by the consignor. Again, the ease of negotiation in this area will depend very heavily on the nature of the property. Three twenty carat diamonds can be sent through the mail even if worth over two million dollars. A large houseful of furniture, located in Sheridan, Wyoming, consigned for auction in New York, could create a shipping charge of twenty thousand dollars. And a castle full of nineteenth-century furniture in Scotland may not be worth shipping all the way to London. The businesslike consignor will acquire an estimate of these costs before attempting to negotiate them off the terms of sale.

Assuming fiendish negotiating ability and unusually attractive property for sale, it is possible though unlikely that all these charges can be negotiated out. The skilled negotiator has one more area upon which to concentrate and that is the selling commission itself. It has already been stated that the auctioneer makes money on his successes. In structuring the selling commission on highly attractive property, it is possible to force the auctioneer to predicate his profit more heavily upon his success than is achieved by a standard commission rate, however low it has been taken.

For example, instead of paying six percent on the hammer price, the consignor may arrange with the auctioneer to pay no commission up to a certain price, then a sliding scale upwards after that agreed price, going up to ten per cent or more in the event of an unanticipated record price. Alternatively, the consignor may agree to pay no commission up to a price and then split the overage thereafter. The major auction rooms can become highly imaginative when the consignment is one they really desperately want to sell. The neophyte should use extreme caution in attempting negotiations of this latter type. It should be noted that, by and large, the greater expertise will reside on the auctioneer's side of the table.

TIME FACTOR
Waiting For the Best Moment to Sell

The amount of time taken to process a consignment at auction will vary considerably according to circumstances. The auction house must continually make a compromise between giving the items for sale the maximum care, research and exposure to potential buyers and the need to sell the property within a reasonable period to satisfy the consignor's need for payment. With this problem in mind, the major rooms have already created secondary auction facilities which sell the less dramatic material more quickly and with less extensive cataloguing. These secondary rooms have become sufficiently popular that even there a time delay may be anticipated. The consignor must accept the fact that there are many other consignors and that, to some extent, it may be necessary to wait one's turn. In order to alleviate this problem, Sotheby's, both in New York and London, have instituted a system of fast, general sales for lesser material, in which the whole process is reduced to a four week period from receipt to collection after sale and settlement with the consignor. This improvement has been achieved by eliminating the formal catalogue; receipting, cataloguing, exhibiting and selling all in the same area; and by including material in sales which are not restricted to specific areas. For minor property, this approach meets several well-established needs, which have a particular attraction to the professional executor, faced with the requirements of raising immediate cash for estate processing expenses and of disposing of entire properties, regardless of individual values. In a phrase, this service makes it possible for the major auction house to offer a "broom-clean" service to the estate. This saving in time makes the auction room much more competitive with the dealer who offers cash for whole properties. Much of the estate hassle has been eliminated.

In the case of works of art having value in excess of two thousand dollars, the time factor takes on a different complexion. It is in the consignor's interest to ensure that a work of art is placed in the correct type of sale at the appropriate time and place. The major rooms specialize in their approach to sales for good reasons. It allows them to employ experts in specific fields who really know their particular subjects; it ensures that, when a sale of a particular category is held, all major interested parties will not only be informed, but will make every effort to attend the sale, thereby increasing the competition and the level of the final bid.

The catalogue, the advertisement and the marketing functions have already been described. The placement of international advertisements and the production of a catalogue of quality require a minimum lead time of two months; the cataloguing, research and photography consume a minimum of another month. Thus it can be seen that, providing a consignor arrives on the day of the cataloguing deadline, he is bound to wait three months until the sale date. When it is borne in mind that most auction houses settle thirty-five days after sale, the elapsed time between catalogue deadline and final settlement is at least four months. Usually, a consignor will not know when the catalogue deadline for a specific sale is to occur. The motive for consignment and the individual needs of the consignor will not tend to coincide with the sale schedule of the auction house, which is provisionally set approximately six to nine months in advance. If it is thus assumed that a minimum time factor of four months is involved, a broad generalization would allow some two months for a specialist to gather together a sufficient quantity of like material to put out a full catalogue. The process has now reached six months, a figure that can be regarded as realistic, as the average time taken to complete a normal consignment procedure. Major sales in the standard categories tend to take place at least three times a year, but this takes into account the classic windfalls, the highly important single-owner properties which make the headlines. The advantage of becoming involved in what appears to be such a lengthy process is not hard to define. By waiting that span of time, the consignor is assured that his works will receive appropriate attention and will, as a result, achieve the best possible price on the open market. The vast increase in the use of auctions as a selling mode is testimony to the numbers who have considered the matter and come to this realization. They have resolved the conflict between cash today and more money tomorrow by selecting the latter.

Aware of the needs of consignors in individual circumstances, major auction rooms do on occasion advance a proportion of the total estimated value on a property to the consignor. This is done typically on the same principles as those exercised by banks in a loan collateral situation. Advances are usually made only on properties containing several major items. The advance will usually not exceed fifty percent of the low estimate. The auction room will retain the right to control the reserve prices on the whole property and interest will be charged at a competitive rate. The auction house is thus acting as a banker, making a bridging loan, using art property as collateral. Where they vary from the normal bank is in that they have experts who can, with a remarkable degree of accuracy, certify the value and authenticity of the collateral.

TERMS OF PAYMENT
Credit Possibilities for Buyers

The buyer should contact an auction house prior to the sale and request a purchaser information form, unless he is already well-known to the auction house. This form can either be obtained by going to the accounts department counter at the auction center or by application through the mail. This form requires bank and credit references together with anticipated spending levels. Account managers will then check this information and provide the potential buyer with a check acceptance facility, which will permit the buyer to bid up to a certain point, to pay by check and remove property within three days of sale. Each catalogue gives the name of the appropriate financial official to contact for this purpose.

Standard terms require payment within three days in local currency, by cash or a certified check drawn on a bank in the country concerned. Credit can in certain circumstances be extended, but only on application to the auction house prior to the sale, since it is necessary for the auctioneer to gain permission for such extension of credit from the consignor. Failure to pay within the prescribed time may involve payment of late charges, as well as handling charges. Auction houses do not thrive on the storage of sold items.

Buyers in New York should remember that they may be liable for sales tax, unless they have a resale number or leave instructions for their purchases to be shipped to a state in which Sotheby's does not have an office. Such shipment must be by a licensed common carrier with an I.C.C. certificate.

In the case of any particular problem with a sale, the buyer should expect the best assistance from the account manager appointed for that specific sale. The treasurer's office will be able to identify the individual concerned. Both in services to the buyer and the seller, Sotheby's, at least, have learned to create continuing liaison between the financial division and the expert departments. This trend toward decentralization follows a period in which lack of communication and expansion of volume left the customer in some doubt as to whether the auction house even wanted to be paid. The efficiency of the accounts receivable function these days has done much to remove such doubts.

FORM OF SETTLEMENT
How and When the Proceeds Arrive

The standard form of settlement made to consignors of property to Sotheby's is to remit proceeds of sale, less commission and any other charges due, thirty-five days after the sale. While payment will normally be made in the currency of the country in which the sale has taken place, arrangements can be made to make payments in the currency of the consignors' choice and to any bank they wish to nominate. Unusual payment procedures should be arranged as early as possible. Most auctioneers will be unwilling to make settlements in cash, but are willing to pay third party nominees upon written instruction.

Payments to the consignor usually require that the purchaser has paid the auction house. However, if the auction house has already released the property to the purchaser, its settlement is made to the consignor, whether the auction house has been paid or not.

While auction houses disclaim responsibility for the collection of funds from purchasers, they will take reasonable steps short of litigation to collect payment as agents of the consignor and will indeed in rare instances initiate joint legal proceedings against defaulting purchasers, providing the consignor is prepared to bear ninety percent of the costs of collection, the percentage being based on the proportionate interest in a successful conclusion to the litigation.

The auction houses retain the right to either cancel the sale and return the item or to cancel the sale and re-offer the item in a future sale.

Problems regarding settlement should be referred to the consignor account manager. Sotheby's in New York alone conducts over one hundred thousand settlement transactions each auction season and the opportunities for clerical error must be admitted. However, the sophistication of modern computerized equipment has done much to ease the problem of remitting the correct amount of money to the consignor in a timely fashion.

RESERVES AND BUY-INS
Protection for the Seller

The reserve price, or limit, as it is sometimes called, is essentially the lowest price at which the consignor is willing to part with a particular lot, remembering that this will be a hammer price, or gross price, subject to the deduction of selling commission and any other charges not already paid. The uninitiated view the reserve as a suspect mystery, an act of conspiracy to defraud the public and an unfair advantage to the consignor. None of these views show an understanding of the function of the reserve.

The auctioneer, in effect, executes a bid on behalf of the consignor up to a predetermined point. This prevents owners from bidding on their own property in the saleroom, a practice in which they are forbidden to engage under the terms of the contract. The reserve price is deemed to be a protective price and is applied at a level which does not artificially inflate auction prices.

To give an idea of the application of a reserve price, an example may serve to clarify the principle. Supposing that the pre-sale estimate on an item is eight hundred to one thousand dollars, the standard formula for the fixing of a reserve is two-thirds of the median auction estimate. In this example, the median auction estimate will be nine hundred dollars and the suggested reserve price will be six hundred dollars, significantly less than the low pre-sale estimate. This limit will serve to protect the client from the proverbial rainy day, though this event in the auction world tends to lead to an assault of bargain-hunters hoping to take advantage of inclement meteorological conditions, thus creating, if anything, higher prices.

This writer remembers one particularly violent snowstorm, in which the city of New York received some fourteen inches of fresh snow. Two inches of snow cripples urban traffic and a walk to work was indicated. An old master paintings sale was scheduled and this conscientious cataloguer braved it across the wastes of Central Park to announce that the sale would be postponed a day, suspecting that no potential buyers could possibly manage to reach the galleries in the near-blizzard conditions. Angrily assembled in the ground-floor lobby were at least twenty-five dealers, many of them from London, insisting that the auction go on at the published time, so they might enjoy the bargain sale of the century. Recognizing that their motives might not have been entirely altruistic, the sale was postponed for twenty-four hours but eventually took place, in spite of continued traffic chaos. The prices were uniformly above estimate, because the real bargain-hunters tend to be highly competitive.

Practices vary from auction room to auction room, but the major rooms are responsible for self-regulation in the matter of reserves. In the case of Sotheby's, the reserve price never exceeds the high estimate. This does mean that, on occasion, the reserve will be between the low and high estimate. While it could be argued that this renders the area between the low estimate and the reserve a fiction, this does not seem correct when a true understanding of the pre-sale estimate is achieved. As expressed in the catalogue, an estimate is described as "an approximate valuation, based whenever possible, on comparable auction values." Thus the estimate is a guideline as to the value of an item based on previous auction experience and is not, in and of itself, a suggestion of what a prospective bidder will have to pay to buy a particular lot. The auction house is in the business of making money by selling art rather than buying it in, so it is in their interest to keep the reserves as moderate as possible. All items having a reserve are identified as such, though the amount involved is confidential. The following three statements, again drawn from Sotheby catalogues, serve to clarify the auction house's position:

"Lots marked with ■ immediately preceding the lot number* are offered subject to a reserve, which is the confidential minimum price below which such lot will not be sold. We may implement such reserves by bidding on behalf of the consignor. In certain instances, the consignor may pay us less than the standard commission rate where a lot is 'bought-in' to protect its reserve."

"As provided for in the 'Conditions of Sale' and as explained in the 'Important Information for Prospective Bidders,' all the property should be assumed to have reserves. In no case, where a reserve exists, will it exceed the range of estimates quoted. . . ."

"Our standard advice to sellers is that reserves be set at a percentage of the mean of the estimates, generally somewhat below the low estimate shown in the estimate sheet."

The reference to a commission rate in the event of a buy-in points to an important controlling factor. A reduced commission is charged to the owner of an item that remains unsold. This commission, which is negotiable, may be as high as five percent of the reserve price, regardless of the level of the last unsuccessful bid in the room. Thus the consignor, bent on squeezing the last penny out of the potential bidder, should he press his luck too far, may well be faced with payment of five percent of an overly ambitious reserve which on a major painting could amount to a sizeable amount of money. The buy-in commission does much to control consignor avarice.

While only approximately ten per cent of the items offered in major auctions fail to find a buyer, it is worth considering the fate of this minority. It must immediately be recognized that a work of art suffers in reputation by failing to sell. In the vernacular, it "gets burnt." The consignor nevertheless is left with several alternative courses of action. He may offer the item, at a reduced figure, to the "underbidder," who, in most

*See pages 25–29 for examples.

cases, will have been noted by the auctioneer. The lot may be offered for sale privately, most likely to a dealer at a reduced price, immediately following the sale. It may be left with the auctioneer to be reoffered after a suitable period of time; in most cases, at least a year is suggested. On some occasions, due primarily to market changes or different attendance at the auction, an item will fetch more the second time around. Finally, the disappointed consignor may decide to take his tarnished property home to enjoy a lengthy period of convalescence in all too familiar surroundings.

While the actual application of reserves in the auction sale will be discussed more fully in the section devoted to the sale itself, two further forms of reserve should be mentioned at this point.

The "global" reserve is used in the case of a multiple property in which a consignor states that he wishes to receive an aggregate total reserve on the entire property. Individual reserves are then allocated to each lot. As the sale proceeds, the auctioneer applies the overage or shortfall on the first lots to subsequent lots, usually with an agreed limit. For the sake of example, take a property of ten items with an aggregate reserve of ten thousand dollars, or one thousand dollars each. Should the first lot realize twelve hundred dollars, the auctioneer may sell the second lot for eight hundred. A limit may have been set, however, so that if the first lot sells for two thousand dollars, the auctioneer may still be prevented from selling the second lot for less than five hundred dollars. In this latter case, the auctioneer will be said to have "fifty percent discretion." When a global reserve is in use, the order in which the lots appear in the catalogue assumes heightened significance. This system is often applied in the case of the estate dispersal, where the last thing in the world that an executor wants is to have a few items remaining unsold and thus unsettled. The second form of reserve to be noted is the discretionary reserve. In this instance the consignor allows the auctioneer a percentage discretion to lower the reserve on any item in a multiple property up to, say, ten percent, based on how the whole property is selling. It is in effect a more loosely structured global reserve and should only be considered where the consignor and auctioneer have a clear understanding of the manoeuverability involved. This sophisticated approach does, however, prevent unnecessary buy-ins, while displaying a trust in the auctioneer's discretion, which should only be applied in the case of the most reputable establishments.

From the above discussion, it can be seen that setting a reserve at the correct level is an important event in the entire sale process. It addresses the consignor's understandable concern over what he may receive as a result of the complicated transaction. The reserve price is best seen as a joint discussion between the consignor and the cataloguer.

The former will be an expert in his financial needs, the latter will be well versed in the educated guesswork of how the market is likely to react to a particular work of art. The final decision is technically with the consignor, but he should bear in mind that the cataloguer has two potent weapons, namely, the ability to charge that five per cent buy-in commission on the reserve and, a more dramatic course of action, the right to refuse to offer the item for sale at all. In spite of the fact that the auction house makes a profit by selling works of art, there are occasions when negotiations become so lengthy and disadvantageous that withdrawal becomes the better part of valor.

CHAPTER THREE
The Role of the Buyer

COLLECTORS
The Private Buyers

WHILE THERE ARE almost as many different types of buyers as there are lots for sale, they may be categorized broadly into three distinct segments: the private buyer, the museum or institution and the commercial dealer. Each of these constituencies will buy for their own reasons. It may be instructive to analyze them briefly.

Depending on their economic comfort range, the private buyer may be anything from a young married couple decorating their first apartment to a dedicated and highly knowledgeable collector in one particular esoteric field. While they practice at different ends of the auction spectrum, they both have discovered the satisfaction of buying at a fair market price items which meet their needs from a wide range of potential offerings. With a few notable exceptions, private collectors are indulging an avocation rather than a professional full-time commitment. For them, collecting is a hobby. It nevertheless requires the expense of much time in study and research. The collector gains much of his satisfaction from the thrill of the chase. With the passage of time, a notable collector who specializes in one area will gain expertise similar to the dealer's or cataloguer's, through continuous connection with an active market. The buying and selling of objects in an active market not only heightens the collector's awareness of market trends and values, it also allows the collector to upgrade the quality of his collection as his knowledge deepens.

The broad variety of knowledge exposed in the buying public among private collectors has led the major auction houses to a wide group of activities to both educate and aid this private sector. Newsletters, lectures, seminars and published works, including extensive annual reviews, all help to serve the private buyer in his thirst for greater expertise. The rooms also have recently increased the availability of advisory services to these private buyers. The buyer may consult a customer advisory service free of charge. "Account executives" are trained to answer the basic questions themselves and provide a conduit to the cataloguers and other professionals. They will also assist in the execution of bids, questions as to condition and any changes in pre-sale estimates. The private buyer, especially if new to the auction method, is strongly advised to seek out one of these customer service agents in each auction room in which they plan to bid regularly. Buyers may, for instance, give such agents a "wish list" of items they are hoping to acquire. The agent will then inform the client when such an item appears. With the great proliferation in the number of sales, this service can be invaluable to the private collector, who typically has his own job to do during the day.

Taken as a broad group and recognizing that each area produces widely varying statistics, the private buyer accounts for at least fifty percent of auction buying. It should not be assumed that only real buyers are welcome, however. Auctions are free and open to the public so that they provide for the private collector an entertaining method of keeping up with current market trends. Auction has increasingly become a popular spectator sport. In a room seating six hundred persons, it is not unusual for only fifty to be actual bidders. The auction houses encourage this aesthetic voyeurism because it adds to the excitement and theatricality of the event, thereby engendering further enthusiasm and higher prices.

The pre-sale exhibitions provide an ideal learning tool for the private collector. Here he sharpens his skills in identification and qualitative comparison, without having to spend a penny. Again the auction houses expect this; the neophyte of today is the hardened collector of tomorrow. Collecting could be described as a chronic, contagious, terminal disease for which no known cure has been established. Auction rooms harbour vast quantities of this contagion!

MUSEUMS

The Institutional Collector

The institutional buyer, be it museum, library, college or other cultural establishment, serves several functions in the auction market. The institution supplies scholarly academic expertise in its field of endeavor.

It thus helps to identify quality in an area of collecting. These institutions, when properly managed, seek to acquire only the rarest and best examples available. In this way, they set an example in quality. From the point of view of the market, this creates an interesting corollary effect. By acquiring the very best examples as they appear on the open market, the institution withdraws them from circulation in the market, thereby reducing the supply of such items and, by their example, at the same time increasing the demand.

Where a particular field has a solidly finite supply, the effect on the prices in the market place is not hard to guess. A prime example of this phenomenon is provided by the field of late eighteenth-century American furniture. Produced in its most desirable form between 1760 and 1790, this beautiful furniture was manufactured in less than ten centers on the eastern seaboard for a few wealthy householders. Bearing in mind a total population of some two million throughout the country at that time, of whom the vast majority could not afford fine furniture, some idea of the small size of the supply is gained. Today, in a population of over two hundred and fifty million, more and more collectors are appearing with an ability to spend considerable sums of money in this popular field. Most major American cities support museums which actively attempt to acquire a fine representative collection of American furniture. This competitive desire to acquire and display decorative examples of cultural roots and ancestry, coupled with the acknowledged technical skill and artistry combined in these rare examples, has led to recent prices for American eighteenth-century furniture in excess of a half million dollars. With the circumstances described above unlikely to change, the chances seem strong that the present trend in prices will continue indefinitely. The great museums are contributing significantly to this trend. Their role as buyers in the auction market should neither be ignored nor underestimated.

DEALERS
The Professional Art Merchants

The extraordinary knowledge and experience of the reputable dealer places him in a strategic position as a buyer in the auction room. The dealer survives economically on the basis of the accuracy of his judgment. The auction room is for him a supply of marketable property which he must buy sufficiently reasonably to pass on to his client at a respectable profit. His clients will be willing to pay the premium or mark-up on a given item because they are paying for the dealer's knowledge, experience and warranty of authenticity. In a reputable dealer, this premium is often extremely worthwhile, especially to the inexperienced collector. The dealer buying at auction may be buying for stock, speculating, in effect, that he has buyers the auctioneer has not reached or who require more time to consider the purchase, or he may be executing bids as an agent for a collector.

In this latter case, the collector's anonymity is preserved. The dealer's professional advice is rendered with regard to bidding levels, quality, condition and other factors affecting the bid. In these instances, it is normal for a dealer to charge a commission for his services. These commissions vary in the range of two to five percent, depending on the extent of the services rendered and, to a degree, on the value of the item purchased. It is not unknown for a dealer to execute a bid on a highly important item free of charge. The successful dealer in these circumstances may expect considerable free publicity and exposure, which can be advantageous to this business activity.

The commission arrangement also recognizes another factor which should not be overlooked. In executing a bid for a client, the dealer may be eliminating himself from competition with that client on a lot in which both parties have a mutual interest. An intelligent collector would rather pay a small commission to a bidding agent than run the risk of battling with a professional in the auction arena. Active collectors can definitely avoid paying higher prices by preserving anonymity. One has heard of occasions in which dealers have bid against private clients to push them into paying higher prices as a preamble to the suggestion that the private client would be well advised to bid through a dealer on subsequent occasions.

Such coercion, while illegal and unethical, points to a feature of the dealers' skills as buyers in the saleroom. Because every judgment a dealer makes has to be backed by a signature on a check, his knowledge of appropriate bidding levels is likely to be extremely accurate. Thus, the dealer comes to the sale with his catalogue already marked with the levels of price to which he is prepared to bid. He cannot afford to risk getting carried away by the heat of the moment. The private buyer would do well to imitate this sound business practice.

It is fascinating to watch a professional dealer view a sale at auction. The inspection is totally thorough and the concentration remarkable. Every facet of an item is noted and a decision reached on the highest practicable bid. Most of the decisions have thus been reached before the auction begins. A dealer will be ready nevertheless to adjust his bidding according to the observed activity on the day of the sale. Consideration of saleroom tactics belongs in another area of this work, but enough has already been said to indicate that the professionalism of the dealer remains a vital factor in the auction process.

THE AUCTION HOUSE AS A
SOURCE OF SUPPLY
The Ability to Handle Quantity

It is often thought that the major auction rooms sell only Impressionist and old master paintings, with an occasional sale devoted to inordinately expensive jewelry. This myth is sustained principally by the publicity generated by these highly visible areas of interest. However, the reason many buyers come to the auction houses is the wide variety of works of art offered in every conceivable area and the extraordinary quantity of works appearing regularly in each specialization.

The international auction rooms sell in some forty different categories, ranging from Ming pottery to antique dolls, from Rennaissance bronzes to jukeboxes, from paintings by Titian to sculpture by Duane Hanson. When it comes to defining works of art for sale, auctioneers take the broadest view. They do so because there are buyers out there clamoring for the material and the auction houses are best placed to provide this material in large quantities. The dealer is limited by economics and restrictions in space to the amount of stock that can be held at any one time. The auction house, by acting as agent on a consignment basis, moves the stock through more rapidly and in greater quantities. To give some impression of the volume moved, the Sotheby Parke Bernet Group worldwide in the 1980–1981 season sold over 450,000 lots, many of which consisted of multiple sets of objects. On occasion, a house will extend itself beyond its standard reach. Computers, airplanes and sunken treasure have all in the past been the subject of "fine art" auctions. The opportunity for profit stretches the imagination remarkably. Were the auction rooms to offer the broad range of material submitted piecemeal on a sell-it-as-it-arrives basis, prices would be notably lower and the buying public would never know when or where to find items within their fields of interest.

It is in the specialization of their sales that the auctioneers provide such attraction to the potential buyer. In each category, the buyer is able to view a large number of comparable items at the same time, weighing their merits against each other, arriving at a determination of their qualitative distinctions and generally finding one or more examples which suit his individual taste. The extent to which taste differs remains amazing and plays a role in the choices made at auction. The old adage that one man's meat is another man's poison has never held truer. When a sale goes on view, there is usually a consensus as to which lots constitute the star items, the popular choices as to salability and quality. More surprising is the fact that the vast majority of items will find homes with buyers who have made a free and independent choice to purchase what many would perceive to be unattractive items. There is no accounting for taste and one is reminded that recently a successful sale was held in which the collector's principal theme was depictions of skeletons and skulls. The buyer should, however, be aware that the more esoteric and peculiar the collecting mania, the more speculative the investment becomes. There is the danger of creating a collection so singular that no one else will ever become intrigued, let alone commercially interested.

It is at the top end of the scale of quality that the supply in the auction rooms becomes truly remarkable. In spite of the withdrawal of masterpieces in every field into the permanent collections of museums, extraordinary items continue to appear regularly, to the relief of the auction houses and the satisfaction of their buying public. There is no doubt that the need to raise funds to pay estate taxes and heavy death duties have made it impossible for all but the wealthiest to pass collections on from one generation to another. Besides which, it is generally true that taste changes from one generation to the next. Children do not always share their parents' collecting mania or tastes. It is often in fact the grandchildren who appreciate their grandparents' choice, but they do not usually have the means to sustain such collections in their original form. Thus, the passing of the generations guarantees recirculation of the best works of art and it has been said with accuracy that each collector is after all only a temporary custodian of the treasures in his possession.

EXPERT ADVICE TO POTENTIAL BUYERS
What the Buyer Should Know in Advance

By now it will be apparent that the buyer at auction needs to do considerable homework before actually bidding on his intended purchase. Even before attending the sale exhibition, a thorough reading of the sale catalogue is suggested. Normal habit sees a buyer proceed to the body of the catalogue to determine which of the lots described attract the attention by description or illustration. Before reaching this stage, the wise buyer should familiarize himself with the policies, conditions of sale and other aids offered by the auction house, starting with the expert.

The heads of the various expert departments are usually listed in the sale catalogues. They know more about a particular item in a sale than anyone else. It was, after all, their responsibility to gather the material and describe it correctly. A collector in a specialist area is denying himself an important resource if he fails to become well known to this individual, who can give answers to questions that could not possibly be answered in the catalogue. How does one object compare with another sold last season? What can be done with the flaking condition on this painting? How much will I have to pay to be absolutely certain to acquire that rug? Has this been tested by technical process for age? The expert is happy to answer these and countless other enquiries because he is providing the type of service that will create longterm client relationships. It surprises new collectors how often an expert will say, "Do not buy this or that!" The chance of a collector finding exactly the right item for his specific requirements at the right price in the first sale he attends is practically nil.

Any collector of some years standing who still has his first purchase will presumably continue to hold it mainly for sentimental reasons. The likelihood of this object having the necessary quality for a refined collection is very limited. The ability to admit mistakes and cull upwards in quality is the sign of sophisticated collecting. The auction house expert can offer sound advice when it comes to instigating this personal deaccession policy, which will serve only to enhance the overall quality of the collection which is retained. Museums and private collectors share the need to improve the quality of their holdings at every opportunity.

Having identified the expert to be consulted prior to the auction, a a return to the forepart of the catalogue is urged. The times and places of the exhibition noted together with the hour and date of sale, an enquiry as to the need for tickets, only for the most important sales, may be appropriate and should be made as far in advance as possible. Unless a decision has already taken place in which actual interest has been proven in a definite lot, conversations with ticket distributors may lead to frustration. Some four thousand applicants seek five hundred seats for a major evening sale. New collectors must expect to have to prove their seriousness in a subsidiary gallery, where bidding is easily achieved. The expert will help the novice even in the accomplishment of suitable seating for the sale. Elevation to the inner sanctum of the main saleroom is readily accelerated by significant purchase in a previous sale.

The buyer should be sure to read the sections in the front of the catalogue described as "Advice to Prospective Buyers and Sellers," "Conditions of Sale," "Terms of Guarantee," "Removal of Property" and "Important Information for Prospective Bidders." All segments of this material will be covered in the course of this book, but for the reader's convenience, examples of these are provided in the Appendices. A thorough reading of these statements will lead to questions which for the buying collector are most likely to be answered by the expert heads of the cataloguing departments. Should any questions arise of a technical nature, the buyer is strongly advised to contact the auction house's legal representative on aspects concerning guarantees or conditions of sale; should these questions bear on financial subjects, the treasurer should be consulted before the sale takes place. It cannot be emphasized strongly enough that the bidder in the saleroom should know what he is doing and precisely under what conditions he is acting. Bidding unprepared on impulse may be fine on a twenty dollar item at a church bazaar. The risks at a high-price fine art auction indicate more thorough preparation.

Having acquired a firm grasp of the procedures of the auction house in question, the buyer visits the exhibition and gives his selected items as thorough an inspection as has been described previously. Having isolated the items of personal interest and formed a personal initial judgment as to the appropriate bidding level, reference should be made to the previously selected expert, who is more than likely in the viewing gallery, answering questions and attempting to gauge both the general level of interest in the sale and any frenzied activity, positive or negative, on specific items. The expert will be called on to go through the sale with the auctioneer prior to the auction, indicating the fine nuances of interest or lack thereof on each lot, based on the expert's observation of the view. If the relevant expert is not to be found, a client service representative can be sought out to make contact with the expert. Once identified, the expert should be asked any and all questions necessary to satisfy the potential buyer that he knows all he needs to know to form a rational decision to bid to a certain level on the object of his desire. This exercise may appear to be aggressive and demanding upon the time of the auction house staff, but it is in fact very much part of their function within what is a service industry. Any residual reluctance to take advantage of this service should disappear when it is recognized that the buyer is paying a ten percent premium on the hammer price. The buyer is thus fully justified in claiming the attention of the expert during the exhibition period. The creation of a friendly relationship at this stage will add significantly to the collector's ability to function within his selected market.

The expert's advice on bidding levels may be safely sought, though it must be realized that experts, being human, are interested in selling the lots in their sales. They are nevertheless more interested in gaining the confidence of clients for posterity so that their advice, while not necessarily totally objective, will be essentially sound. The buyer, however, is cautioned to learn to interpret this advice on the basis of his own findings and the opinions of other professionals, which will become more available as the collector becomes familiar with the field of his collecting endeavor. The final decision on bidding level must rest with the individual; the expert is not in a position to evaluate the potential buyer's economic background.

The buyer should never forget that the first principle in purchasing remains what has been termed the psychic dividend. Works of art should be bought for the pleasure they provide the purchaser. All other criteria and factors in the decision, important, and indeed vital, as many of them are, must remain subordinate to that original selection. The buyer should never be persuaded to buy a work of art he does not like personally, regardless of the motives for the purchase. Even those who like to treat art as an investment need to apply this essential fundamental test, for it aids in the establishment of qualitative judgment, without which no purchase should be contemplated.

REPUTATION

Longevity and Fair Dealing

An auction firm is only as good as its reputation. This reputation is based on many factors but can vary rapidly in the face of an auction house's failure to instill in its employees a thorough understanding of the importance of reputation in a service industry.

Length of time in business helps. Several of the leading houses can claim corporate ancestors from the eighteenth-century. Sotheby's, founded in 1744, claims to be the oldest auction house in the world. Christie's, their archrival, began sales twenty-two years later, in 1766. Phillips, the third oldest room, was founded in 1796. It is interesting to note that all these three rooms make a habit of mentioning the year of their foundation in their institutional advertisements.

In America, Freeman's of Philadelphia have the edge in longevity, having remained in continuous family ownership since their founding in 1805. Sotheby's American operation began life in New York as the American Art Gallery in 1880. Five years later, its name was changed to the American Art Association. In 1900, John Anderson started a small book auction room, modelled on Sotheby's in London. And, in 1929, the American Art Association and Anderson Galleries merged. Two employees, Otto Parke and Hyram Bernet left the merged firm in 1937 to form the Parke-Bernet Galleries. Their first sale was held in 1938 and, within two years, they were able to acquire their former employer. In 1964, Sotheby's acquired Parke-Bernet. And both Christie's and Phillips now have New York salesrooms.

Longevity is seen to inspire confidence but, in and of itself, does not in fact guarantee a standard of competence. The reputation of an auction house is in fact only as good as the current standard of operation. As the big houses grow larger, the risk of loss in standard of performance increases. It is in the maintenance of a high quality of personal service that good reputations will survive.

Assuming that this standard of personal service can be maintained, the next most important elements in a reputation are the accuracy of the expertise and the willingess of the auction room to stand behind its descriptions, particularly as they relate to authenticity. The extent to which an auctioneer will guarantee the statements in a catalogue will vary significantly from room to room. Examination of any statements on this subject in the catalogue is essential. The degree of guarantee not only differs from auction room to auction room, but also from one category of art to another. For example, the degree of guarantee in the area of painting will depend on whether the work was created before or after 1870. Paintings created before 1870 are often impossible to guarantee, but become subject to the auction house's "best efforts" as can be seen in the glossary of terms in the appendix. Authenticity in many areas of the fine and decorative arts is often at best a consensus. There can be no final proof that Rembrandt painted a particular subject but, if the leading scholars on the artist agree that in their opinion the work is authentic, such opinion will hold until such time as their scholarship is replaced by either convincing technical testing to prove them wrong or the emergence of new, more respected scholarship.

An auction house which is prepared to stand behind the scholarship of its experts and those outside experts whom the cataloguers choose to consult is likely to retain a more satisfactory reputation than the house which makes no such claim or, even more disturbingly, takes refuge behind the traditional defense of *caveat emptor,* proclaiming that each lot is sold "as is," and that no guarantee, implied or warranted, is intended by any definition or statement within the catalogue. This situation, typical of many auctions which take place under tents or on boardwalks, only offers opportunities to buyers who are convinced that they know more than the auctioneer or any other bidders present.

All the legal waivers, definitions and small print notwithstanding, the reputable auction houses are likely to stand behind their catalogue definitions, to the extent that they would rather take back a misdescribed lot than risk the loss of reputation involved in costly and publicized legal proceedings. The intelligent auctioneer will admit genuine errors with good grace and absorb the consequent loss in income, rather than attempting to recover from a consignor, long since the happy recipient of a settlement check. All the reputable house has to offer in competition is the superiority of its expertise and service to both the buyer and the seller. On the rare occasions that this breaks down, the sooner the reputation is repaired by conscientious remedy on the part of the house, the better.

CHAPTER FOUR

Anatomy of a Sale

THE CATALOGUE

A Most Important Reference Work

**CONDITIONS OF SALE: RULES TO BE STUDIED
BEFORE BIDDING**

As HAS ALREADY been suggested to potential buyers, a thorough understanding of the conditions of sale is necessary before becoming involved in an auction. These will vary from room to room and will even change from sale to sale. If it is possible, the potential buyer will know precisely the conditions under which a particular lot is sold. The catalogue, in conjunction with the published conditions of sale, will do much to inform the customer of his rights and what he should expect on the occasion of the sale. As can be seen from the Sotheby's conditions of sale reproduced in the appendix, these conditions cover a wide variety of matters.

It will be noted that the conditions of sale may be "amended by any posted notices or oral announcements during the sale." Auction-goers should listen carefully to the announcements at the beginning of a sale. Withdrawn lots will be noted by the auctioneer. This will avoid the frustration of sitting in the salesroom for two hours, eagerly awaiting the arrival of a chosen lot number, only to discover that it has been withdrawn. If one is unable to be present at the beginning of a sale, placing a telephone call could prevent this inconvenience. Withdrawal is not a common practice and rarely takes place between exhibition and sale. Items withdrawn by their consignors do not usually reach the exhibition stage of the process. The pre-sale announcements will usually also include a statement to the effect that all lots are sold "as is," a repetition of one of the standard conditions of sale. This, notwithstanding the terms of guarantee, points to an important limit for the bidder. The first condition states: ". . . neither we nor the Consignor make any warranties or representations of the correctness of the catalogue or other description of the physical condition, size, quality, rarity, importance, provenance, exhibitions, literature or historical relevance of the property . . ." This statement is followed by a cardinal rule for bidders, which cannot be emphasized sufficiently: *PROSPECTIVE BIDDERS SHOULD INSPECT THE PROPERTY BEFORE BIDDING TO DETERMINE ITS CONDITION, SIZE AND WHETHER OR NOT IT HAS BEEN REPAIRED OR RESTORED.*

In the event that a bidder is making a bid on the basis of an illustration in the catalogue, it is strongly urged that a telephone conversation take place with a customer service representative who is able to offer professional opinions on all of the factors defined above. While it is difficult to render an opinion on size, the buyer should be aware of the possibility of printer's errors; such facts are better checked than assumed. It should also be remembered that, in the field of painting, for instance, only the painting itself is measured and not the frame, which is probably not the original and is thus subject to considerable variation. Exact measurement can be a major determining factor in the establishment of authenticity.

Continuing a study of the Sotheby's conditions of sale, the second condition refers to a buyer's premium of ten percent of the successful bid price. This premium, which has become general practice among the principal auction rooms, continues to raise considerable opposition from the art and antiques trade. The auction houses take the position that they are acting as an agent between seller and buyer, offering a service to both parties. They are finding a market for the seller and supplying available material to the buyer. In that the dealer is in competition with the auctioneer, naturally hoping to acquire the property as inexpensively as possible, it is unlikely that a premium on the bid price would come as an attraction. The resulting argument continues.

The bidder should therefore calculate an additional ten percent into his bidding limit so that this charge does not come as an unhappy surprise at the time of payment. While this premium does not affect the bidding levels on less valuable property, it obviously does require more careful consideration when bidding on items worth several thousand dollars or more.

The third condition of sale refers to the right to withdraw property from a sale. As mentioned previously, this is not a widespread occurrence and the reasons for withdrawal either by the consignor or by the auction house are more often than not practical or straightforward. For example, the property may be discovered to be incorrectly described in the catalogue. If the error is sufficient to be detrimental to the sale or if it cannot readily be corrected by a salesroom notice and announcement, the auctioneers have a clear responsibility to withdraw the lot. The item may have been significantly damaged or broken during the exhibition. The policy of allowing clients to inspect property physically during the pre-sale exhibition creates such a risk. Withdrawal is then mandatory because, once again, the catalogue description becomes seriously inaccurate. Withdrawal is also inevitable if a consignor refuses to agree to a reserve below the high estimate, because the statement is published that no reserve exceeds this high estimate. And withdrawal will automatically follow the failure of a consignor to return a signed contract of sale. The auctioneer cannot possibly afford the risk of selling an item without contractual approval. It can thus be seen that withdrawal from sale does not necessarily mean that the lot involved is a fake, though this possibility must to some extent affect the reputation of a withdrawn lot. Auction houses do not encourage unnecessary withdrawals and in most cases charge a percentage fee for withdrawal to discourage wanton abuse. This can often arise where a nervous consignor attempts to sell an item privately after the catalogue has gone to press, an unpopular habit with the auction houses.

The fourth condition of sale refers to the fact that the lot numbers in the catalogue are the lots to be bid upon. This confirms that the bidder should know what each lot consists of, in some cases several items or a set. The auctioneer retains the right to adjust the number of items from the figure mentioned in the catalogue. This could happen because an item in a multiple lot had become damaged or was missing or because of an error in the catalogue. The condition also indicates the auction house's lack of willingness to combine several lots or take the lots in an order different from that in the catalogue, two practices to be found in less reputable auction environments.

The fifth condition of sale establishes definitively the auctioneer's right to accept or reject any bid, with total discretion. In the event of a dispute the auctioneer retains the right to determine the successful bidder. In the heat of an auction sale in which lots are being sold in rapid succession, it is possible for two bidders, both believing that they are being acknowledged by the auctioneer, to assume that they are the rightful purchasers. The normal procedure, when this confusion arises, is to reopen the bidding until one bidder drops out. Should a dispute of a similar nature arise after a sale, the auctioneer's decision remains final in that he supplies the name of the buyer to the sale clerk who maintains the sale record. In most auction rooms, a buyer will be asked to fill out a "bid card" immediately after each lot is sold. If this is seen to be the practice and if a bid card is not brought to one who presumed himself to be the successful bidder, enquiries should be made to the sale clerk or one of the bid-spotters immediately, rather than after the sale. Auctioneers much prefer to reopen a disputed lot when all those interested are still present. Prevention being better than cure, it is important to ensure that an auctioneer has seen a bid and acknowledged it. However, if paddles are used, bid cards are not. This matter will be more fully addressed when techniques in bidding are explored.

The auctioneer is empowered to reject any bid which he believes lacks validity. He may doubt the seriousness of the bidder, as when a six year old child waves at him. More often, however, the auctioneer may be in possession of facts regarding the bidder's ability to pay for a purchase. The salesrooms are open to the public and provide immediate limelight for the adventurous spirit, so it is occasionally necessary to recognize that a bidder is acting under false pretenses. Staff from the accounting departments are specifically trained to handle such circumstances with a minimum of embarrassment to those concerned. In the discretion achieved by this condition of sale, it is possible for the auctioneer simply not to acknowledge the bidding signal from one who has gained notoriety and finds himself on the auction room's "no-bid list."

This condition of sale also contains a caveat regarding bids by telephone. This service, offered as a convenience to absentee bidders, is liable to significant risks of error. Telephones can be temperamental; long distance connections may be severed without warning; and, because of the time lag in communicating the decision to advance the bidding, the auctioneer may simply be moving too fast for the party at the end of the telephone line. Arrangements to bid by phone are made only for major lots and the prospective telephone bidder is responsible for discussing his requirements with the bids department in advance. Recognizing the need for speed, such a bidder should limit his remarks to "yes" or "no" as to his desire to advance the bidding, responding to the bidding level in the saleroom relayed to him by the bids department staff member. This technique of buying is not considered reliable and does not remotely compare to actual presence in the salesroom for efficiency. The warning in these conditions of sale reflects the experience of difficulty in this procedure. However, it should not be forgotten that the world record price for any American painting at auction, the $2.5 (£1,063,830) million paid in 1979 for Frederick Church's *Icebergs* (see illustration), was bid by telephone from Texas.

The sixth condition of sale addresses the situation in which the lot being presented elicits no interest or insufficient interest. It also gives

Frederic Church, ICEBERGS.

the auctioneer the right to reject a particular bidding advance. Should the auctioneer opening the bidding find no response from the bidders in the room, he may "pass" the lot. He will announce this prerogative by saying, "Passed," and the auction will proceed with the next lot. While the increments in bidding are more or less standardized, bidders who may be acting as agents will on occasion offer a lesser advance to respect a limit they have been set or to satisfy their bargain-hunting pride. This can also happen to break a tie. Should two bidders, for instance, both be bidding at self-imposed limits of one thousand dollars, it can be resolved by a bid of one thousand and fifty dollars, rather than the more standard increment of one hundred, which would raise the bid to eleven hundred. The auctioneer retains the right to refuse such advances and will usually make his decision on the basis of the perceived motive behind the nominal advance. In that the speed and rhythm of the sale are important contributions to its successful conduct, the good auctioneer will not allow his audience to gain too much control of incremental advances and will do his utmost to prevent a group of bidders or an individual bidder from slowing down or disrupting the process.

The next and seventh condition speaks to the passage of title and the expectations of the auction house with regard to payment and the removal of property following purchase. The right to title passes to the highest bidder acknowledged by the auctioneer. This moment is normally reached at the fall of the hammer. Title passes once the full purchase price is paid. However, in that the auctioneer retains the right to reoffer a lot in several circumstances, the bidder should not operate under the impression that the fall of the hammer is final or absolute. It certainly signifies that, all factors being satisfied, the highest bidder has the right to purchase the item in question at the price quoted by the auctioneer, plus any further commissions and charges due. The banging of the gavel on the rostrum constitutes the auctioneer's acknowledgement of this right. At this moment, therefore, the *bona fide* purchaser assumes risk and responsibility for the lot. It should be noted that risk and responsibility thus pass some time before the purchaser gains possession of his new acquisition. This fact has important connotations in the event of loss or damage.

The successful bidder may be asked to sign a confirmation slip immediately after a lot has been "knocked down." This confirms the correct identity of the buyer and the price at which his bid was successful. It becomes a vital document in the event of a dispute over who was the successful bidder. It also helps when confusion arises over the actual level of the final bid; memories can become erratic when a purchaser inspects his new property and has a change of heart regarding its desirability. The buyer agrees to pay the full purchase price. Unless special credit arrangements have been made in advance, the agreement to purchase carries with it the understanding that property will be paid for within three days and removed within the same period. A late charge of 1½ percent per month may be imposed together with a property handling charge of 1 percent per month, with a minimum of 5 percent after sixty days. In addition, the auction house retains the right to remove any uncollected purchases to a warehouse at the buyer's expense. Anyone having experience with fine art shippers and warehouse facilities will think seriously before allowing this expensive proposition to become a reality.

Payment is not considered made until actual funds have been collected. In the case of a local check, this obviously does not create any difficulty; a standard three day clearance period is anticipated. But problems arise with the international collection of funds. Buyers with banks in countries other than those in which the sale is held are urged to discuss the mode of payment with the treasurer of the auction house concerned. With interest rates as high as they can be, an understanding in advance can forestall later inconvenience and fiscal pain.

The auction room retains two sanctions beyond the late charges and warehousing costs described above. It may cancel the sale and sell privately to another party or cancel the sale and reoffer the property at a future sale without reserve, in both cases holding the original buyer responsible for the first hammer price, the buyer's premium on the first sale, the seller's commission on the second sale, and the additional costs and expenses on both sales. Thus, an unsatisfactory final price on the subsequent sale will leave the original buyer liable for the shortfall between the two hammer prices. These perfectly reasonable but apparently punitive arrangements point to a fundamental concept in buying at auction. One must be absolutely sure what he wishes to buy, be certain to have inspected the property thoroughly prior to the event of sale and be ready, willing and able to pay the full price plus commissions, under the conditions set forth by the auction house concerned. It is little wonder that many auctioneers operate on a "cash or certified check only" basis. Those who find these conditions onerous would be amazed at the difficulties encountered in collecting payments from otherwise perfectly respectable citizens.

The eighth condition of sale identifies the system for the identification of lots bearing a reserve. The subject has been previously covered in the section devoted to consignors. In all but the most mundane sales, the buyer should assume that there is a reserve but that it has been fixed at a level that will not impair the bidder's ability to acquire an item at a reasonable price. In the Sotheby's conditions of sale, mention is also made of the consignor who is either indebted to the auction house or "has a monetary guarantee from us." In both these cases the auctioneer retains the right to "protect such interests." This, in effect, means that the auction house may place a reserve on items in which they have an interest. On occasion, an auction house will guarantee a proportion of the estimated value of a work of art. Certain consignors are unable, for valid reasons, to commit an item for auction without such a guarantee. As with other special arrangements, the auction room is unlikely to consider adding this risk to its arrangement with a consignor unless the property is highly desirable and of considerable value. The guarantee is not to be confused with the advance, in which a percentage of the estimated value is advanced against the proceeds of sale to a consignor needing immediate cash. The advance is closely comparable to an interest-bearing loan from a bank using the property as collateral. The guarantee, however, eliminates a large proportion of the risk for the consignor and therefore is most likely to be considered by the auction house where a successful sale will involve a larger than usual share in the success beyond the agreed figure.

Before deciding on a final level of bidding, the buyer has already been warned of the need to consider the buyer's premium where it is levied. An additional consideration is raised by the ninth condition of sale, concerning the levying of state and local taxes. In New York the company is obliged to collect New York State and City taxes which create a combined tax of 8¼ percent in New York City. By virtue of the fact that they do business in other states, Illinois and Pennsylvania for example, Sotheby's is also required to collect sales taxes on behalf of some other states. The prospective bidder is strongly urged to discuss his liability for such taxes prior to the sale. Certain classes of buyer, for instance the dealer with a resale number, are automatically exempt from these taxes. Individuals living out of New York State may be exempted, but must have their purchases delivered out of state by licensed common carrier. Buyers with two homes are thus encouraged to resist the urge to pick up their purchases in person immediately following a sale and to arrange for shipment to the domicile in the least burdensome state from a sales tax point of view. Not all sales are subject to these requirements, so the buyer should ascertain the particular conditions in advance. The Andre Meyer collection, sold at Sotheby's in New York in October 1980 was free of sales tax because the consignor was a charitable foundation. The absence of sales tax certainly added to the already considerable attraction of this collection, giving private New York collectors the rare sensation of bidding on a par with commercial and out of state participants.

In London, the V.A.T. (value added tax) applies to all purchases, unless exempt by law. Foreign buyers may have this tax refunded or waived by executing documents which demonstrate the purchases are being taken out of the country. As in other charges and terms of sale, changes occur frequently so it is wise to inquire in advance about current charges and taxes, which will vary from auction house to auction house and from country to country.

The tenth condition of sale places the purchaser firmly under the jurisdiction of the laws of the State of New York and the federal courts sitting in that state. An interesting feature of this provision provides that telephone contact or any other means of bidding constitute willingness to treat the transaction as taking place in New York. As the auction process enters the twenty-first century, this writer enjoys the prospect of lawyers inventing conditions of sale to cope with the bids via satellite from a wide variety of planets and space vehicles not yet under the jurisdiction of the courts of New York. It is assumed that no responsibility would be assumed for errors and omissions due to malfunctioning laser beams or intergalactic traffic jams!

The final condition of sale excludes responsibility for malfunction by carriers or packers of purchased lots, those operations being at the entire risk of the purchaser. The purchaser would, however, be well-advised to seek the advice of the auction room in question as to the name of a reputable specialized art packer and shipper. It is definitely worth the extra cost to ensure that a work of art receives appropriate treatment. The major rooms have shipping or "art transport" departments whose function it is to aid purchasers with these important logistical details.

They should be consulted and will remove much of the anxiety from this often complicated procedure.

PRE-SALE EXHIBITION: VITAL INSPECTION OF
THE MATERIAL

The need to make a thorough inspection of any property before bidding upon it has been previously emphasized. The catalogue is a source of information with regard to the exact hours and location of the public view. This period may last a week or more and will generally last at least three days. In sales of international interest, traveling pre-sale exhibitions may be arranged to give a sale or a section of it wider exposure. Thus, it has become common practice for items to be sold in New York to be shown in London, Hong Kong, Miami and elsewhere, catering to the tastes of the international market. This practice is obviously expensive and therefore only involves the most important items. It is, nevertheless, always worth inquiring about the pre-sale exhibition plans for a major sale.

The pre-sale exhibition stage, apart from affording an opportunity for thorough inspection, also offers a chance to estimate the strength of interest in various items in a sale. Not only will dealers and collectors be available for inquiry and subtle research, but the very tempo of the sale can be prejudged by the atmosphere during the view. It is worth a potential buyer's while to spend some time just "floating" on the exhibition floor.

The departmental experts do this to gauge the interest in a sale. The collector is urged to join the crowd. He may glean some vital information and thus determine to bid or not to bid. Collecting is an active occupation and should not be done from behind a desk with a catalogue. The more total the involvement in the process, the more professional the results.

ESTIMATES: A GUIDE TO PRICE LEVELS
BASED ON EXPERIENCE

The pre-sale estimate has been covered earlier where it relates to the evaluation given to a potential consignor. But prior to the auction, it assumes a different significance. A printed caveat should however be repeated here:

NOTE: AS A CONVENIENCE TO ITS CLIENTS, SOTHEBY PARKE BERNET INC. FURNISHES PRE-SALE ESTIMATES FOR ALL PROPERTY INCLUDED IN THE AUCTIONS. THESE ESTIMATES ARE OUR APPROXIMATE VALUATIONS BASED, WHENEVER POSSIBLE, ON COMPARABLE AUCTION VALUES EXCLUDING THE 10% PREMIUM.

In that these estimates are based on "comparable auction values," it must be realized that estimates in the catalogue reflect activity in a previous sale, which will have taken place at least three months and possibly as much as six months earlier. They cannot therefore reflect completely current market conditions and, of their very nature, must be three months out of date because of the production cycle of the catalogue and the four week circulation period after it is published. The conscientious buyer will, therefore, seek an oral estimate from the relevant specialist department, during the view. Estimates are adjusted as interest is elicited and current market conditions change. To give an example; suppose a Cézanne landscape is listed in an auction catalogue with an estimate of $600/800,000. After the catalogue is printed, a closely comparable work is sold to a dealer at another auction house for $1,200,000 and the dealer then sells it to a client for $1,500,000. These events will modify the original estimate substantially and the department head should have an adjusted estimate available as his auction approaches.

Where an item is either extremely valuable or so rare that no comparables are available, the printed estimate list will contain the cryptic message: "Refer department." Interested parties should, without exception, accept this invitation to at least establish the price range that they should be considering. In these instances, the facts established during the presale exhibition period become vital to the auction house in offering potential bidders reasonably reliable information.

RESERVE: THE PRINCIPLE OF A MINIMUM BID

The final fixing of a reserve may not take place until immediately prior to the auction sale, because a change in either direction may be indicated by the response to an item during the public view. Changes are not made unless considered essential and they will usually be in the nature of a reduction rather than an increase. While some auctioneers can be accused of beating the client down at the last minute, a responsible auctioneer will exercise his judgment in informing the consignor of a desirable adjustment. The object of the exercise is to sell the object, not to buy it back and the professional auctioneer will have a finely tuned ability to determine how a sale is likely to proceed, given all the circumstances obtaining on the day of the sale. The customer is urged to heed such advice and react accordingly, remembering that the high reserve is more likely to prevent a sale than to encourage a high price.

THE ROLE OF THE AUCTIONEER

STYLE, SPEED, PURPOSE, CONTACT
THE PERSONAL TOUCH OF THE AUCTIONEER

It hardly needs to be said that the role of the auctioneer is pivotal to the success of the auction process. All the preparation discussed so far is in vain should the auctioneer not do his or her job effectively. The auctioneer must literally pull everything together and give each lot its best opportunity to achieve the highest possible price.

To the untutored eye, the job of the auctioneer appears to be simple in the extreme. He merely gives out the lot number and waits until his audience has stopped bidding, at which point he bangs down his gavel and proceeds to the next lot. It is not however nearly that simple. Each auctioneer must develop a personal style and this style must be consistent with the image of the auction room and its location.

London auctioneers do not sell in the same manner that New York auctioneers employ. In England, bids are received in the ultimate low-key fashion. In America, the auctioneer continually reminds the room of the price that they have reached. Nevertheless, the neophyte should not expect the indecipherable gibberish of the horse or tobacco auctioneer. In spite of the melodramatic approach of these latter two exponents of the art, they conform to the general axiom that the more noise from the auctioneer involved, the slower the sale. A competent fine art auctioneer will sell an average one to two lots per minute; this will not allow for a large quantity of excess verbiage. Even in the instance of the most expensive items, the time involved in the sale of a particular lot is not prolonged. John Marion, by any standards the leading auctioneer in America, sold the record-breaking Turner, *Juliet and Her Nurse* (see illustration), for $6.4 million in just over six minutes, a million a minute providing a satisfactory "rate of exchange."

There is no doubt that one of the prime tasks for the auctioneer is to keep the sale moving along at a good pace. The sale must acquire a good rhythm so that the bidders are encouraged to enter the bidding smartly and be urged along by the speed of the bids as they are enunciated. There is nothing more depressing than an auctioneer who is selling too slowly. An infectious lethargy steals across the auction room, and the apparent boredom of the auctioneer lulls the assembled company into soggy inertia. This unwelcome situation can be severely exacerbated when the saleroom is a little warm; the effect then rivals the second act of a second-rate opera. Warm, dark and soporific, accompanied by a somnolent monotone from the rostrum, the saleroom assumes the aspect of a waiting room, all excitement vanished. To avoid this disastrous result, the auctioneer must remember that the purpose of his task is to sell the lots in the sale before him as expeditiously and efficiently as possible. His audience should have already seen the material. It is fully described in the catalogue, so that he does not need to give a lengthy description of the item that is assuming its position at the center of the stage. To be sure, it is his duty to check that the item is indeed the one described as the next lot in the catalogue, but this is not the time for a string of superlative adjectives or a doctoral dissertation on the merits of the School of

J. W. M. Turner, Juliet and Her Nurse.

Fontainebleau. Any action which distracts either the auctioneer or his listeners from the principal purpose of the exercise should be taken advisedly. The occasional humorous remark may help to relax a tense saleroom appropriately but a continuous string of off-the-cuff one-liners is not a good idea. Consignors tend not to appreciate a lack of seriousness when it comes to informal definitions of their merchandise. The auctioneer should do everything within his power to prevent bringing the auction to a standstill. Interruptions and unanticipated disturbances put the bidders off their stride and thus are to be kept to a minimum.

One of the chief objectives of the auctioneer in selling is to establish personal contact with the bidders in the room. Eye contact with the individual creates a bond which will literally lead to a decision to continue bidding, not as a result of cajolery but more because of the feeling that the auctioneer wants the bidder to be successful. That this involves salesmanship is not to be denied. The auctioneer must achieve an atmosphere in which he has made this contact with as many bidders in the room as possible and makes it evident that he will help each reach his goal of being the successful purchaser. At the same time, the auctioneer must convey politely to the audience the insinuation that he cannot sit there in the rostrum all day and the sooner the next bid is registered, the better off all concerned will be.

Above all, the auctioneer must retain control of the proceedings. His or her presence must, by definition, be commanding. The apologetic stance is not conducive to successful handling of the gavel. The audience must respect the auctioneer and accept his role as final arbiter. To this end, the auctioneer must be aware of the dramatic ingredients of his role. Auctions have a theatrical element which gives them their appeal and creates what has been called auction fever. The auction houses succeed to the extent that they harness this element effectively without proceeding beyond reasonable limits and thus creating a counter-productive circus atmosphere.

STAGING: AUCTIONS AS THEATRE

As in any theatrical production, the manner of staging has considerable effect on the results. The auctioneer is placed either at center or just to one side of center in a raised rostrum, closely akin to a church pulpit. The auctioneer must be clearly visible and audible to each member of his "congregation." He must also be able to look down upon the assembled participants to aid in establishing his controlling function and to assure him of full visibility of any bidding signals. A highly efficient sound system remains a *sine qua non* for the auction room. Less than perfect acoustics will lead to a loss in the contact with the bidder that has just been described as vital.

Most major auction rooms in America work with a stage. The more refined rooms in London are satisfied with an easel or a table, once more underlining the distinction in style between the two nations. Sotheby's, in New York, have adapted their use of the stage so that it has become a giant turntable. This innovation adds to the drama, efficiency and speed of the process, though this writer remembers the first trial runs when the revolving stage was cranked by hand, creating an alarming wobble in the works of art as they circled into view. The immediate remedy was to have a saleroom attendant stand on the circulating platform, holding each valuable work of art. Unfortunately, these embarrassed stage crew members also wobbled, doing little to ease the apprehension which pervaded the prospective bidders, who became more intrigued with the technical logistics than the works of art on offer. Long since perfected and now mechanically propelled, the revolving stage is here to stay as an auction technique.

Over recent years, the requirements for security and greater visibility in the auction room have led to the selling of many smaller objects through slides projected onto a screen by rear projection. In such areas as jewelry, netsuke, paperweights and other small objects, this improves the efficiency of the sale considerably, without diminishing its dramatic content. Certain items are sold entirely from the catalogue without being placed on view or illustrated by slide, books being a notable example, where no one would consider bidding without careful prior inspection, where most of the bidders are professionals or knowledgeable amateurs and where a stream of volumes most bidders could not see would in no way engender added excitement.

The current advances in technical equipment make it inevitable that auction rooms will soon employ videotape instead of slides and videotape catalogues await only the more general possession of equipment by collectors. It is not hard to envision the collector sitting down after dinner to flip through his latest Impressionist and modern paintings sale video catalogue on his Betamax, inserting his art credit card into his home phone and punching out his bid on a selected lot to be transmitted to a central gallery where his credit will be automatically cleared and a bid executed as cheaply as possible against all competition when the appropriate lot comes up for sale. The technology exists. It is only to be hoped that this buyer of the future will not forget the essential need, emphasized throughout this book, to make a thorough personal inspection of any item intended for purchase or to ensure that a reliable agent has performed this function on an absentee bidder's behalf.

In that auctions contain a dramatic element, it is likely that the true afficionado will continue to prefer to attend his auctions "live." The atmosphere of an auction in progress cannot be reproduced on the screen or over a telephone wire. To miss this element is to forego the thrill of the chase. The auctioneer understands this thrill and harnesses it in the same manner in which a competent actor carries an audience with him. The comparison is valid; the need for such synergy is vital to both professions. As in the theatre, no two houses are the same; no two auctions have exactly the same mood. The auctioneer, however, does not have the advantage of rehearsals and a trial run. He must attempt to score a hit every performance.

THE AUCTIONEER'S CATALOGUE: AN ESSENTIAL RECORD

In order to maintain control of the sale, the auctioneer must have at his finger tips a mine of information, much of it confidential, all of it essential to the immediate task of selling the particular lot. This information will consist of the following: the lot number and the catalogue description in its entirety; the pre-sale estimate; the agreed-upon reserve price; order bids submitted in writing prior to sale expressed by price level and in chronological order of receipt; the name of the consignor of the lot; any adjustments to the catalogue description or estimate after the catalogue has gone to press; the text of any saleroom notice made concerning the lot. The bids and reserve price will be in a confidential code, which will have been memorized by the auctioneer to such a degree that he will think in the code as he conducts the sale, translating in and out of the code as he directs the bidding. Because much of this information is not only confidential, but is generated right up to the time the sale begins, the creation of an accurate auctioneer's catalogue is a full-time task in a major auction house, involving the continual entering of information as it becomes available and a considerable amount of cutting and pasting from the regular catalogue that reaches the buying public.

The purpose of providing all this information gives an instructive insight into the actual role of the auctioneer. It is obvious that the auctioneer must ensure that he is selling the lot number which applies to the item being displayed at a given time. Sales progress by numerical order in all major rooms; the cataloguers have worked to create a rhythm in a sale, aiding the auctioneer in keeping a flow going, as described previously. The auctioneer needs the full description in case any question is raised during the sale itself regarding any part of this description. The more the auctioneer knows about what he is selling, the better equipped he becomes to sell the lot successfully. Since all the bidders in the auction room also have the description, there is no need to repeat it in full when each lot is produced. At this point the lot number itself generally suffices, though the skilled auctioneer will emphasize an important lot by giving the artist or craftsman as well as the lot number, together with the briefest description, for instance, "Lot 42: the Goddard Townsend kneehole desk" (see illustration). The use of the definitive article also aids to define this lot as something special. It is not just another kneehole desk, it is *the* kneehole desk. This technique has to be used sparingly to be effective.

The pre-sale estimate reminds the auctioneer of the price level to be attained on the lot. It will also form the basis of his calculation of the level of the opening bid. As a general practice, auctioneers will begin the bidding at approximately one-third to one-half of the low estimate. This will vary however, in circumstances in which the auctioneer realizes that there is sufficient interest to warrant starting the bidding higher, circumstances which will be discussed during study of the sale process itself.

The reserve price is entered next to the lot description in code, in red, to make this essential information clearly distinguishable from any other bids—the absentee, written-in bids already in the auctioneer's book. The auctioneer will have to execute this reserve against the order bids recognizing that the reserve price is the lowest price at which he may sell the lot. Failure to execute a reserve correctly leads to immediate consignor dissatisfaction and potentially disagreeable economic consequences. A "missed bid" or a "missed reserve" remain classic sources of

The Goddard Townsend kneehole desk.

embarrassment to the auctioneer who regards himself as competent. Too many of these will lead to critical adjustment in a career pattern!

The order or absentee bids are also placed next to the reserve and are executed against the reserve and the bidders in the room. The name of the order bidder is written beside the order bid so that it can be given to the sale clerk in the event that the order bid is successful. Auctioneers will on occasion either announce this name or say, "Sold to the order." Order bids are executed as inexpensively as possible against the reserve or the live bidding in the room. An absentee bidder who consistently finds himself purchasing lots at exactly the top limit of his bid is either an acute judge of the market or is being abused by an unscrupulous auctioneer.

The consignor's name is written in the auctioneer's catalogue primarily to remind him of any special instructions he may have been given by that consignor. It also means that, should the consignor engage in the illegal procedure of bidding on his own property, when it is already protected by a reserve, the auctioneer will be aware of this and take steps to prevent it.

Corrections, saleroom notices and adjustments to the estimates are all entered into the auctioneer's catalogue, for it is the auctioneer's responsibility to ensure that all competing bidders are in possession of the same facts, so that the public auction is conducted on an equitable basis. The business laws, as they relate to auction, clearly seek to protect the buyer so that all enter the bidding on an equal basis. However, no law can be created to impose equal quantities of experience and specialized knowledge on each bidder so that the neophyte is once again warned to recognize that he will be bidding against professionals.

Saleroom notices are only made when absolutely necessary and should be carefully heeded. The auctioneer is obliged to make such announcements when a lot varies materially in any way from the catalogue description. Because such announcements tend to concern the downgrading of a lot, they will often dissuade bidders from entering the bidding. Care should be exercised in being certain that such announcements are clearly understood. On other occasions, additional information will be supplied which will enhance the value of a lot. Additional provenance, statements concerning inclusion in a forthcoming *catalogue raisonné* and other complementary facts may lead to additional bidding. The full possession of all of these facts can be seen to be vital to the proper conduct of an auction sale.

ABSENTEE BIDS: PARTICIPATION IN AUCTIONS WITHOUT ATTENDANCE

The presence of order or absentee bids in the auctioneer's catalogue has just been described. Because of the pressure of business and the limitations of space in the auctioneer's catalogue, these order bids may also be executed by one of three other figures in the auction room. The sale clerk may receive written order bids up until the very moment that a lot is offered. The department responsible for receiving bids and entering the facts in the auctioneer's catalogue may also have a representative seated at the sales desk, executing bids which have either arrived too late to reach the auctioneer's catalogue or which require the exercise of human judgment. This latter situation is illustrated by what is familiarly called the "either/or bid." A client will call and instruct the bids department to buy lot 10 or 12. If the client succeeds on lot 10, then the bid on lot 12 is withdrawn. The amount of the bid may vary so that this could take the form, "Bid $10,000 on lot 10 and $12,000 on lot 12 if the bid on lot 10 is unsuccessful." This illustration is one of the simpler forms of bidding undertaken by the bids department. It would be impossible for the auctioneer to exercise these instructions while conducting the sale effectively, in the light of his already highly complicated function. A client may also instruct the bids department to exercise a degree of discretion, expressed either as a percentage or in the phrase, "one bid over." Quite correctly, absentee bidders assume that the bidders in the auction room itself have come to the sale with a fairly rigid idea of what they are prepared to bid and these limits tend to be at standard increments. Thus a bid of "one bid over $10,000" may be a highly effective bid.

The third potential executor of the order bids other than the auctioneer will be the client services representative, who literally acts as an account executive for individual clients. These experienced personnel are available to any client who requests their help and they will execute specific instructions for their client.

Any of these three categories of personnel may also be executing bids over the telephone for clients who wish to bid in this manner. As described in the section covering the conditions of sale, bidding by telephone has its risks, but it remains a viable option for the absentee bidder who has made arrangements with the auction room in advance.

The standard form of absentee bid remains the written bid, submitted well in advance of the sale to the bid department. Every catalogue contains a bidding form, which can also be obtained independently from the auction house. These bids form a considerable segment of the total bids submitted and auctioneers will execute them efficiently and free of charge, in recognition of the contribution that such bids make to the overall success of a sale.

The bid form does much to clarify the process involved in absentee bidding, especially when the "Advice to Order Bidders" on its reverse has been carefully noted (see appendix). Many of the points covered in this advisory declaration have been touched in treatment of the buyer's role. However, in the context of absentee bidding, these points assume an added significance and dramatically underline the risks involved in not being present at an auction sale in person.

The execution of order bids is offered by an auction house as a service to its clients. Auction houses much prefer to have their bidders participate in the sale in person. In certain areas, notably stamps, coins and books, order bidding has been a traditional form of participation. It is to be noted that the service is free. Auctioneers would face charges of conflict of interest should they charge for this service. The buyer's premium places the auction house in a position of providing such services to the buyer. The exercise of order bids as cheaply as possible imposes on the auction room the responsibility of treating all order bids confidentially and performing this bidding function honestly. Any attempt to take advantage of absentee bidding to inflate the final auction price can only be regarded as unethical and such behavior would destroy the reputation of an auction room rapidly. The auctioneer, as agent, remains in a position of trust. Bids on the book, reserves and bids by telephone and from the saleroom itself must be treated with equal consideration.

The "Advice to Order Bidders" addresses some of the risks involved. No auction room is prepared to accept responsibility for errors or failures in order bidding. Mistakes can occur and are often caused by technical problems with the telephone systems, so that it is reasonably suggested that telephone bids be made as early as possible and that they be followed by letter or cable confirmation. Use of the bidding slips provided by the auction house eliminates some of the risk of misinterpretation or loss, because both the sale number and date of the sale are printed on it. Such bidding slips should be filled out clearly and concisely. It is amazing how badly many bidders write, when considerable sums of money are at stake.

Quotation of the sale number is extremely important, for although the individual may be concentrating on one sale on a day, in frequent cases major auction rooms may have as many as three sales in one auction center, not to mention the various international centers. The suggestion of bidding as early as possible gives the first bidder chronologically an advantage in the event of identical bids. The complication of mail delays can cause disorder when order bidding is left until too late.

"Buy bids," bids in which the client requests that the auction room buy an item whatever it brings, are not accepted by responsible auction houses, because the bidder cannot possibly foresee the potential dangers of this approach. For example, if there are two agents present in the saleroom, each with a "buy bid," where will the bidding stop? This has happened on occasion, producing ridiculously high prices, cancelled sales, annoyed consignors and embarrassed auctioneers. The alternate bids, discussed as "either/or" bids, are perfectly acceptable and work best when the client's first choice of item appears numerically first in the lot order of the catalogue. Instructions on alternate bids must be totally clear and should be discussed on the telephone prior to written confirmation in all but the simplest circumstances.

As the bid form suggests by asking for a bank reference or deposit, if the bidder is unknown to the auction house, credit needs to be established prior to sale to expedite clearance of purchases following a sale. The establishment of credit is not complicated and, once achieved, makes subsequent buying at an auction house much easier.

Successful absentee bidders are informed of their purchases by mail or telephone within a few days so they can make arrangements for payment and delivery. Unsuccessful absentee bidders can either assume that no news is bad news or arrange to have price lists sent after the sale. Establishment of a close working relationship with a member of the bids department in an auction room can do much to eliminate the risks that have been described and give an absentee bidder access to sound professional advice which may not be contained in the sales catalogue.

The absentee bidder should remember that, where an auction house adds a buyer's premium to the hammer price, this premium will be added to the amount bid accordingly. Failure to take this premium into account can cause surprise and irritation when the invoice arrives.

THE SALE PROCESS
AUCTION FEVER: SYMPTOMS AND PREVENTATIVES

In treating the role of the buyer at auction, it has already been emphasized that the wise bidder comes to a sale with a predetermined limit above which he will be unwilling to bid. The lack of such wisdom is the stuff of which auction records are made!

There is no doubt that the combination of the theatricality of the salesroom and the natural human disposition toward competition creates an atmosphere which breeds "auction fever," that condition in which one or more bidders abandon all preconceived ideas and determine to win at any cost. It is for this reason that "buy bids" are not accepted. It must also be conceded that it is this element which not only makes auctions exciting but also creates their reason for existence. People are inclined to spend more at an auction than they would sitting rationally at an office desk or browsing slowly at a gallery. The momentum of an auction is designed to excite the potential buyer and carry him along with the thrill of the chase. The sense that just one more bid will capture the prize presses the competitive bidder onward. The very idea of allowing another bidder to successively run off with an item becomes almost absurd. Auction fever has struck.

Only on the rarest of occasions will a dealer or a professional succumb to this disease, for it tends to eliminate profit margins. The intelligent bidder knows when to stop and does so. In its most violent manifestations, auction fever leads literally to the desire to purchase entire sales, lot after lot. When a buyer shows evidence of bidding on each lot, regardless of value or competition, the competent auctioneer takes immediate steps to prevent the party in question from bidding further. All of this may sound melodramatic and incredible, but the auction-goer should be aware that it can and does happen.

Such aberration should not be confused with the conscious design to eliminate the opposition on a major purchase. The purchasing power of the possible opposition should be considered on every occasion, The Louis XV encoignure by Dubois (see illustration), purchased by the Getty Museum in 1979 for $1,712,088 (£835,165) from an auction in Monaco provides an example. While exact details are not published, it is generally recognized that the Getty Museum has unusually extensive purchasing power in the art market. Indeed, the fear has been expressed that it has so much money that the markets in the areas of interest to the Getty

Museum will become inflated if not exploded by this legendary amount of money. The piece of furniture in question was sold to the museum bidding against an extremely wealthy private collector. The actual price was not important to either party compared to their desire to own the piece. The last bid by a dealer, one who knew the extent to which he could reasonably bid, was in the region of one million dollars. The museum, which houses a superb collection of French eighteenth century furniture, was correct in buying this piece for it added a significant jewel to its crown. It obviously has no intention of turning round and selling. It will not be long before the price paid will seem reasonable; the market for the finest French eighteenth century furniture must be growing at a rate of more than ten percent per annum. But the best advice to one

Lous XV Encoignure by Dubois.

who finds himself bidding against the Getty Museum or its equivalent is to stop.

Dealers also pay what appear to be excessive prices for individual lots. This can be for a number of reasons. The item may be needed to fill the specific needs of a client. For example, this writer remembers a Meissen lemon, sold in the late 1960s for $11,000, which appeared to be a ridiculous price. The dealer who bought it already had one, in less good condition, for which he was asking a significant price. He was in effect maintaining and supporting his own market. In this instance, the dealer also had a client who collected Meissen fruit forms and needed a good lemon. In this situation, the victim of auction fever was the under-bidder. The dealer knew precisely what he was doing.

New collectors with evident purchasing power in a field should guard against the possibility that one or more dealers will bid against them to encourage them either to bid through a dealer or purchase direct from a dealer in the future. A dealer may risk having to buy an object expen-sively to convey this message, which can serve to line his pockets in the future. Even should the dealer find himself the buyer, there is a good chance that he will sell the item at a profit to the underbidder who may yet have a desire to possess the object on which he ceased to bid.

A further manifestation of auction fever is seen when an individual, usually totally without means, comes to an auction as a spectator and, carried away by the atmosphere or possibly in a momentary desire to achieve the limelight, bids on a major item. Flashlights pop, television cameras whir and the buyer appears on the front pages of the newspa-pers. Once again incredible, but it happens.

The lesson remains clear. The potential bidder must decide in advance what he can afford and respect such limit regardless of any and all circumstances in the saleroom. The fact that this advice will continue to be ignored by a significant segment of the buying public is what makes auctions succeed. The competitive spirit is alive and well.

BIDDING SIGNALS: CLARITY VERSUS ANONYMITY

The popular belief exists that one of the major risks in attending an auction is that one who unconsciously scratches his nose will find himself the instant owner of the lot which is on the block at that moment. The spontaneous greeting to a friend entering the auction room is a variant on the same theme.

Clearly, it becomes confusing to an auctioneer if half his audience is either scratching their noses or waving to each other but, by and large, a serious attempt to bid is easily recognized by a competent auctioneer, whose responsibility includes the determination of whether an action is meant to be a bid or not. Hence, the auctioneer will sometimes ask, "Are you bidding?" before accepting a bid. In the same desire for clarity, a good auctioneer will identify the location of the bid being received on a frequent basis, "It's your bid, sir, in the back row seated next to the column," or "It's against the lady in the red hat." Just as it is important for the auctioneer to make eye contact with the bidders to encourage their continued participation, so it is important for a bidder to establish eye contact with either the auctioneer or his delegate, the nearest bid-spotter. In that a bid-spotter places the bidder at one remove from the auctioneer, it is suggested that neophyte bidders place themselves as near to the auctioneer as possible, thus obviating the need for a signal through a bid-spotter.

The signal that one has entered the bidding should be firm and easily identifiable. The traditional raising of the hand or, where in use, the numbered auction paddle is the most easily recognizable signal and renders the auctioneer's task simpler. By its very nature, however, this form of signal announces to the competition that one is in the bidding and leaves the bidder open for identification. The well-known private collector, the dealer or the institutional buyer may have perfectly valid reasons for seeking anonymity in the bidding process. Once the initial bid has been recognized, the auctioneer will be aware of the interest and subsequent bidding can take the more subtle forms of a nod of the head, a wink of the eye, the jerk of a pencil and any one of many forms that have been adopted through the years. Once this discreet but clear form of bidding is started, the bidder is encouraged to remain consistent. Thus, if the signal selected is the wink of an eye, this form of signal should be maintained or else the risk of confusion on the part of the auctioneer is increased. Vocal bidding is not suggested unless the bidder wishes to alter the bidding increment. The auctioneer reserves the right to reject such vocal suggestions, but the bidder should be aware of four situations in which a vocal modification of the increment may have an advantage.

First, when two bidders are deadlocked at a limit of their intended bidding, a lesser increment may break the deadlock and secure the prize. Thus, if the bidding is deadlocked at ten thousand dollars and the previous bid was nine thousand five hundred, it is appropriate to say clearly to the auctioneer, "Ten thousand, one hundred!"

Secondly, the auctioneer will often accept a smaller increment if he has a sole bidder in the room against a reserve price in the book. That last small increment may make the difference between selling or not selling the lot. The seasoned bidder will sense when even the most accomplished auctioneer is struggling against a reserve and take advantage of the situation. It should nevertheless be remembered that, if an item is encountering difficulty in reaching its reserve price, it may either have too high a reserve or there may be a good reason why no one else in the saleroom is expressing any interest in the lot.

The third occasion on which an articulated vocal interruption of the auctioneer's incremental pattern is suggested involves what can best be described as a power play or even a bluff. The auctioneer has started the bidding low and the bidder is under no illusions concerning the probable final price. As the bidding proceeds along its normal course, but before it has gone too far, the bidder jumps the bidding by a significant amount, even on occasion doubling the current level of the bid. This maneuver is intended to indicate to the rest of the saleroom that the bidder in question has unlimited funds and every intention of securing the lot at any price, neither indication being likely to be true in fact. However, the impression gained often discourages hesitant competition and this observer has never seen an auctioneer refuse such a bid. The risk taken in this instance is that the bold bidder might have secured the item for less, but this is generally not the case because the jump is made very early on in the bidding.

The fourth type of bidding adjustment, beloved of professionals and bargain-hunters, is the signal which cuts the bidding increment in half. This is achieved either by enunciating, "Twenty-five," when the logical increment would be fifty, or by signalling a horizontal cutting motion with the hand, as if beheading the auctioneer. This last bidding signal is the preserve of hardened professionals who thoroughly enjoy causing the auctioneer discomfort, know precisely what an item should bring and gain pleasure from demonstrating their ability to refine the auction process. The auction room would be a dull place without these regular adherents. The neophyte, however, will achieve less sympathy from an auctioneer should be attempt to emulate these saleroom antics.

To return to the desire for anonymity, it is clear that an easily identifiable opening signal will destroy any possibility that such anonymity can be retained. The secret signal, a favorite of writers of fiction about auctions, has a place in the auction room, but requires careful preparation. The failure to have such signals fully agreed upon prior to auction, resulting in missed bids, has even led to a considerable lawsuit over a major painting. The auctioneer and the bidder should discuss such signals immediately prior to the sale and should establish ultimate limits to avoid any misunderstanding. The forms of secret signalling run the gamut of human creativity.

A few examples serve to illustrate the imagination brought to bear on this subject. This writer remembers a painting dealer who arranged with the auctioneer in advance that, on the particular lots in which he was interested, he would be bidding as long as he was not in the saleroom. Thus, when an item he wished to purchase appeared, he stood up ostentatiously in front of his competition and left the saleroom, much to their relief. Once the lot had been knocked down to him in his absence, he would reenter the room, to be informed by his smug competitors that he had missed the particular lot. This ultimate of "anti-signals" displays a highly sophisticated understanding of the auction process. However, should it be adopted on a broad basis, the resulting "non-sales" would lose much of their excitement and effectiveness.

Among other signals that have been employed successfully are the wearing of spectacles when bidding and their removal when the bidder wishes to withdraw, the grasping of coat lapels and the crossing of arms. One imaginative customer conducted his bidding by pretending to inspect an antique mirror hanging in the back of the saleroom and at the same time keeping in eye contact with the auctioneer. The secret signal must be easily identifiable and capable of abrupt and recognizable termination. Due to the complexity of most of these arrangements, auctioneers will tend to accept such conditions only in the case of valuable lots. In discussing the role of the auctioneer, it is evident that complicated signals are a less than welcome addition to an already onerous task.

TECHNIQUES OF BIDDING: STRATEGIES IN THE SALEROOM

As with bidding signals, there are as many theories as to the most successful techniques for bidding as there are bidders. Does the bidder come in at the first opportunity to scare away the opposition or wait inactive until the last moment to snatch the prize away from the unsuspecting contenders who have battled their way up from the opening bid? Is it better to sit in the room with the arm stolidly raised, apparently unmoved by the amount of the bid, the identity of the opposition or the blandishments of the auctioneer?

There is no simple answer and the factors which govern the appropriate course of action will vary not only from sale to sale, but from lot to lot. In the normal circumstance, in which the bidder has decided the extent of his interest ahead of time and has set his bidding limit, there is no great advantage in holding back and the quicker the lot is sold the less likelihood there is of another party changing his mind and joining the bidding at the last moment. Those who prefer the technique of joining the bidding at the last moment run the risk that the auctioneer will bring down the hammer slightly sooner than anticipated. This latter form of bidding also negates to a large degree the possibility of anonymity because the late bid will be the bidder's initial bid and he will have to make it sufficiently apparent to be recognized.

Those with considerable experience will adjust their technique to the mood prevailing during the selling of the individual lot. Such consid-

erations as the number of bidders displaying interest, the speed at which
the increments are progressing and the identity of the principal bidders
all have a decisive part to play in the decision. In certain sales strong
bidding by one or more dealers on an item may give private collectors
that needed additional amount of confidence to increase their bidding
or, guided by the dealers' interest, to bid where they had hesitated to
back their judgment as to quality, condition, authenticity or value. In
such instances, the private collector can usually afford to outbid the dealer,
who has to consider the profit he wishes to make and the costs of conducting business.

Those who are new to the auction world might well consider the
possibility of having a professional agent conduct the bidding on their
behalf, either through a dealer, who will charge a small commission, or
through a customer service agent representing the auction house, free
of charge. The dealer's charge reflects his ability to advise the client on
specific bidding levels and the sacrifice which may be involved in not
bidding on the specific lot for his own purposes. The auction house agents,
in reputable operations, are reliable and act in complete confidence. They
cannot, on the whole, become involved in the complicated nuances of
bidding discussed above. They are simply too busy but will do their best
to execute bids as cheaply as possible.

After the initial experience, it will be found that the actual process
of bidding does provide a satisfaction which the enthusiast will be loath
to delegate. Surrogate bidders should only be used when time and geog-
raphy render attendance impractical or when total anonymity is mandatory.

BIDDING INCREMENTS: HOW THE SALE ADVANCES

While the auctioneer has complete discretion over the amount of
each bidding increment, most auctioneers will follow a logical progres-
sion, which involves increments of approximately ten percent. Thus, they
will raise the bidding in increments of ten up to two hundred dollars.
After two hundred dollars, the increment will be raised to twenty-five
until five hundred is reached, at which point the increment becomes
fifty. At one thousand the increment becomes one hundred, at two thousand the increment will increase to two hundred and fifty, at five thousand, five hundred and at ten thousand, the increment reaches one
thousand. This sequence holds good all the way up to ten million and
beyond.

Because the auctioneer has discretion, part of the skill of the auctioneer's role is seen in his ability to vary the pace of the bidding, to
accept lesser increments to encourage participation and to raise the level
of bidding up to the reserve price. As has already been stated, the auc-

tioneer will usually start the bidding at approximately one-third to one-half of the low estimate. However, if there is a plethora of bidding right at the beginning, the auctioneer may increase the increment substantially, to weed out the less serious bidder and in the interests of time. If, for example, there are more than three or four bidders on an item at the opening of a bid of, say, five hundred dollars, an efficient auctioneer will immediately raise the increment to one hundred and keep it there up to two thousand. If the competition is still heavy, there is nothing to stop the auctioneer from raising the increment to two hundred and fifty at the one thousand level, in spite of the general principles enumerated above. It is interesting to note that an opening bid of five hundred will normally indicate a pre-sale estimate of between fifteen hundred and two thousand. Thus, up until the two thousand mark, the presence of several bidders remains logical and reasonable. Should the cataloguing department have underestimated the lot, always a possibility, this situation becomes even more probable. Additionally, increased interest at the opening bid level may well be a reflection of an increase in the market level since the catalogue and the estimates went to press. When this latter condition is persistently present in a sale, with heavy bidding on every lot, the auctioneer has two options which he would be wise to adopt. First, he should commence the bidding much closer to the low estimate, thus preventing the waste of time and effort at the lower level of bidding. Secondly, he should increase the increments on each lot significantly. Auctioneers welcome both these opportunities. Bidding audiences, who are in the mood to spend money, easily become bored and impatient with a rigid auctioneer who solemnly plows along with the standard increments apparently unaware that the sale is so popular that it is virtually selling itself. Such an auctioneer can sometimes be awakened from his lethargy by persistent bid-jumping from the room.

BID-CALLERS: SPOTTING THE BIDS

Most auction rooms employ bid-callers or bid-spotters to assist the auctioneer in identifying bidders. The need for this function depends on the size and shape of the auction room and the number of the bidding public. In that most salerooms did not start as salerooms, but have been converted from other uses, the chances of their being ideal for the purposes of auction are slim. If the room is too long, the auctioneer will have difficulty in seeing bidders at the back of the room. If the room is too wide, the problem for the auctioneer involves continual horizontal scanning similar to that involved in a tennis match and a risk of missing a bid at either extreme of the room. Further to these two endemic problems, it is amazing how often auction rooms contain columns which obviously prevent total visibility for the auctioneer.

The solution is the bid-caller. An employee of the auction room and usually in the major rooms identified by the wearing of a uniform, he is available to call a bid to the auctioneer. In effect, he bids on the bidder's behalf, relying on a signal from the actual bidder. The principal difficulty arises when a bidder raises his hand, intending the signal to go directly to the auctioneer, and both the auctioneer and the bid-caller pick up the signal and execute it. The bidder is then, often unconsiously, bidding against himself, an act of self-abuse with less than happy fiscal consequences. A good auctioneer will make sure that the bid-caller identifies the location of the bid to avoid this duplication.

A practical bidder may very well wish to take advantage of the anonymity gained by bidding through a bid-caller. Should this be the case, it is advisable to sit at some distance from the auctioneer and close to a bid-caller. After attracting attention initially, the bidding signal can be extremely subtle. Over the years, clients will develop a relationship with a specific bid-caller, who will ensure that the client is placed in his or her favorite seat. The bid-callers, in fact, become quite possessive of their clients and the relationship broadens until the bid-caller almost achieves the role of account executive to a particular client, aiding that client in many of the functions necessary to purchase and facilitating such logistical matters as pick-up, packing and shipping. In addition to their function of calling bids in the salesroom, the bid-callers are responsible for the distribution and collection of confirmation cards.

In lesser auction rooms, the bidder should be aware of the distinction between a bid-caller and a bid-puffer or shill. In situations where there is a possibility of confusion between these two functions, the former being legal, the latter not, it is suggested that bidding directly to the auctioneer has certain advantages.

CONFIRMATION CARDS: CORRECT IDENTIFICATION OF
THE BUYER

When paddles are not used, as soon as a bidder has successfully outbid his competition and the hammer has come down, the purchaser will be approached by a gallery attendant, usually one of the bid-callers, and asked to sign a confirmation slip or card. This document performs several useful purposes.

First, signing of a confirmation card to a large degree eliminates confusion and dissension over who was the actual buyer. It is not uncommon for two bidders, sitting close to each other, both to believe they were the successful bidder. This will become apparent when only one of them is asked to sign a confirmation; the fair-minded auctioneer will, at that point, reopen the bidding until one is definitely successful.

Secondly, the confirmation document will identify the lot number and price bid on that lot number. Memories as to exact prices paid have a habit of becoming fuzzy between the auction and that moment at which payment is to be made. The confirmation card, signed by the bidder, can help to establish the facts when such lapses occur.

Thirdly, the confirmation card will indicate the name and address of the purchaser which are then recorded, correctly spelled, in the auction house records. The sale record will record the name; the address is available to the accounts division for later contact if required. Bidders acting as agents can identify themselves as such, protecting their clients' anonymity.

Some auction houses will forego this process in the case of well-established, well-known clients, whom they believe are sufficiently familiar not to require such confirmation. The feeling exists that it is insulting to ask a dealer who has bid for over twenty years to sign for his purchase. The intelligent bidder will realize early that he is protected by this procedure from any claims by another bidder to the lot in question. Any sensitivity should be easily outweighed by the protection afforded. With familiar clients, the bid caller will often fill out everything on the card except the signature. This sensible step takes only a few seconds and can prevent many hours of argument later on. The confirmation card protects all parties and is evidence of an efficient saleroom organization.

THE EXERCISE OF THE RESERVE:
REACHING THE PRE-SET MINIMUM

The purpose and various forms of the reserve, including "global" reserves, have already been discussed. As far as the sale process itself is concerned, the bidder should remain aware that it is extremely likely that a reserve price is in operation. This should not deter one from bidding but underlines the importance of bidding to a set limit. For, in so doing, the bidder will not be prevailed upon to bid artificially high against an unreasonable reserve price. If the reserve has been set reasonably and intelligently, the bidders in the room will normally proceed past this figure without effort. Conversely, if the reserve is too high, the seasoned bidder will watch for telltale signs of distress in the auctioneer's manner: heavy repetition of the price being bid, exaggerated scanning of an unresponsive audience, a break in the momentum and rhythm of the bidding, threats to knock down the hammer and so forth. The writer remembers an auctioneer in London who raised his eyebrows involuntarily when he reached the reserve, an action which soon became recognized by his regular customers. Another auctioneer inserted the words, "sold then at" into his announcement of the increments once he had passed the reserve, which announcement while being factually correct, indicated to many professionals present more facts than the auctioneer intended to convey.

The good auctioneer, in the interests of keeping the sale process flowing, avoids these pitfalls and thus does not allow his audience to identify the moment at which the consignor would be willing to settle, the minimum price at which the item may be sold, the reserve. Arguments have been advanced that the reserve should be announced in advance. This would destroy the competitive nature of an auction sale and can only be justified if bidders were prepared to announce their upper limits beforehand, thus leaving both buyer and seller in possession of the same facts. The notification in the catalogue of the existence of the reserve is mandatory in New York State and is common practice in other places. This warning, in this writer's opinion, goes sufficiently far in consumer protection. The seller has rights which also need consideration.

CURRENCY CONVERSION: AN AID TO THE FOREIGN BIDDER

Sotheby's, in both New York and London, have installed currency converters, which give bidders the equivalent of the amount being bid in various national currencies, such as French francs, German deutschmarks, Japanese yen and British pounds or United States dollars. The converter keeps pace with the bidding, as well as recording the final price. This technical aid undoubtedly helps the foreign buyer, who is having to make rapid decisions in a short space of time. The existence of such a machine is in itself a notable indication of the international scope of the art market, a comment on the frequent participation of the Japanese in the occidental works of art market and a reflection of the importance of considering exchange rates in major purchases abroad. Skillful buyers and sellers will arrange to buy money forward if they predict an unfavorable change in the rate of exchange obtaining in the country where the sale is being held. Major auctioneers can make arrangements to help in this transaction. The currency converter also adds measurably to the atmosphere of a major sale, a factor which did not escape the proponents of its use at Sotheby's.

RECORD KEEPERS: FIRST STEP TOWARD
THE BUYER'S INVOICE

While the auctioneer's catalogue is considered the official record of the auction sale proceedings, the records kept by the sale clerk at the desk beside the auctioneer are a vital element in the sale process. The sale clerk enters the amount of the winning bid, the name of the purchaser and the source of the bid. The source may be the auctioneer, a bid-caller, a customer service agent, a telephone bid, or an order bid from the bids department. Not only does the clerk record this information as the sale proceeds, but also keeps a running total of the sale results. This information is entered on bid sheets which are taken to the accounts division as the sale continues, so that credit may be checked and invoices prepared. This action makes it possible for purchasers to collect their new possessions within minutes of executing the winning bid. Smaller auction rooms may not have either the staff or the equipment to offer this service and it is not unusual for auction rooms to insist that no purchases be picked up until the end of the sale. This has the advantage for the auctioneer of creating a captive audience that might be tempted to bid again while it waits.

The record keeper and the auctioneer work closely together and information has to pass rapidly between them during the sale. An experienced auctioneer will know the names of many of the buyers and will thus give the record keeper the desired information long before the bid-caller has collected the confirming bid card. The experienced record keeper will also come to know a vast array of bidders and thus the task becomes less awesome with familiarity. One of the worst nightmares for a record keeper is to work with an auctioneer who is selling so fast that the record keeper falls behind, thus losing track of the bids and the buyers. This error compounds as the auctioneer continues and the running total drops behind. Newcomers to this task have been known to burst into tears and finally bring the sale to a grinding halt in order to sort out the resulting chaos. Merciful auctioneers will recognize the extraordinary pressure exerted on these unsung heroes and heroines and make sure that they are keeping up with the pace of the sale.

CUSTOMER SERVICE REPRESENTATIVES: HELPING THE BUYER IN THE SALEROOM

The customer service representatives who will be present at a sale are likely to be of two types, the bids department representative and the special client representative. The former will be member of the bids office who will be executing absentee bids received too late to place in the auctioneer's catalogue or sufficiently complicated to require careful interpretation as the sale proceeds. "Either/or" bids or bids with discretion would both fit into this latter category. The special client representative will be bidding for clients who have viewed the exhibition and discussed their bidding intentions ahead of the sale. Once again, a degree of discretion is usually present. Either of these types of customer service representative may receive telephone bids, which have been discussed previously.

One does not have to possess a vivid imagination to suggest the problems which could occur should an auction house attempt to use such representatives to raise the bidding under false pretenses. How does the bidder in the room know that there is anyone at the other end of the telephone? The only possible response to such a question is that a major auction house has a reputation to uphold based on trust and fair-dealing. The auctiongoer should form his own judgement as to the reliability of the auction room he is attending and determine whether or not that employee on the telephone is indeed a *bona fide* customer service agent or an old-fashioned shill in disguise.

The dangers of telephone bidding have been described in previous discussion of advice to bidders. The remoteness from the saleroom and the risk of technical failure far outweigh the advantages of anonymity and convenience. When telephones eventually contain video screens, many of the risks will be eliminated, but this eventuality is some way down the technological road.

THE USE OF PADDLE NUMBERS: POSITIVE IDENTIFICATION OF BUYERS

Most minor auction houses and even major ones make use of a numbered paddle system for bidding. The paddle will usually take the form of a disc of either plastic or cardboard, approximately ten inches in diameter, on which is printed a large and distinct number. The paddle system has several advantages. In a sale in which bidding is by paddle only, every bidder must register with the auctioneer's agent to secure a paddle. Thus the name and address of every potential buyer is recorded at the beginning of the process. Any credit problems can thus be identified before bidding commences. Paddle sales are often conducted on a cash or certified check basis, thereby initially eliminating the risk of bad checks or extended credit. Bidding by paddle makes identification of the buyer much less prone to error. The successful bidder holds up his paddle, the auctioneer calls out the number which he records in his catalogue and the sale clerk takes that number and also records the name under which that paddle number is registered.

After the sale has been in motion for a while, the active bidders and their numbers become familiar to the auctioneer and the process becomes extremely efficient. Regular customers become attached to a specific number and their requests to reserve such a number are usually honored. Paddles are almost universally used at on-premises sales and in tented auctions, where many bidders unknown to the auctioneer are likely to be present. In its very efficiency it is not inconceivable that the day will come in which many more sales will employ this system.

REASONABLE PRICE: HOW HIGH TO BID

In much of what has already been said, the need to bid only to a reasonable level has been emphasized. The auctiongoer has been advised to arrive at the sale with a predetermined bidding limit in mind. How then can a reasonable price be defined? Auctions are made by the fact that people will come to a sale with different opinions as to what constitutes a reasonable price and many of them will be perfectly justified, for the reasonableness of the price will vary according to the motive for purchase.

One who buys for commercial purposes, the dealer, will have to stop bidding at a point where he can still add a markup when re-offering the item in his gallery and be assured of his operating costs and a reasonable profit. A private collector may need a specific item to round out a collection and be prepared to pay a little over the current market value for that item to enhance the overall value of his collection. While the principal motive of the private collector will probably be the enjoyment his collection affords, he would be unwise not to consider the economic factors. Thus, in making a purchase, it is not inappropriate to consider the eventual resale value of an item or a particular area within the art market. Collectors tend to hold their possessions for a lifetime, but their heirs appreciate the formation of a collection which has appreciated in value at a higher rate than the cost of living. The collector who restricts himself to the best possible quality within a field of collecting will achieve this objective. To pay a little over fair market value for a superb item is to act within the bounds of reason.

An institution such as a museum, whose principal interest is to restrict its purchases to the very best quality and which does not have to consider the possibility of eventual resale, can, subject to fiscal capability, afford to pay an even higher price; yet it could be reasonable. Museums rely on visitors for their survival. Visitors come to see the spectacular and the best in quality. It may benefit a museum to invest in such items and outbid the rest of the market. Such purchases were the Velasquez *Juan de Pareja* (see illustration) for $5,500,000 (£2,300,000) in 1970 and Rembrandt's *Aristotle Contemplating the Bust of Homer* (see illustration) for $2,310,000 (£821,000) in 1961. There can be little doubt that both these works have significantly added to the attendance figures of the Metropolitan Museum of Art in New York, which bought the paintings. It is also interesting to note that, should the trustees of the Metropolitan decide to place the Rembrandt back on the auction market today, there can be little hesitation in accepting the fact that it would realize well in excess of ten million dollars.

Thus, when contemplating a purchase at auction, the bidder must be aware of what constitutes a reasonable price in his particular instance.

There is a danger in assuming that all other bidders in the room are operating under the same criteria. In addition to the motives for purchase, the bidder must also consider his own fiscal capability. Historically, Europeans have invested approximately ten percent of their net worth in tangible assets, excluding land and housing. Any one who exceeds this figure should do so only when in possession of particular skills and knowledge, acquired only with the investment of considerable time and energy. It hardly needs to be said that investment in art is usually restricted to those in an economic position of having spare funds to invest. The purchase of art should be complementary to other forms of investment, rather than replacing them.

The ability to discern reasonable price levels and adhere to them is thus a prerequisite in the auction market. By its very meaning, "reasonable price" denotes the careful consideration of all factors before the commitment of funds. The whole subject can be summarized in a single instruction: *Do not get carried away!*

SYNDICATES AND RINGS: GROUP BUYING— LEGAL AND ILLEGAL

To the outside observer, syndicates and rings have a peculiar fascination. Conspiracy, fraud, covert assemblies, mystery, and intrigue all help to fan the flames of possible scandal within the imperturbable framework of the established art market. Some examination of the facts is in order. Distinction should be made between a syndicate, which is legal, and a ring, which is not.

With the ever-increasing rise in the value of major works of art, it is often not possible for a dealer to purchase a lot from his own resources. Hence it is completely logical that two or more dealers should pool their resources and buy a particular item in partnership. This syndication is legal, providing that the partners share in the eventual profit upon resale, in proportion to their share in the purchase. In such an instance, it cannot be claimed that either competition has been eliminated or that the consignor has been cheated of rightful gains for, if it were not for the syndication, none of the dealers involved would have been able to bid. Thus competition has been increased by the presence of a syndicate and

Velasquez, JUAN DE PAREJA. *The Metropolitan Museum of Art, Fletcher Fund, Rogers Fund, and Bequest of Miss Adelaide Milton de Groot (1876–1967), by exchange, supplemented by gifts from Friends of the Museum, 1971.*

Rembrandt, ARISTOTLE CONTEMPLATING THE BUST OF HOMER. *The Metropolitan Museum of Art, purchased with special funds and gifts of Friends of the Museum, 1961.*

the consignor has, in fact, gained additional bids through the existence of a syndicate. A law requiring syndicates to register with auction rooms prior to sale has been the recent subject of testing in the British courts. One can appreciate the benefits of such a requirement in the light of possible abuses in the syndication method, but must also appreciate the resistance on the part of the trade to such a restrictive measure. Dealers are naturally hesitant to announce their interest in a certain lot to an auctioneer before the bidding commences.

The operation of a ring involves the creation of a syndicate with the specific intent of eliminating competition. In its simplest form, the arrangement works in the following manner: A group of professional bidders, acknowledging their common interest in a lot or a series of lots, agree not to bid against each other at the public auction, arranging for one to bid on behalf of the group. In the event that this representative is successful, the group meets after the sale and holds an auction among themselves, familiarly known as a "knock-out." Participants in this second, unofficial auction share the difference between the public sale price and the knock-out sale price among themselves. Thus, the member of the ring who abstains from the public auction and who fails to secure the lot at the knock-out is rewarded, often handsomely, for his abstinence. The losers in this arrangement are the consignors, who will have received less than the price that should be realized in open competition, and the auctioneer, who will receive diminished commission on the sale. While the practice is illegal, it flourishes under certain conditions. If neither the consignor nor the auctioneer knows the identity or value of an object, the ring can operate freely. This can often be the case in a country estate sale. If the property is sold without reserves, the chances of successful operation by a ring are greatly enhanced. If a sale is attended almost entirely by professionals, there being few or no private buyers or institutional buyers, the chances of successful ringing are increased. Certain areas of the fine arts are thus more prone to this practice than others.

One of the chief difficulties in controlling, not to mention eliminating, this illegal activity is the extreme unlikelihood of ever proving the pre-existence of such an arrangement. The agreement to enter a ring is always made informally and orally. There are no written contracts and thieves' honor prevails. Knock-outs take place in the neighborhood bar and, if interrupted, assume the appearance of a friendly drink after the sale. On occasion, the more blatant offenders have been known to conduct the knock-out in the back of the actual saleroom, a practice which should make every other bidder aware of the ring's existence and which should hint at the advantage of outbidding the ring, who presumably are not prepared to bid as high as fair market value.

How then does the auctioneer deal with a ring? First and foremost, he guarantees a good mix of private and dealer bidders. Secondly, he fixes reasonable reserves on property to protect items from selling below their value. Thirdly, he lets the ring know that he is aware of its existence. Such remarks as, "Which of you are bidding on this one?" will do much to dissipate any security a ring feels it may have through anonymity. In more extreme instances, advanced techniques may be employed. The placing of a photographer next to the participants in a ring can do wonders in the cause of fair play. Participants in a ring tend to sit together to control the action. A good auctioneer will acknowledge their presence early on. Rings tend to operate in sales where merchandise is commercially saleable, but not first class, merchandise that a dealer can turn over quickly, but which might not appeal so readily to a sophisticated private collector. Bidders should therefore never bid against a ring on the assumption that the item is of the best quality. The dealers are involved in a different market. Nevertheless, they are hoping to buy cheaper by forming a ring and should therefore be watched.

In items of high quality, two factors mitigate against a ring. First, it is highly unlikely that the ring will achieve sufficient solidarity among all dealers present to be effective. This will be particularly true where dealers from several different countries are involved. Secondly, the best protection against a ring is the greed of its individual members. Dealers have been known to enter the ring to eliminate competition and then to send an anonymous agent to bid on their behalf against the ring. Thus there are rings within rings and seldom are they effective in a properly advertised and marketed sale. The best items achieve their true market value at auction in spite of any efforts to eliminate open competition and, the new price level once achieved, the same dealers who have attempted to form a ring will race back to their galleries to raise the price on their stock to levels they were seeking to prevent in the saleroom. From the auctioneer's point of view, one of the most entertaining features of this phenomenon is the reaction which occurs when members of a ring get their signals confused and start bidding against each other. Needless to say, they cannot object if the auctioneer receives both bids and yet strenuous efforts have to be made to correct the situation, without giving the game away. At this point it is fascinating to watch an industry regulate itself. With all that has been said about rings, a subject which intrigues the public, it should be understood that ringing is neither omnipresent nor effective in the conduct of reputable auction sales. It adds to the spice of less well-regulated auctions at which the old adage must apply: *caveat emptor!*

TERMS FOR BUYING

BUYER'S PREMIUM: AN ADDITIONAL CHARGE TO CONSIDER

Most major auction houses now charge a buyer's premium. In Europe this premium varies, but reaches its highest point in Amsterdam, where it is sixteen percent. This charge, common practice in Europe for a long time, has created considerable opposition both in England and the United States. The principal source of disquiet is the professional dealer, who has two concerns. By reducing the selling commission, the auction house can offer terms which are more competitive with the dealer's cash offer. By placing a buyer's premium on the hammer price, it is costing the dealer more to purchase his stock at auction. The buyer's premium is usually ten percent. This obviously is a large enough amount that it should be carefully considered in bidding.

Much has been made of the disadvantage this premium gives the dealers. Nobody likes to spend more money or to encounter more competition. In New York, at least, the dealer had always enjoyed an advantage over the private buyer in that the latter, if a New York resident, was subject to a sales tax, from which dealers are exempt. The private buyer, resident in New York City, now faces surcharges of eighteen and a quarter percent on the hammer price. It is interesting to note that the private sector has accepted this as inevitable and has presumably adjusted its bidding accordingly.

Once one auction room had instituted the buyer's premium, it became only a matter of time before the others followed, in spite of comments likening the charge to a return to the Stamp Act. Cries of "Never!" had to be swallowed when the economic reality became apparent.

Competition for property dominates the art market. Both dealers and auctioneers cannot conduct business without property. In charging a buyer's premium of ten per cent, the auctioneer was enabled to reduce the seller's commission dramatically, if not totally. While it is impossible to make a profit as an auctioneer on a commission of ten percent, it is possible to succeed at a combined commission rate of something less than twenty percent, provided one is conducting his business effectively. Prior to the introduction of the buyer's premium, auctioneer's selling commissions ranged from twenty-five percent on lesser property to around eight percent on major property. With the buyer's premium, commission to the seller is a maximum of fifteen percent on lesser property, is reduced to ten percent as the norm and becomes negotiable on any major property. Because the price achieved at auction may well exceed any offer that a dealer can profitably make, it is not hard to understand the dealer's reluctance to accept the buyer's premium. However, a vindictive and punitive campaign to eliminate the auction function might well destroy the very function which allows the dealer both to find sufficient material and to charge competitive prices for it. The interdependency of the two constituencies has already been noted. A solution to the existing animosity may well be found with a further reduction of selling commission to the dealer, who already has an advantage of six percent in most salerooms.

The economics of running an auction room dictate that the buyer's premium or its equivalent is here to stay. As the costs of doing business rise, a service industry dependent upon skilled staffing for its successful operation and the maintenance of its reputation will face inevitable rises in costs. The salary bill alone for a major auction room accounts for millions of dollars each year. The need to expand continuously to meet such demands increases with the concomitant necessity of controlling expenditure. A service industry is particularly vulnerable to the economic forces which create such conditions. The buyer must remain prepared to contribute in exchange for the convenience of being able to use a source of supply for his collecting which makes more material available on a regular basis than can possibly be located privately.

ESTABLISHMENT OF CREDIT: A NECESSARY PRELUDE TO BIDDING

While the traditional mode of payment for the auctioneer has been cash on the barrelhead, this sound principle of stewardship tends these days to apply to the less stable practitioners of the profession. On-premises sales conducted out of town, on Sundays or in a tent cannot afford to offer the same sophisticated credit facilities as an Impressionist sale on Bond Street. Just as a successful sale requires sellers, so indeed does it require buyers. The more bidders, the higher the price, the more successful the sale. Thus, it is to both the consignor's and the auctioneer's advantage to extend reasonable credit to a potential buyer.

Any bidder who is unknown to an auction house would do well to establish credit in advance. This could be as simple as giving the treasurer of the auction room a bank reference and establishing the limit amount for which that auction house is prepared to accept a personal check. To achieve this, it is not necessary to identify interest in a particular lot, but it will expedite the process of collection of the purchase following the sale. Failure to establish such credit in advance will mean that the auction house will retain the item purchased until the check has cleared. This is not a complicated process within the city of the purchaser's residence. Check clearance in New York City, for instance, usually is completed in three banking days. The problem becomes more significant with out-of-town and international clearance, which can take

three weeks or more, leading to considerable frustration for the purchaser who has not established credit in advance. A banker's or cashier's
check can prevent much or all of this inconvenience.

Most auction houses demand payment within three days of purchase. Customers should realize, however, that arrangements can be made
to extend this period for reasonable cause. The important factor is to
make those alternative arrangements. The auction house will usually make
payment to the seller after thirty-five days. This period between the three
days given the purchaser and the eventual settlement date to the consignor gives the auction house floating capital, which obviously can earn
interest. It also allows the auction house to extend credit to its buying
customers. Such decisions are made on an individual basis and may well
involve charging interest, but the availability of such credit can on occasion make the difference between a decision to bid or not to bid. A competent dealer is thus placed in the position of being able to buy on credit,
speculating on his ability to turn around and resell his purchase at a
profit within the period of the allotted credit. The auction house in this
situation is acting as a banker to the dealer, but is also assuring itself of
a higher price and thus, presumably, of a higher commission.

Another form of credit exists and is available mainly in cases of major
property, often from estate consignors, who may not need to receive the
entire proceeds of the sale immediately following the sale. Often, extended
credit may be sought and given by the consignor to encourage fuller
bidder participation. An example will clarify this mode of credit.

A major collection of French eighteenth century furniture and decorations comes to auction, worth, say, fifteen million dollars. The major
private collectors, museums and dealers are universally interested in purchasing from the sale. A private collector decides that three items in the
collection, estimated at half a million dollars each, belong in his home,
but has difficulty in producing one and a half million dollars between
the time he views the exhibition, two days before the sale, and the time
in which payment should be made, within three days of the sale. This
collector can go to the auction house and indicate his interest in the three
lots. If they are all from the same estate, he will not have to specify them
individually. If they are from different consignors, he may have to identify the specific lots. The auction house will then contact the consignor
and offer the consignor the opportunity to extend credit to this potential
buyer. The terms which are often suggested in this procedure are for
payment to be made in three parts, thirty, sixty and ninety days following the sale date, with interest charged at the current bank rate. Thus,
the collector in question makes three payments of half a million dollars
plus interest each, is given time to raise this money and has the satisfaction of acquiring the three items. Quite clearly, the auction house will

encourage such arrangements when they lead to increased bidding on important property. Most consignors, when not pressed by immediate cash needs, will share the auctioneer's enthusiasm for heightened sale prices and will readily accede.

The establishment of credit can be seen to aid both buyer and auctioneer in the smooth transition of property. A few moments spent in advance of a sale can prevent days or even weeks of frustration later on.

SALES TAX: CONSIDERATION OF LOCAL TAXES

Potential buyers should be aware of the possibility that they will have to pay sales tax in addition to the hammer price and the buyer's premium. The conditions of sale will indicate in general terms whether or not sales tax is being charged. The New York Sotheby's sales catalogues usually contain the following condition:

Unless exempted by law, the purchaser will be required to pay the combined New York State and local sales tax or any applicable compensating use tax of another state on the total purchase price. The rate of such combined tax is 8.25% in New York City and ranges from 4% to 8.25% elsewhere in New York State.

Not only do such taxes vary from state to state, but from country to country, so that it is strongly urged that a prospective buyer ascertain the local situation before bidding. Exemption from such taxes is usually extended to dealers holding a resale number and in the case of a sale for charitable purposes. Thus, the Andre Meyer collection, sold at Sotheby's in New York in October 1980, was not subject to New York sales tax because it was the property of a charitable foundation.

Some or all of these taxes may be avoided by buyers from out of the state, but, to prove non-residence, it is necessary to ship purchases by licensed common carrier out of the state. Buyers with more than one residence in different states should consider which residence offers the least tax burden. Because of the existence of operations in several states, such as Illinois and Florida, Sotheby's may well be obliged to collect state sales tax on purchases made by residents of such states. Once again, it becomes clear that a potential buyer should seek a statement from any auction house where he intends to bid, clarifying the situation.

CHAPTER FIVE

Further Services of the Auction House

WHILE THE PRINCIPAL FUNCTION of the auction house remains the sale of fine art property at auction, the skills required for the operation of an auction house can readily be applied to other services in the art world. The larger rooms compete with each other to provide the fullest possible service to the art collector and in certain cases imagination appears to be the only boundary. This section is intended to cover the more logical extensions of the auction houses' business but it should be remembered that, in their desire to win new clients, the auction houses are anxious to respond to any of the collector's needs and to offer advice as to where help can be found, should it not be available from the auction house itself.

APPRAISALS

The art of appraising comes naturally to one who is suitably qualified to put together an auction catalogue. The making of an evaluation for whatever purpose is but the expression of an opinion and the opinion is only as good as the expertise of whoever makes this evaluation. A pre-sale estimate is thus seen to be an informal appraisal with the limited use of conveying to both the potential buyer and seller the range of value that an item can reasonably be expected to bring in normal saleroom circumstances. In the auction world, these pre-sale numbers are known as "estimates" to distinguish them from appraisals, which can take several forms, but are not directly related to a sale. The values placed on items in a formal documented appraisal will vary according to the spe-

cific purpose of the appraisal, a purpose which should be clearly understood between client and appraiser before the individual expert or experts
arrive on the site to make their inspection. Most appraisers insist on a
form of contract (see appendix), which will demand clarity as to purpose. The reasons for having the purpose of the appraisal clearly defined
will become apparent as the different forms of appraisal are described.

In seeking the services of an appraiser, whether from an auction
house or a professional appraisal company, the collector is advised to
observe certain precautions. Appraisal has become a highly specialized
business. Gone are the days of the gifted generalist appraiser who will
enter a collector's home and appraise everything from the Remington
bronze to the Remington electric razor. The collector should ensure that
the appraiser is qualified in the particular field or fields involved. A
number of years experience is desirable and it should be recognized that
a broad collection may require several different experts, a factor which
will probably affect the cost. Appraisers should be prepared to list their
qualifications and give references to past satisfied clients. If there should
be any hesitation, such references are worth pursuing.

Because the appraisal business has no official licensing system,
membership in professional organizations may help in determining an
appraiser's qualifications. However, potential clients should be advised
that belonging to a professional body does not necessarily indicate that
the member intends to subscribe to the particular code of ethics published by such an institution. In America, the principal appraisal organizations are the Appraiser's Association of America (A.A.A.) and the
American Society of Appraisers (A.S.A.). The latter group requires an
examination for qualification as a senior member, but the standards of
knowledge required for the examination are far from rigorous. The writer
knows of an appraiser of American furniture who was given the examination in European paintings as a result of a clerical error. Not wishing
to waste his journey, he settled in and wrote the paintings examination,
passing it with no difficulty. The Appraiser's Association requires pro-
posal and seconding by two existing members, followed by payment of
dues. It can be seen that membership in these bodies is not an uncondi-
tional guarantee of quality in appraising. The reputable auction houses
not only contain a wide choice of qualified appraisers; they will also
be willing to recommend appraisers in fields in which they have no
specialist.

Having ascertained that the appraiser is indeed qualified to render
an evaluation, the collector should be aware of the minimum requirements for an appraisal description, which are not dissimilar to those of
a catalogue description. However, in normal practice, appraisal descriptions are shorter and are not usually accompanied by extensive lists of

provenance, literature and exhibition history, although much of this information may be necessary to substantiate a particular evaluation. In the interests of practicability, appraisal descriptions will contain an item number, a brief description, notation of any signatures or marks, measurements, weight where applicable, date and country of origin, where appropriate. This description should be followed by an individual value of each item, since groupings of value are of little use in the event of a claim. Each description should be sufficiently detailed so that the item described could not possibly be confused with another. As long as this objective is achieved, unnecessary verbiage should be avoided. In the case of many appraisals, a listing by room location is desirable, so that items can be identified more readily. It is, in fact, considered good practice for an appraiser to describe a room in a clockwise direction starting to the left of the natural entrance. This becomes a little complicated in furniture and decorations, but works well with paintings and other items displayed on shelves and in cases.

The number of copies required of an appraisal should be made clear at the time at which the contract is signed. Collectors are advised to ask for a few extra copies. They cost very little and can be useful in unexpected situations. Executors should certainly be in possession of such a document, to name one obvious example.

INSURANCE APPRAISALS: ESTABLISHING REPLACEMENT VALUE

The most common form of appraisal is at replacement value for insurance purposes, sometimes called "insurance value" or "replacement value." This value requires further amplification, for it is often misunderstood. In this instance, the appraiser seeks to determine precisely what it would cost to replace a particular item with another as closely similar as possible. Given that many works of art are absolutely unique, this opinion is bound to contain a degree of subjectivity. Nevertheless, a qualified appraiser should be able to arrive at this hypothetical value without much difficulty. Put a different way, the replacement value is the price that one would pay if he walked into a knowledgeable dealer's gallery and purchased a totally similar item. This value is relatively easy to determine at the low end of the price scale, where similar items tend to re-appear on the market with a consistent degree of regularity. The problem becomes more complicated at the other end of the market.

What, for instance, would be the current replacement value of Rembrandt's *Aristotle Contemplating the Bust of Homer,* sold to the Metropolitan Museum in New York in the Erickson sale at Parke-Bernet in New York in 1961 for $2.3 million dollars (£821,000)? It is not possible to walk into a commercial gallery and ask the price of a similar item. There are no similar items available. However, a professional appraiser will take the current highest price paid for a similar painting at auction and make a qualitative judgment between the two works, bearing in mind the relative importance of the different artists involved and the logical difference between an auction price and the dealer's retail price, explained earlier in this work. This exercise might bring one in 1981 to a figure of around ten million dollars, which fairly reflects the movement in the old master paintings market over the last twenty years.

In insurance appraisals, a careful distinction should be made between works of art, which usually appreciate, and furnishings which lose value from the moment they leave the showrooms. The eighteenth century carved Philadelphia wing chair (see illustration), whose dilapidated upholstery did not prevent it from realizing $85,000, should be distin-

Philadelphia wing chair.

guished from the overstuffed sofa, purchased for three thousand dollars, and worth not more than five hundred dollars the moment anyone has sat in it. For insurance purposes both items must be valued at retail price or the price at which they were purchased. Collectors should not, however, fall into the trap of believing that this replacement value is synonymous with auction value, thereby gaining the illusion that should they change their minds and submit the overstuffed sofa for auction, they will receive the three thousand dollars the appraiser judged to be replacement value.

Before moving from insurance to other forms of appraisal, a word of warning is appropriate on the habit of overvaluing for insurance purposes. There are those who believe an inflated insurance evaluation will lead to greater satisfaction in the event of a claim. This is potentially true, but the immediate result of this activity is to raise the premium. To gamble on greater gain in the event of loss is to stack the deck against oneself. A further instance of overevaluation is occasioned by what can best be described as "owneritis," a potentially fatal disease in which the collector is incapable of accepting that his particular items are not either unique or the finest possible example available. This disease, whose prime symptom is the question, "What do you think this is worth?," tends to manifest itself in a desire to work with the appraiser, second-guessing him at every item, in spite of the fact that the appraiser has been retained for his professional knowledge and skills. In its terminal stage, the disease will reach the point where the collector's nineteenth century copy of the Mona Lisa becomes the original and the Louvre is credited with possession of an inferior imitation. The need to massage the collector's ego should not be indulged at the time of insurance appraisal. In spite of what has been said on the subject of overevaluation, the vast majority of collections remain underinsured, since most collectors do not keep their evaluations up to date and values are constantly changing, usually in an upward direction. Thus, in an economic climate in which reappraisal is suggested every three years, an insurance appraisal which is over five years old is not only inaccurate but far from effective in the event of a claim.

In seeking to insure works of art, collectors should be certain to use brokers with experience in this specialized field. The major auction rooms are happy to provide the necessary names.

FAIR MARKET VALUE APPRAISALS:
ESTATE AND GIFT EVALUATION

In the United States, any estate containing a significant quantity of works of art will require an appraisal and this form of appraisal is second only to insurance appraisals in demand, no cure having been found for the precipitating event. Tax authorities in most countries require an appraisal at "fair market value," which will be seen to differ, in some instances widely, from the value described above as replacement value.

The Internal Revenue Service in the United States defines this value as "the price at which the property would change hands between a willing buyer and a willing seller, neither being under compulsion to buy or sell and both parties having reasonable knowledge of relevant facts. . ." A discussion of this definition of fair market value will follow, but for the purposes of estate tax appraisals, it should be realized that what the authorities are looking for is a reasonable value.

It has in certain quarters long been the practice to do the client a supposed favor by valuing estate property extremely and artificially low, thereby reducing the estate taxes due. Several factors make this an inappropriate activity. First, such underestimation constitutes tax fraud. Assuming this factor is overlooked, the consequences for the beneficiaries of an estate can be complicated. The I.R.S. has created an art advisory panel, composed of scholars, museum officials and dealers, who examine all tax appraisals of art works in excess of twenty thousand dollars and who accept referrals from regional offices at any value. This advice, together with the readily available current auction records, means that the tax authorities are usually well aware of the range of value of a particular art work. Any attempt to undervalue radically will thus be easily identified. Should the authorities suspect a case of conscious underevaluation, the taxpayer is liable to punitive fines, not necessarily restricted to the fine art property. Thus an entire estate may be penalized on account of an attempt to conceal value in a small proportion of it. The best course, not to mention the ethical one, is to treat the situation as honestly as possible, though no one is suggesting that, in creating appraisals for estate tax purposes, the appraiser is obliged to view the property through rose-tinted spectacles. In considering the evaluation of unique works of art of major value, the appraiser is advised to consider the actual requirements, laid down by the I.R.S. in its regulations. These place a considerable burden on the appraiser and the estate, but skillfully selected comparative material at the early stages can prevent much time-consuming activity either at conference or tax court levels later on. Because the art advisory panel works entirely from photographs, it is suggested that these be professional and accompanied by comparable prices from recent sales.

While the I.R.S. maintains that the panel does not know the particular purpose of an appraisal, seeking only to establish true "fair market value," it should be remembered that the art world is relatively small and the chances of no individual member of the art panel recognizing a particular major work of art in a field in which he or she specializes are minimal. The practice of submitting extremely poor photographs in order to veil the quality of the works of art would on the whole have the adverse effect of warning the panel that the estate is attempting to hide its light under a technical bushel.

Some executors prefer to hold back some of their substantiating material, to produce it as an ace from the sleeve later in the process, when specific demands are made. This assumes an adversary role on the part of the I.R.S., an assumption which, in certain cases, appears to be warranted. This writer, however, believes that the more complete the original appraisal can be, within the bounds of reason, the more likely it is that the tax authorities will take the appraisal seriously. This does not mean, however, that it may not be necessary to conduct further research on individual works, should questions arise. In practice, the I.R.S. would appear to accept the working limitations imposed upon the estate appraiser. Were he to follow the regulations to the letter on every item in every appraisal, not only would it be impossible to complete any estate appraisal, but the I.R.S. advisory panel could not possibly complete its task of review. Meeting twice a year, the panel is faced with a considerable backlog of material for review. Adherence to regulations in detail would make the review process a full-time occupation. The expertise simply would not be available at any price the government is willing to pay.

In that estate tax appraisals are rendered at fair market value either at the date of death or at the alternative date months after that date, the need to have completely accurate current values is apparent, because accurate appraisal can have a direct effect on the taxes due. By its observation of the market place on a daily basis, the auction house is unusually qualified to render such appraisals.

The requirements for capital gains taxes in the United Kingdom are covered by guidelines. As with all matters concerning tax liability, the reader is encouraged to seek qualified professional counsel at the earliest opportunity.

The tax authorities in the United States also require an evaluation at fair market value when property is donated to qualifying institutions for tax deduction purposes. As with the estate tax appraisal, the requirements of the regulations are drafted to prevent fraud and excessive abuse in an area in which the unscrupulous have in the past made monstrous claims. The potential for giving away a worthless painting to an institution in return for a vastly inflated appraisal is popular and has been curbed only by the creation of a reasonable review process in the form of the art advisory panel. Far from perfect though this system might be, the taxpayer may draw comfort from the fact that excessive abuse has been radically curtailed.

In spite of the claim, previously discussed in relation to estate appraisals, that the advisory panel is unaware of the specific purpose of an appraisal under review, it is suggested that, in gift tax appraisals, substantiating material performs a vital function because every penny of tax relief gained relies upon the ability of the appraisal to withstand government review. It is more than ever necessary to place as much information as possible before the tax authorities at the earliest opportunity.

Because of the likelihood of challenge, appraisers are often loathe to undertake these "gift appraisals" and certain informal rules of operation are liable to apply. Sotheby's in New York, for instance, will only perform these appraisals for clients who are already known to them. Further, they will not take on the task unless the institution for whom the gift is intended has already formally accepted the gift. They will only proceed if they are satisfied that their expertise is sufficient in the area in question and, as with all appraisals, insist on a signed appraisal contract before commencing the appraisal. Failure to observe these commonsense rules has, in the past, led to lengthy and sometimes costly litigation with potential donors who have become disappointed with realistic determinations both as to attribution and genuine fair market value. Museums are rightly becoming more particular concerning the quality of gifts which they are prepared to accept and will normally tend to accept only unrestricted gifts.

Reasonable adherence to the regulations is not only desirable in terms of the common good, but also will encourage the government to maintain the program of tax relief for donations to museums, a program which has contributed significantly to the extraordinary growth of museums in America, assuring these institutions of a supply of the very best available on the art market. American donors have a distinct advantage over their international competition, whose best chance is that a gift of a major work of art will be accepted in lieu of death taxes, a rather late opportunity to enjoy the rewards of generosity.

The ability of the major auction rooms to produce extensive substantiating material and their willingness to stand behind their opinion in the face of official challenge make them a natural place to turn for tax appraisals.

APPRAISALS FOR OTHER PURPOSES:
VARIOUS NEEDS FOR EVALUATION ARISE

The need for appraisal at fair market value is not restricted to estate tax and donation situations. A fair market value appraisal is sometimes used by two parties who wish to conduct a sale by private treaty and are either unwilling or unable to agree on a price without the aid of a neutral professional authority. Family division, that process by which a property is divided equally among heirs, either before or after the demise of the owner, is often accomplished by means of a fair market evaluation. Where an estate does not need to raise capital, much anguish among beneficiaries can be eliminated by the creation of a competent appraisal, regardless of the tax implications. The distribution can then proceed in a number of ways, including selection by rotation or a cashless auction in which participants have an allowance up to their proportion of the appraised total. Executors have been known to refine such methods with sophisticated points systems and the major appraisers are prepared to assist estates on these occasions, even should no sale be contemplated, for a reasonable fee.

Fair market value appraisals perform an invaluable function in the matter of estate planning, which is obviously best carried out long before the terminal event. Knowing the current value of a collection can obviate major problems for the professional adviser in estate management.

Division of tangible assets in divorce proceedings also calls for an accurate and up-to-date inventory and evaluation, which can withstand the rigors of often fervid challenge in the courts. Once again the auction house appraiser stands ready to perform an unbiased professional evaluation based on fully current knowledge, independent of any consideration of sale or other disposition.

It could indeed be said that regardless of the particular purpose of the appraisal, from the informal, oral, over-the-counter estimate to the highly detailed, formal, documented appraisal of a major work of art, the auction house is a good place to initiate an enquiry.

APPRAISAL FEES: WHAT AN APPRAISAL SHOULD COST

Auction houses and independent appraisers vary considerably in the manner in which they charge for their services. The two principal approaches that will be encountered consist of a percentage-based fee and a fixed fee based on time and the number of experts involved. The public's natural cynicism when encountering a percentage rate in appraisals has led to widespread adoption of the fixed fee system. While reputable appraisers should be immune to appraising highly for the sake of an enhanced fee and a victim of such practices would be unlikely to return with further business, it must be stated that the percentage fee basis recognizes an important factor, namely, that the higher the value placed on an item, the more responsibility the appraiser must undertake to support that evaluation. Notwithstanding this justification, the fixed fee system has many advantages. A competent appraisal service will be able to determine in advance how many experts will be involved and how long they will take, so that the client will have a clear idea of the expense to which he is committed before the appraisal takes place. The hitherto undiscovered million dollar heirloom will not, thus, leave the client happy, but penniless. In negotiating a fixed fee, an appraiser will usually take into account the nature and value of the property, in addition to the time and number of experts involved. To appraise a Renoir oil worth one million dollars may take an acknowledged expert twenty minutes; to appraise a collection of ten thousand items, each worth one hundred dollars—a collection of buttons, for instance——could take an appraiser six months. The Renoir appraisal will not be charged strictly on a per diem rate nor will the button appraisal fee be based solely on the number of experts involved. Fees are likely to be adjusted to the occasion and should be understood to be negotiable.

In negotiating an appraisal fee with an auction house, where a sale is contemplated, a rebate should be negotiated in the event of sale within a reasonable period. The normal system for rebate in these circumstances is for the auction house to rebate a portion of the appraisal fee, in proportion to the amount consigned. The degree to which the auctioneer-appraiser will be willing to engage in this largesse will be in direct proportion to his desire to obtain the property for sale.

Most appraisers will charge for travel and accommodation and this should not be considered inappropriate, because fine art appraisers may have to travel considerable distances and spend time away from other work. These additional expenses should be negotiated at the time the contract is discussed and can usually be set at a maximum limit. Clients should not be obliged to underwrite the nocturnal whims of the more ebullient members of the appraisal fraternity, but should also bear in mind that appraisers are not hired on a round-the-clock basis and thus may prefer the local motel to an invitation to pass the night in the collector's guestroom, performing as guest of honor to twenty local friends at an elaborate dinner, at which he is expected to value four hundred objects both *gratis* and *in absentia,* in the same manner in which doctors are expected to render free consultations at cocktail parties. The writer recalls one unorthodox appraiser who quoted a reasonable per diem rate, but qualified his quotation with the provision that he would charge an additional fee, if he was required to make conversation or answer questions of a professional nature during luncheon.

Since the appraisal business is highly competitive, a customer should be reassured that the reputable firms are likely to quote a reasonable fee for the services offered. A call to the most obvious competitor will determine whether or not the appraiser of choice has temporarily engaged in commercial optimism.

DEFINITION OF FAIR MARKET VALUE
An Educated Opinion as to Value

The definition of fair market value provided by the I.R.S. regulations, contains the essential elements of what constitutes this sometimes elusive value. It must be remembered, as stated before, that an appraiser is only expressing an opinion and the sales which frequently follow estate tax appraisals demonstrate the vulnerability of opinion when weighed against fact. The concept of fairness between any parties concerned, be they seller, buyer, or tax authority, lies at the foundation of this value. Any attempt to adjust values up or down from a conscientious opinion, based on expert knowledge and reasonable possession of relevant facts, is patently unfair.

The precise nature of the "market" at any given time is not readily grasped. The appraiser who is attempting to consider "all relevant facts" must constantly be aware of current market conditions. These conditions are subject to change on a daily basis, in spite of the fact that the art market tends to move more slowly than other markets. This resilience to economic factors is, however, by no means an immunity; the art market is liable to adjustment in the face of such common twentieth century phenomena as recession, inflation, changing interest rates and the vagaries of foreign exchange. To the extent possible, the appraiser should consider these factors when arriving at his conclusion as to fair market value at a particular time. By being placed at the center of his particular market, the auctioneer-appraiser stands a better chance of having this necessary awareness.

The I.R.S. regulations speak of a willing buyer and a willing seller in the open market. The auction environment provides these by definition. Auction sales being free and open to an international market and dependent upon willing buyers and sellers for their very existence, satisfy the requirements totally. The rule that all parties must be in possession of relevant facts is met by the very detailed disclosures provided in a competently compiled catalogue. As has been demonstrated earlier, any facts not contained in the catalogue are readily available through inquiry to the experts at the auction house.

A further element tends to reinforce the suggestion that auction price meets most effectively the requirements of the I.R.S. definition of fair market value. In reviewing values submitted, the authorities are heavily committed to comparisons with comparable prices. The only records which are available to the tax authorities and the public are the published auction records. The art advisory panel and the I.R.S. are free to consult with dealers at any time, but the very nature of the art trade makes it extremely unlikely that a dealer will make his financial records available, thereby indicating both his cost and selling prices. These facts have traditionally been held to be confidential and the *modus operandi* of the trade makes it likely that this situation will remain unchanged. Thus, if the authorities are using prices obtained at auction to establish fair market value, it stands to reason that a median auction estimate will most truly approximate the elusive fair market value. This does not mean that the appraiser is bound to exercise excessive optimism in an estate appraisal, nor should he be expected to view a prospective gift appraisal in a mood of pessimism. A degree of reasonableness is the key to responsible appraisal; open and notorious greed meets the severe penalties it assuredly deserves. A difference in expert opinion can provide variations of up to approximately twenty percent and this is generally accepted by the authorities. Variations of greater degree can lead to time-consuming confrontations which soon cost more to pursue than the advantage theoretically to be gained.

THE CRITERIA OF VALUE
The 'Ten Commandments' of Value

Having established the principal forms of value sought in various situations, it would seem appropriate to attempt to establish the factors which determine value in the art market. Every market functions subject to its own particular nature and the art market is no exception. It appears to this writer that there are ten criteria, any or all of which may apply in a given situation to a greater or lesser degree. These factors will be weighed, probably subconsciously, by an expert in a field of art in reaching his opinion as to value. In no order of priority, because this priority will change with each item considered, these "Ten Commandments of Value" are:

1) Authenticity	6) Medium
2) Condition	7) Size
3) Rarity	8) Subject matter
4) Historical importance	9) Provenance
5) Fashion	10) Quality

So vital is a full understanding of these criteria to any grasp of value that it is proposed to examine each of these criteria in some detail and to provide specific examples from the last twenty years, to illustrate the validity of each criterion.

1) Authenticity • It is perhaps stating the obvious to remind the reader that a work of art that lacks authenticity will cease to have the value ascribed to it as an authentic work. However, in forming an opinion as

to value, genuineness must be the first consideration. Not only must a work of art be seen to be genuine, but it is necessary that its authenticity can be established with a fair degree of certainty. The appraiser-cata-loguer faces the same dilemma that he confronts in preparing a cata-logue entry. Authenticity may often be a matter of opinion. Value then can depend on opinion.

The outright, obvious fake, the mechanical reproduction, the straight copy are relatively easy to identify and, once identified, to value as some-times interesting, but commercially of nominal worth in the market place. A Van Meegeren fake "Vermeer" has value as a fascinating document of an attempt to deceive the public, but would not command much of a price at public auction, certainly more than a Van Meegeren portrait in his own style, but less than any genuine seventeenth century work by a moderately competent artist of that period. There are those who collect fakes intentionally, but the demand is limited and usually confined to educational institutions who require examples for study purposes. Many a collector has acquired a fake unintentionally and this experience tends to educate informally. The very best fakes are presumably yet to be iden-tified and thus carry the value of their genuine counterparts.

Copies, as opposed to reproductions, can have considerable value, providing they have sufficient quality. Copies have been part of the artis-tic heritage of the world since the first artist-teacher told his pupil to attempt to reproduce one of his works as an academic exercise. In the original and subsequent act of artistic creation there is no conscious attempt to deceive, which may not occur until centuries later, when a scholar becomes over-optimistic in his opinion as to attribution or one with a commercial interest deliberately describes the work as that of the master, rather than the pupil.

Roman copies of Greek statuary have value. Genuine Centennial copies of eighteenth century American furniture have risen remarkably in value in the past ten years. A nineteenth century imitation of an eigh-teenth century French desk by Linke, a highly skilled Parisian cabinet maker, sold at auction in 1981 for $48,000 (£23,188).

In the matter of copies it should be understood that the existence of value will depend to a large extent on the identity and skills of the copyist. A copy of Sir Peter Paul Rubens's *Lion Hunt* by an unknown twentieth century artist will have little or no value, except as a decoration for the wall. On the other hand, a copy of an Isaac Von Ostade village scene by Jean Honoré Fragonard will have more value than a genuine Isaac von Ostade. The New York market saw this situation illustrated well when a copy of Emmanuel Leutze's *George Washington Crossing The Delaware* (see illustration) sold in 1980 for $370,000 (£178,743). The rea-son for this apparently high price for a copy was not hard to establish

Eastman Johnson after Emmanuel Leutze,
GEORGE WASHINGTON CROSSING THE DELAWARE.

because the name of the copyist was Eastman Johnson, who enjoys greater popularity than Emmanuel Leutze.

A careful distinction should be maintained between a copy made with artistic integrity and a mechanical reproduction. In the latter case, quality is sacrificed totally in the interests of quick, cheap, mass production and, in most instances, materials will differ from those used in the original. To take an extreme example, a plastic, life-size reproduction of Michelangelo's *David* should only be of interest to the collector of "kitsch," but it has no artistic integrity and deserves no attention from the serious collector. Many forms of reproduction, less apparently offensive than the above example, are advertised widely as investment opportunities, masquerading as "collectibles" or even as "antiques," a technical impossibility if they are not over one hundred years old. These offerings, in spite of opulent color work and cunning copy in serious art periodicals, should be seen for what they are, an attempt to coax large sums of money from unsophisticated buyers. This writer has recently seen an advertisement for "Antique Forgeries," which were neither antique nor forgeries but reproductions. Clearly, the collector is well-advised to steer clear of this *demimonde* of the less than authentic, and concentrate on what the Coca-Cola Company would describe as "The Real Thing."

If value is to some extent determined on the ability to establish and indeed prove authenticity, the ability to weigh the quality of expert opinion becomes a necessary tool of the appraiser's trade. Certificates of authenticity, discussed in an earlier chapter, are only as good as the knowledge of the authority who signs them. In fact, in determining authenticity, the art market eventually has to depend on the consensus of the leading authorities of the moment. Value is thus directly affected by the current opinions of leading experts, a factor that any one entering the art market for the first time should not overlook.

It will be seen that, in the criterion of authenticity, there is little compromise between the value of the authentic and the fake. This factor provides the collector with the thrill of the chase, with its concomitant agony of error.

2) Condition • For a work of art to retain its full value, it must remain in perfect condition. Even the smallest departure from this state will have its effect. What constitutes perfect condition will vary from one field to another and in some instances will involve active maintenance, as in furniture and silver, whereas in others perfection only will be preserved if the object remains untouched by human hands, as in stamps and coins. The scope of this work does not allow a full description of perfect condition in every area of the fine arts, but a few examples will serve to illustrate the extreme importance of this criterion of condition, when considering value in a work of art.

Old master paintings, usually defined as paintings created before the nineteenth century, are seldom in perfect condition. If one considers the fragility of the various elements which are combined in them, this is easy to understand. The base material, the gesso ground, the delicate pigments of the paint and the various varnish layers all react to temperature and climate in different ways. This inevitable movement will lead to expansion and contraction of the painted surface, blistering and eventual paint loss, unless conditions are carefully controlled, a less than common practice in most collectors' households. When a deteriorating condition eventually declares itself, the collector quite naturally submits the painting to a conservator for repair. Current materials are then added to restore the painting to an approximation of its original condition. However, with the passage of time, the ongoing process of deterioration will continue and the new paint will age and discolor in an entirely different manner from the original. After some twenty years, the restored areas will be totally obvious, because they will have become a totally different color from the original. The percentage of restoration will have a direct effect on the value of a painting, regardless of the location of that restoration. Clearly, if a portrait is involved and the principal restoration occurs in the face, the effect will be more disastrous than if it were in a curtain in the background, but the mere presence of restoration and evidence of past damage will have a profound influence on the market.

Those with limited experience in this area express disbelief that an expert would demand perfect condition in a painting three hundred years old. It is remarkable testimony to the technical skills of the old master painters that this standard can apply, for sixteenth and seventeenth century paintings in perfect or near perfect condition are to be found in the market. Occasionally, an old master painting of great antiquity and in perfect condition will appear in the market and confound the *cognoscenti* by its seemingly absurd high price. Such was Dirk Bouts' *Resurrection*, which sold in Sotheby's London rooms for $3,995,000 (£1,700,000). Dirk Bouts is normally considered a relatively minor follower of Hans Memling. In this instance, he not only surpassed his stereotypical studies of "Christ as the Man of Sorrow," but painted on fine linen rather than oak panel. The combination of this and the fact that the painting had been maintained in ideal climatic conditions through the centuries of its existence led to its continued perfect condition and the extraordinary sale result.

In the realm of furniture, condition remains a vital consideration. With the availability of similar materials, it is possible to simulate almost any condition and the furniture market is notorious for its ability to manufacture convincing fakes as well as to engage in illicit marriages and conversions to upgrade the appearance of a particular piece. Every square inch of a fine example must be scrutinized and any hint of the irregular must be followed up with extreme care.

An interesting comparison can be made between two apparently similar pieces from the Goddard Townsend workshop in Newport in the last quarter of the eighteenth century. One kneehole desk (see illustration p. 86) sold in May of 1980 for $250,000 (£120,772), having previously sold at the Lansdell Christie sale in 1973 for $120,000 (£48,979). A second similar desk (see illustration) sold in 1983 for $687,500 (£450,000). While the first desk would appear to be in better condition, the reverse is the case, since the second retains its original patina. The first desk has been completely refinished, having been painted over in white lead enamel paint during the nineteenth century.

A certain amount of wear is expected in furniture; the patina of the years is a distinct advantage. Perfect condition remains such an elusive quality in furniture that it assumes the greatest importance in establishing the value of the finest pieces.

Both in European and Oriental porcelains, condition plays a vital role. The presence of the finest hairline crack can reduce the value of a major piece by fifty percent or more. The collector in these areas can ill afford to compromise in the matter of condition and those responsible for auction catalogues must be consulted, if any doubts are present. In preparing a catalogue entry and creating a sale estimate, the cataloguer

The Gibbs Family Chippendale block-and-shell carved
mahogony kneehole dressing table.

will be most cautious concerning condition because a failure to make a
correct assessment is likely to promote the return of an item by a dissatisfied purchaser, an event which leaves everyone concerned unhappy.

Particular care should be exercised in the area of silver and other
precious metals, because skillful repairs and alterations can be all but
impossible to detect. Hallmarks may be false, engraving may be added
or removed and shapes can be radically altered. Silver will deteriorate if
left uncared for, but overzealous cleaning will lead to inevitable wear
and so a compromise must be reached. Items should be inspected closely
for any hint of alteration or repair, any presence of soldering or damage. Early silver has a quality about it which survives the effects of normal wear to be expected in metal over the years. Comparison with modern
silver will quickly lead to an understanding of this point.

Works of art on paper, such as drawings and prints, are susceptible
to numerous forms of damage and lose value quickly if their condition
is questionable. Tears, stains, foxing and fading, all take their toll on the
value. Repairs can be highly effective and a magnifying glass may be
necessary to establish a particular condition. There are specialists in the
conservation of works of art on paper who, through bleaching and other
methods, are able to restore works which one would assume to be lost

without hope. Condition assumes an enormous significance in the area of prints. Any departure from perfect condition can be catastrophic to value and he who aspires to print collecting needs to be thoroughly grounded in the techniques before presuming to judge the actual condition of a work. As in all areas, there is no substitute for regular consultation with an acknowledged expert in the field.

These few examples make it clear that the criterion of condition can have a major effect on value. In each field it is vital to learn what constitutes good condition and to accept little compromise. Bad condition can sometimes be checked or reversed to some degree. It is never possible to return an item to its original perfect condition, which fact accounts for the premium registered when such a condition is encountered.

3) Rarity • While the importance of good condition in any art object has been appropriately stressed, there are occasions when extreme rarity will lead to unusual value, in spite of less than perfect condition. Examples of this situation occur regularly in the auction rooms and in most cases the prices realized astound both cataloguer and public because the very rarity of the object makes it unlikely that anything similar has been sold in recent auction memory. Three examples serve to illustrate the importance of this criterion of value.

In 1973, Elizabeth Seton College in Yonkers, New York, requested sale estimates on a series of old master paintings, most of which were in poor condition and considerably over-painted. However, before leaving, experts were shown a cabinet, which contained a small blue and white bowl (see illustration). Appearing to be eighteenth century oriental export

The Medici bowl.

ware, no great excitement was felt, because it was quite worn and slightly lopsided. However, in turning the bowl over, an activity no art expert can resist, an unusual mark was seen. This mark revealed the bowl to be one of a few examples of late sixteenth century European porcelain, created for the Medici family, still in private hands. The Medici bowl realized $180,000 (£73,469) at auction. No other piece has been seen on the auction block since. It is interesting to note that it had been purchased by the gentleman who gave it to the college, along with his house and other property, in 1916 for $200 (£42). Under one hundred pieces of Medici porcelain survive and the great majority of them are already encased in museums.

A lady brought a small carving, which she believed to be in wood, to Sotheby's office in London. Inspection by an expert soon revealed that this "wood" carving was, in fact, ivory. There are plenty of ivory carvings to be found and this one was not in perfect condition. However, when it was established that it was in fact a Carolingian ivory carving, of the ninth century from Aachen, the minor damages sustained over eleven centuries assumed less significance and the plaque, measuring 7½ inches, was sold for $471,750 (£255,000) in 1977, a remarkable testimony to the rarity of this intriguing object.

In one of their regular Heirloom Discovery Days, occasions upon which a group of experts will visit a community and offer informal oral appraisals on individual art objects to benefit a local cultural institution, Sotheby's experts encountered the dagger (see illustration) illustrated here. This dagger, made of sheep's horn and copper, was correctly identified as a Tlingit work, from the Indian tribe of that name in the Pacific Northwest. Had the dagger been found in its native British Columbia, it is possible that it would not have been permitted out of Canada. However, this heirloom discovery day took place in Scarsdale, New York, and thus the dagger could be consigned for auction without inhibition. The rarity of such pieces on the market accounts for its significant price of $72,000 (£30,638) in 1979. The fact that similar pieces are readily accessible in museums does not alter the fact of its rarity in the market, which combined with its remarkable quality, contributed to its value.

Caution should be observed, however, in the matter of rarity, for it is possible for an item to be sufficiently rare that it falls outside the realm of collector's interest. Should there be any hesitation in a specialist's ability to identify an object due to its extreme rarity, difficulties can arise. Such was the case with the bird form pectoral (see illustration). Most experts were prepared to accept its antiquity; most were agreed on its quality. The problem which arose was based on a lack of consensus as to its origin. Was it or was it not Egyptian? So rare as to be unique, the riddle which hung over its identification proved its undoing in the auc-

Tlingit dagger of sheep's horn and copper.

Pectoral bird pendant.

tion event. It failed to find a buyer during the auction, a classic example of being too rare. However, several months after the sale, it was purchased by a prominent American museum, where it is on exhibition in the galleries of Egyptian art.

A converse example, illustrating the need for some rarity, is seen in the small terra cotta oil lamps of classical antiquity. They can be as much as five thousand years old, fully authentic and in perfect condition, and yet one hundred dollars would be a fair price for one. The reason for this apparent anomaly is that, each time an archaeologist digs a spade into the desert, another one hundred of these oil lamps pop up like seed potatoes. The total lack of rarity thus negates any other criteria of value. Familiarity with a specific field will soon lead to knowledge of what constitutes rarity within it.

4) Historical Importance • Items of historical interest do not always conform to any classic definitions of works of art. They nevertheless are sold at fine art auctions and will be classified in a variety of ways: documents, memorabilia, ephemera, etc. Distinction should be made between the item whose only value resides in its historical importance and that which, while being historically significant, has intrinsic artistic value. The former category would include President Abraham Lincoln's opera hat and the binoculars which accompanied him on the fateful visit to Ford's Theatre; the latter category is well represented by Jean-Antoine Houdon's sculptured marble bust of Benjamin Franklin (see illustration), created from life during the statesman's stay in Paris. The $10,000 (£4,545) paid for the hat and the $24,000 (£10,909) paid for the binoculars in 1979 have nothing to do with the values of one hundred year old hats and antique optical equipment. The value resides in the historical significance of these two examples, which is utterly dependent upon the possessor's ability to substantiate the historical connection with convincing documentation. The historical value of the Houdon bust adds to the already considerable value based on artistic merit. Were the bust to have been of similar quality of an unknown eighteenth century French gentleman, the value in 1976, when it was sold, would have been approximately thirty thousand dollars. However, because the sitter is unmistakably Benjamin Franklin, this particular Houdon bust sold in the bicentennial year for $310,000 (£180,232). Thus, in this instance, nine-tenths of the value lay in the work of art's historical significance. The danger of assuming that any or every Houdon bust is subsequently worth in excess of three hundred thousand dollars is apparent. It is this writer's belief that American historical items will tend to have greater value than comparable European material. The reasons for this are straightforward. America's history is comparatively short and thus there is a limited sup-

ply of historical material. Secondly, America's staggering growth in population, coupled with its extraordinary wealth and the consequent willingness, desire and ability to collect, render the demand for historical material much stronger than in European counterparts. Thus it would appear that the criterion of historical importance adds a form of assurance to the collector of art. While in no way negating the attraction of the purely historical object, it seems worthwhile considering the added value of an art object, which not only pleases aesthetically, but will appreciate at a significantly greater rate because of any genuine historical association it may have acquired.

A further distinction should be made between the Houdon bust of Benjamin Franklin and a hypothetical Houdon bust of a French gentleman, once owned by Benjamin Franklin. This becomes a matter of provenance and does not have as great an effect on the value of a work of art. As will be seen when the criterion of provenance is discussed, the effect of ownership can be considerable, when the owner has outstanding importance. The form of the historical association will vary and must be carefully analyzed. A posthumous depiction of an event or a personage will have minor value compared to one that is contemporary with

Marble bust of Benjamin Franklin by Jean-Antoine Houdon.

the event. A portrait from life has more appeal than one created at third hand.

In other instances, the precise contribution to value made by historical association can be hard to quantify. For example, silver made by Paul Revere commands a higher price than silver of equal quality created by his contemporaries. How much of the $64,000 (£27,234) paid for a Paul Revere coffee pot in 1980 can be attributed to a midnight ride in which this patriot announced to sleeping New Englanders that the British were coming?

It cannot be emphasized strongly enough that historical importance is only as significant as the proof thereof. Family hearsay being notoriously inaccurate and optimistic, it is not sufficient that an ancient great-aunt claims on her deathbed that George Washington slept in the very same piece of equipment. Should she possess a letter from George Washington thanking her for her hospitality and should that letter transpire to be genuine, then the bed will have an enhanced value. In general terms, a genuine historical association can only benefit a work of art and thus such associations should encourage the collector in his pursuit of the worthwhile.

5) Fashion • The tenets of fashion are likely to have some influence on the value of any work of art. The motives for the purchase of art will vary but so long as the collector has the intention of allowing others to view his possessions, he will, to some extent, be swayed by what he thinks these observers might like to see. Enter fashion. Even the specialized area in which the collector engages his passion will be the subject of fashion and current trend. Occasionally, a leader will appear and set a new fashion in collecting. William Randolph Hearst in America, in building his dream castle, San Simeon, and filling it with baroque furnishings, set a style. In the nineteenth century, Sir John Eastlake, who initiated the National Gallery in London, made collecting of old master paintings fashionable. The difference between these two is that the taste for old master paintings has flourished while Hearst's baronial pretensions have lost their charm for the modern collector and his remarkable domain is viewed principally out of curiosity.

In seeking to establish the effect of fashion upon value, the appraiser is placed in the difficult position of judging to what extent fashion is responsible for current market value. He has, in effect, to form a judgment as to the lasting value of an object. To accomplish this, it is necessary to look at past performance, compare it to current price and then to project any trend into the future. An instructive comparison can be made here between two different fields of collecting, both of which have seen spectacular rises in value during the last ten years, namely Tiffany glass and American eighteenth-century furniture. Until recently, the world record in price for these two categories was identical, $360,000 (£173,913). A Goddard Townsend chest and the spiderweb lamp by Tiffany (see illustration), both sold in 1980, reflect ultimate quality in their respective areas. The question the appraiser must address is which of these objects is likely to be most valuable in the year 2000. It is this writer's belief that the majority, faced with this decision, would opt for the Goddard Townsend chest, because it would appear to have a more lasting value. This decision must be guided by the vagaries of fashion and assumes that while Tiffany glass is currently very popular, it is less likely to remain so than eighteenth century American furniture. It so happens that the market has recently reacted in a manner which vindicates this hypothesis, because Tiffany glass suffered what is euphemistically described as a price adjustment in the autumn of 1980.

Sudden price rises can often point to a change in fashion as can sudden price declines. In the jewelry business, the diamond market will observe an unpredictable change in fashion with regard to a particular cut. Emerald cut diamonds will overnight lose popularity for no apparent reason and be replaced by pear-shaped examples. Fashion is the logical explanation, although supply may also play a part. The astronomic

Spider web lamp by Tiffany.

rise in French Impressionist paintings from 1958 to 1968 might have been ascribed to a change in fashion in collecting in that period, which coincided with the taste for fine French eighteenth-century furniture. The two styles appeared harmonious and the wealthy vied for the best examples of both. However, a study of both these markets will reveal that the values for the best examples have continued to rise steadily until today and that the markets are behaving in a similar manner to the more conservative fields, such as old master paintings. A Wall Street analyst sees only one percentage point distinction between Impressionist and old master paintings over the last ten years. It may thus be posited that Impressionists have risen above fashion and have themselves become "old masters" with the passage of time. To observe the effects of fashion in the area of paintings, it is more appropriate therefore to look at the truly modern painters of the 1960's and beyond. Here, indeed, taste may change, though it should be remembered that the best examples of any period will continue to be collected as a record of the development of art in a country's cultural history. Andy Warhol's *Soup Can* (see illustration) will remain important for it signified all that was happening in the New York school in the early 1960's, a period in which New York led the international art scene. The cynical should not forget that, in the seventeenth century, the royal family in England collected works by an

Andy Warhol, Soup Can.

out-of-fashion, bankrupt, contemporary Dutch artist, whose collection was sold at auction to meet his heavy and continuing debts. His name was Rembrandt. It should also be pointed out that until a French collector named Thoré Burger revived interest in his work in the nineteenth century, Jan Vermeer of Delft had become a totally unknown artist. When his previous champion, Jan Dissius of Delft, died at the end of the seventeenth century, his Vermeers were sold at auction in Amsterdam for nominal sums, even for that date. Fashion may thus have an influence on even those areas which today's observer would regard as immutable. Nevertheless, rapid price growth does not necessarily denote the action of fashion. Activity in the area of nineteenth century American paintings has been intense over the last ten years, but this may not be wholly attributable to fashion.

Edward Hicks, the Quaker coach painter turned naive artist, left an accurate method of determining movement of price in this particular area, for he painted no less than sixty-three versions of his popular subject, the *Peaceable Kingdom* (see illustration). Given some variations in

Edward Hicks, THE PEACEABLE KINGDOM.

condition, size and the number of animals depicted, the similarity is sufficient for comparisons of sales to lead to valid conclusions regarding the
performance of the market. The figures speak for themselves:

1959 $8,500   (£3,035)
1973 $65,000   (£26,530)
1978 $125,000 (£62,500)
1980 $270,000 (£130,434)

No one would seriously deny that American nineteenth century
painting is currently fashionable. However, it may be argued that the
historical nature of the subject matter, be it figural or topographical, the
dwindling, inelastic supply and the burgeoning demand of both museums
and private collectors make it unlikely that prices will do anything but
increase in the foreseeable future. Notwithstanding this last example,
both the appraiser and the collector would do well to consider this flighty
criterion of value. The chic and the trendy may not in the long run
prove to be the most satisfactory and the serious collector should ponder
more worthwhile values than the superficial popularity of a current fad.

Fashion may well dictate the most advantageous location in which
to sell because taste differs quite considerably from nation to nation. An
auction house expert will be able to offer advice in this area; observation
of the market in action makes such trends readily apparent. For example, post-impressionism finds favor in Japan and abstract expressionism
is popular in West Germany. Such factors could well influence a decision
to sell appropriate paintings in more than one location. Expert guidance
in the selection of the sale location is essential and can prove rewarding.

6) Medium • The medium, or material, in which a work of art is
created, will have a considerable effect upon its value. While rarity will
often account for the desirability of a given material, durability may also
be a factor.

Thus, in the realm of the fine arts, an oil painting will tend to be
more valuable than a watercolor, a watercolor more valuable than a
drawing and a drawing more valuable than a print. On the basis of supply, it stands to reason that an artist will produce fewer oil paintings than
watercolors or drawings and that he will produce many more prints
because they usually come in multiple editions. On the basis of durability, pastel drawings are generally the least popular of all media, because
they react badly to climatic changes and are easily damaged by contact,
regardless of steps taken to "fix" them appropriately. But the appraiser
must beware of creating rigid formulae. No sooner is the principle established than a pastel by William Merritt Chase of *Gravesend Bay, Gloucester*,
(see illustration) sells at auction in 1981 for $820,000 (£396,135), consid-

erably in excess of a typical price for an oil by the same artist. Such exceptions do not invalidate the rule, but once more point to the fact that the criteria of value will operate in different proportion in each instance. In the case of the Chase, most of the criteria, except for its medium, showed it to be a truly remarkable example and, most important, its quality was second to none.

Study of other areas will reveal consistent patterns with regard to values in different materials. In European, English and American furniture, the type of wood employed will have a profound effect on value. The same basic design but manufactured in mahogany, oak, maple or pine will have vastly different values, to state the principle in its simplest terms. The rarer the material, given an equality of craftsmanship, the more likely it is that the object will have greater value. The pine forests of New England guarantee that furniture in imported mahogany is accorded greater attention in the market. It is difficult to discern whether mahogany has a greater aesthetic appeal, but the collector is subconsciously conditioned to believe that this is the case. Correct analysis on the basis of medium in furniture obviously becomes more complicated when the appraiser is confronted with the more elaborate confections of the eighteenth century French *maîtres ébénistes,* where many different materials were employed, especially in the finer examples of marquetry. Why, for instance, is red lacquer preferred to black lacquer? One has to

William Merritt Chase, Gravesend Bay.

assume that collectors prefer the color red to the color black, a reasonable assumption. Why then is green lacquer less popular than red? One has to continue to assume that red is the most popular of all colors in lacquer.

Having thus established a preference for the color red, attention turns to the jewelry world, where it is discovered that emeralds are more sought after than rubies. One is forced to conclude that, having established the relative value of a work of art by medium, one must then examine the distinct characteristics of the criteria within a specific field. If jewelry collectors prefer green and furniture collectors prefer red, could it be that collectors of Meissen prefer yellow-ground ware?

The danger in pronouncing broad generalizations is evident. The need to establish the relative values of different media remains. Study in detail of each market will elicit the necessary guidelines.

7) Size • The factor of size affects value in works of art principally in its extremes. Connoisseurs deplore the attitude of the buyer who walks into an auction room or commercial gallery and demands a painting of particular dimensions to accommodate the gap left between the mantelpiece and the ceiling. However, in considering the purchase of a work of art, it is necessary to take into account its intended location. A tapestry that is ten feet high cannot be suitably displayed in a hall with eight foot ceilings; a carpet measuring twelve feet by eighteen feet will not happily occupy a ten by fourteen foot floor space. Cabinet paintings, small drawings and miniatures do not satisfactorily fill the walls of large drawing rooms, unless they are amassed in great quantity and, even then, the effect of their detail is lost. Appraisers must consider size in weighing comparative values, not only from the point of view of practicability but also in relationship to the normal output of the artist or craftsman and the expected proportions in the field involved. As with all the criteria considered previously, hard and fast rules of operation are dangerous, because in certain areas magnitude accounts for increased value, whereas in others the degree of miniaturization can be of consequence in creating enhanced value. Size is no barrier in top grade gemstones, while miniaturization tends to increase value in objects of vertu and Fabergé, where craftsmanship is at a premium.

The field of old master paintings once more provides an interesting comparison between two works which span the extremes. Beyond a certain size, paintings will usually decrease in value because of the limited number of locations suited to their display. The average private buyer will be eliminated from the competition to acquire any painting whose longest measurement exceeds approximately six feet. By the time allowance has been made for suitable framing, the six foot dimension will have increased to eight feet and that takes care of many ceiling heights in average homes. Thus, the Rubens *Adoration of the Magi* sold by the Westminster Estate at Sotheby's in London in 1959 and measuring 12 feet 9 1/4 inches by 8 feet 1/4 inches, without the frame, was not likely to attract extensive bidding by private collectors. At this size, it is natural to presume that the bidding would be restricted to major institutions and, more specifically, museums or dealers acting on behalf of museums. The Rubens was bought by a dealer, Leonard Koetser, on behalf of a private collector, Major Allnatt, who originally intended to give it to the National Gallery, but gave it eventually to King's College, Cambridge where it now resides, forming a reredos to the high altar. The price of $825,000 (£275,000) established a new record for old master paintings and, in this instance, the extreme size contributed to the value. Almost needless to say, the quality had to be superb to maintain competitive interest at this price level.

By comparison, supreme quality and condition may overcome the problem created by lack of size, as evidenced in a small, fifteenth century painting, *St. George and the Dragon*, measuring 5 5/8 inches by 4 1/8 inches attributed by Sotheby's to Hubert van Eyck and sold for $660,000 (£250,000) in 1966 to the National Gallery in Washington, which now ascribes the work to Rogier van der Weyden (see illustration). Regardless of the apparent indecision as to attribution, understandable for a work of this period, it is the very detail of the miniaturization which makes this work so attractive. There are those who even doubt the existence of Hubert van Eyck and yet the quality of this work demanded a price not far below that of the massive Rubens, though allowance must be made for the advance of price levels in the old master market in the seven years which separated the two sales.

These two exceptions illustrate how supreme quality, even in extremes of size, will overcome the logical dictates of the criterion of size, one best applied with liberal doses of common sense. The appraiser with experience recognizes that art cannot be valued by the square foot, any more than land. One square mile of the Mojave Desert continues to be less valuable than one square mile of downtown Dallas.

The demands of space and a natural appreciation for good craftsmanship in miniature combine to give an impetus to collection of works of art in small scale. The great expansion in interest in dollhouse furniture and furnishings in recent years has not been restricted to children. It is their parents and grandparents who are making the purchases for their own enjoyment. This phenomenon has made itself felt in the auction world and auctioneers are becoming happily accustomed to the sighs of longing which accompany the appearance on the block of miniature cabinetry, be it designed for the dollhouse, the nursery or for roving

Rogier van der Weyden, St. George and the Dragon.
Photograph courtesy of the National Gallery of Art, Washington, D.C.

Miniatures from the Garbisch Collection.

cabinetmakers in the eighteenth century, who used miniatures to encourage orders for a particular model. A spice cabinet in the form of a miniature highboy realized a price of $65,000 (£31,400) in 1980, which would have been a highly satisfactory result for its adult counterpart. The prices realized by three miniatures from the Garbisch collection sold in the spring of 1980, reflect the same attitude (see illustration). The appeal may, to some extent, be an emotional reflection of childhood, but the appraiser cannot afford to ignore it.

8) Subject matter • The subject depicted by a work of art can have a beneficial or detrimental effect on its value. This criterion can in a sense be described as the demands of taste. While an artist or craftsman may find inspiration in a certain subject, his enthusiasm may not be shared by the art-buying public. No matter the extreme technical skill employed, a depiction of a dead ox by Rembrandt will not command the same price as a portrait of his wife as a young woman. Nature being what it is, portraits of women tend to command a higher value than portraits of men. Animal depictions in most fields of art are more popular than those of humans. Still life subjects are preferred to landscapes. Religious subjects take second place to mythological scenes in this secular age and church interiors do not usually find buyers as readily as other interiors. In the French Impressionist field, Manet proved to be a consummate exponent of the still life mode. However, his *Still Life of Fish* (see illustration) experienced considerable difficulty in finding a buyer in the early

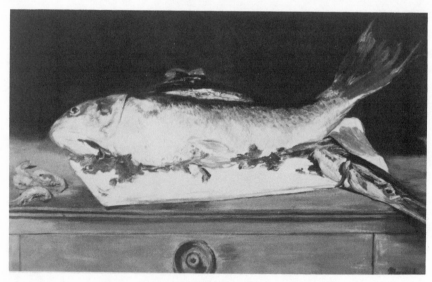

Edouard Manet, NATURE MORTE AUX POISSONS
(STILL LIFE OF FISH).

Jean Richard Goubie, PARIS ZOO.

1970's. It is obviously important that the animals remain alive in their depiction and the benefit of this is well seen in the painting of the Paris Zoo by Jean Richard Goubie (see illustration), which realized $90,000 (£43,902) considerably more than the market will normally pay for this artist's more mundane treatment of equestrian subjects.

On occasion, the subject of a painting will raise its value far beyond the anticipated level. Such was certainly the case in the sale of the now well-exposed Frederic Church of 1861, *The Icebergs* (see illustration p. 75). Not only massive in size, which, as previously discussed, is not necessarily an advantage, this painting's subject distinguished it from the main body of the artist's work. The painting, lost from the public for a century, together with his treatment of the Andes, marks the high point of this artist's output and provides an outstanding example of American Luminism in the nineteenth century, commanding a purchase price of $2,500,000 (£1,136,364).

In another example, that of Joaquin Sorolla's *Triste Herencia* (see illustration), the extreme painterly skill and sensitivity of the artist's work outweighed the awkwardness of the subject, once again in spite of heroic dimensions. It realized $240,000 (£115,942).

In the decorative arts, the form and subject will have similar effects.

Joaquin Sorolla, Triste Herencia (Sad Inheritance).

Meissen *singeries,* or monkey orchestras, appear to be more popular than groups of human figures. Porcelain fruit and vegetables have acquired a cachet all their own. Tang horses are preferred to Tang humans. They are certainly more dramatic.

In every area, the nuances of subject matter play their part. Not only will the attraction of the subject be relevant, but the form of the composition of a picture or a work of art requires consideration. The subject matter of two apparently similar works can be identical and yet the market will distinguish between them, on the basis of both composition and quality.

A fine illustration of this is provided by two watercolors by Winslow Homer, each depicting two boys in a boat. They are in the same medium, of the same size and from the same period. They are both in fine condition (see illustrations A and B). They were put up for auction at the same time. Watercolor A failed to find a buyer and was bought in for $72,500 thus making the last authentic bid $70,000. Watercolor B sold easily to a purchaser for $150,000. The difference in the two drawings is, in fact, considerable. Drawing A has little color in it, the sea is rough and there is no land in sight; one cannot see the faces of the boys and one is left with a sense of anxiety. A skillful drawing leaves the observer unhappy. In drawing B, the sun is shining on a calm sea, the shore is visible, as are the faces of the two young oarsmen and the observer is left with no doubt about their safety. Thus the subtle differences in subject matter and composition directly affected the value of the drawings and, in this case, made the significant distinction between selling and not selling. It is then little wonder that the appraiser must be sufficiently versed in his subject to make these distinctions and that the unwary buyer will, on occasion, be led into a purchase without having taken account of what on the surface might appear to be minutiae, but what are in fact vital considerations. This criterion, when combined with historical importance, can, for instance, lead to the value discovered in the Houdon bust of Benjamin Franklin, discussed earlier. It was the fact that the subject was Benjamin Franklin which added two hundred and eighty thousand dollars to the value of this work of art.

9) Provenance • In an ideal world, it might be supposed that the history of the possession of a work of art should have little effect on its value. Surely the work of art should stand for itself and not compromise its integrity to the circumstances of its ownership? Unfortunately or not, the case is exactly opposite to this ideal. The "provenance," or history, of the individual work of art can have a vast influence on its value. As might be suspected, the more important the owner, the greater the enhancement of value. The importance may be earned, as in the case of

A. Winslow Homer, ROWBOAT.

B. Winslow Homer, ROWBOAT (the more popular version).

a great collector or patron. Drawings are enhanced by collectors marks of such as Joshua Reynolds or Peter Lely. Currently, an English painting which joins the illustrious ranks of Paul Mellon's collection at the British Art Center at Yale is considered to have received the final accolade as to quality. Importance may be hereditary, as in the royal collections of Europe, but the effect is nevertheless substantial. An example from the decorative arts will serve to emphasize the efficacy of this criterion.

In 1958, a private collector bought a console table by J. H. Reisner (see illustration) from a major commercial dealer in New York for $40,000 (£14,285), a remarkable price for that time. In 1972, the table was submitted to Sotheby's in New York for sale at auction. In the cataloging process, it was discovered that the piece bore the inventory mark of the royal collection at Versailles and subsequent research revealed that this very console table had been delivered to Marie Antoinette's suite on September 24, 1781. Thus was the piece not only royal, but its provenance could be traced to the very day upon which it had been delivered by the

Console table for Marie Antoinette by J. H. Reisner.

maître ébéniste. The solidifying of the provenance led to the sale of the console table at auction for $400,000 (£160,000). Certainly, the table would have doubled in price during the intervening years, but the remaining $300,000 can only be attributed to the royal connection.

The more complete the provenance, the more satisfactory will be the result in the marketplace. Every fact of a work of art's history has value and appraisers should be informed of such background before coming to any conclusions as to value. Collectors, for the same reason, should not only seek to acquire as much knowledge as possible of the provenance of their possessions, but should also do everything in their power to ensure that any provenance is satisfactorily documented. As in the case of George Washington's bed, previously discussed, it is little use claiming that a prized item came from the personal collection of Tsar Nicholas, if there is not one jot of evidence to support such a claim.

10) Quality • The appraiser, or indeed the collector, having considered all the previous nine criteria, is then left to make the most demanding judgment of all in seeking to establish the relative quality of a work of art. Impossible to define accurately, quality in works of art is nevertheless not a matter of entirely subjective opinion. A group of qualified experts will reach a consensus in determining the quality of one object against another. The example cited above of the two watercolors by Winslow Homer speaks to this issue. While subject matter and composition remain decisive factors, the quality of the more valuable drawing would not have escaped a specialist. No dealer in American paintings and drawings would have encountered any difficulty in selecting the drawing with the greatest quality. They did precisely that by their participation and lack thereof in the bidding at auction on these two drawings. It can then be claimed that there is to a degree an objective, quantifiable quality in a work of art. It is also suggested that the measurement of this quality takes the expert appraiser far beyond the nine previously defined criteria of value. Here one is forced to consider such ethereal qualities in the appraiser as his "eye." Does he see works of art with a correctly developed judgment? Is an expert born with this eye or can he acquire it? To what extent should the appraiser allow his personal tastes and reactions to enter his subconscious deliberations and sway his final determination?

As the appraiser mentally compares a specific art object with any and every similar object he has ever encountered, he makes a decision as to the relative quality of the object in question. It is vital that he become used to the process of making that decision, having weighed many factors in coming to it, and that, having made his decision as to quality, he must be prepared to stand by it and substantiate it satisfactorily. Neither clients nor tax authorities are likely to be favorably impressed by such comments as, "It just seemed so beautiful to me!" The professional is required to have an educated opinion of what an object is worth and to be able to justify that opinion. The hardest task which faces the appraiser is that of convincing any interested parties that a major proportion of a work of art's value lies in its quality and that such quality rests on the reliability of the appraiser's opinion. Experience of the market is the only way to acquire this reliability. It cannot be taught from slides in a classroom and the learning process never ceases.

Judgment as to quality then may contain factors from some or all of the other criteria that have been outlined, but it must then go beyond them and render a final summing up. The skill of the appraiser involves placing his judgment as to quality alongside a scale of values which recognizes the precise level of the current market of the time. It is impossible for appraisers to travel in the field with their complete reference libraries, so it is necessary for this information to be filed mentally, available for use at any time. Constant study of the market as it moves is required for the appraiser to maintain any degree of accuracy. The auction house appraiser is uniquely placed to monitor the market for this purpose. He sees the value of quality daily, he operates in continuous association with the criteria of value. For him there would be little difficulty in deciding which of two Renoirs (see illustrations) is the more valuable, the *Woman in Oriental Costume* or the *Young Girl*. While, in many opinions, the first painting is a better Renoir, more what one is looking for in the artist, the second has the sentimental attraction of a sweet, innocent young girl. The first painting realizes one million dollars in the same season that the second sold for $1,600,000. Is it possible that it would have been more welcome in the drawing room, while the first might have more happily resided in the master bedroom? Was the quality of the painting of the little girl significantly higher that that of the woman?

Such are the questions which confront the appraiser daily. It is the accurate responses to these questions which determine the reputation of the auction house, not to mention its profitability.

THE AUCTION HOUSE AS
AN EDUCATIONAL RESOURCE

DOCUMENTS AND EXPERTS: SOURCES OF KNOWLEDGE

The constant flow of a wide variety of property through the auction rooms provides the public with an opportunity to educate itself in every area of the fine arts. In contrast to studying objects in a museum, the browser in the auction gallery is encouraged to handle the material and to ask questions. The catalogue information, correctly interpreted, provides a fine basis of knowledge. Reference is made to standard literature in each area and this literature can give the collector a foundation of connoisseurship upon which to build. *Catalogues raisonnés* of major artists are mentioned in catalogue descriptions and these can become vital

Renoir, WOMAN IN ORIENTAL COSTUME.

resources in authenticating works of art. Major auction rooms support
specialized libraries. These libraries have the great advantage of being
working facilities and, therefore, tend to contain only necessary and reliable material. But most major reference works will be found within an
auction room of international stature.

One of the most vital possessions of an auction house is its records.

Renoir, YOUNG GIRL.

As has been emphasized throughout this book, the ability to make valid comparisons with a range of sales in a field lies at the heart of sound estimating. Auction rooms therefore maintain extensive, accurate and up-to-date records of their own sales and of the sales of competitors throughout the world. The computerization of records has aided greatly in this task. The public cannot expect to be given access to the confidential records of an auction house, the names of sellers and buyers, the registered reserve prices and the agreed terms of sale contracted with the seller, but most records regarding prices reached at auction and past sale information are available to scholars and collectors, providing an invaluable resource to both.

Photographic records form another area of great interest to the collector and scholar. The widespread use of illustrations in auction catalogues guarantees the availability of photographs of works of art and these can often aid the collector or the cataloguer in the identification of a like object.

The intelligent use of a sale catalogue coupled with the price list published shortly after each sale can teach the collector much about his market. By studying the prices realized against the sale estimates, the collector can not only learn about price trends for individual items, but can also gain a grasp of any movement in the market as a whole. The serious collector will also acquire the ability to view a sale preview, marking his own estimates against each lot and then comparing his estimates against the auction house's official estimates and the final results. This system, employed by the auction houses to train their own personnel, improves perceptions efficiently and quickly. The ability to·explain one's own error is the beginning of wisdom!

In order to emphasize the availability of its expertise, Sotheby's in America has developed an event which they call the "Heirloom Discovery Day," a phenomenon peculiar to the company's American operation. This derives from the old travelling expert who, like the itinerant portrait painter, would travel the country announcing his intended arrival in each city for the purpose of inspecting property in his particular category of expertise. The old practice, "sweeps," conducted by one or more experts, continues to function as an importrait source of material for consignment. But the Heirloom Discovery Day addresses a slightly different audience and serves a triple purpose. On a selective basis, the auctioneer agrees to provide a museum or cultural institution with a group of at least five experts in different fields. They agree to give oral appraisals on up to five objects in return for a donation of five dollars per object to the institution. Thus, for much less money than they would pay for an expert visit or a formal appraisal, the curious can discover the value of that "strange object in the attic." Should the object transpire to be a fantastic rarity and should the fortunate owner decide to commit it to auction, the institution receives a portion of the commission earned by the auction house. The mystique of a search for hidden treasure provides endless spectator satisfaction; the public becomes better informed of the value of works of art and the local cultural institution receives much needed funds.

Collectors not domiciled close to a representative office of a major auction room would do well to inquire as to the date and location of one of these events most suited to their situation. Experts are not averse to arranging subsequent visits to persons who bring in objects of better quality. Since Heirloom Discovery Day is a registered trade mark, other houses use different nomenclature, but the concept is readily identifiable from the publicity which surrounds it.

SEMINARS, LECTURES, PUBLICATIONS, ETC.:
SPREADING THE WORD

Because of their extraordinarily practical grasp of their subjects, auction house experts tend to make good lecturers. Immersed as each expert is in his field, he will nevertheless be able to describe a facet of the market in the context of the market as a whole and add the fascination of monetary value. The art market is of particular interest in that it provides aesthetically pleasing illustrations almost automatically. An illustrated slide lecture on Georgian silver is more attractive than its counterpart on current trends in the stock market. Public fascination with the art market and the obvious marketing advantages of lectures have led the major rooms to offer a wide variety of educational experiences. These include individual lectures by experts on specific topics, walking tours of sale exhibitions where individual examples are discussed, panel discussions at seminars on current trends in the art market and extended courses on the fundamental aspects of art and antiques. These last courses vary from training schemes, aimed to create potential employees, to broad courses designed to give the collector an introduction to a wide variety of topics. Those responsible for communications, marketing and public relations in the major houses should be consulted to ascertain what opportunities are being offered. Few days pass without some form of seminar or lecture taking place, often free of charge. There is little more fascinating than to hear an established expert talk about the subject he knows and enjoys. Those who doubt the depth of the auction house experts' expertise have probably not taken the trouble to hear some of them speak on their fields.

Outside London and New York, it is very possible that an auction house expert will appear as a guest lecturer at a museum or with another institution. Such organizations as the English-Speaking Union, the Young

Presidents Organization, the American Bar Association and local security analysts groups often provide a forum for presentations on the art
market. Once again, a call to one of the major houses can easily establish
the schedule for the interested collector.

Both Sotheby's and Christie's are also involved in the publication of
books at several levels of scholarship. These may be as basic as an introductory guide to print collecting or as esoteric as a monograph on one
specific historic firearm. Sotheby's publishes a list of their scholarly publications and this should be of interest to the established collector.

All the major auction rooms publish an annual review of highlights
of the past season. These attractive publications not only contain copi-
ously illustrated examples of major works of art, together with the prices
realized, but also feature articles of interest by both auction house experts
and outside scholars. These annual volumes are a vital resource for the
serious collector in that they provide an accurate record of current price
levels, with the great advantage over most of the published price indexes
in that they are well-illustrated. Of immediate interest when they appear,
they gain in usefulness with age and have become a major source of
information since they began to appear, in much more modest form, in
1958. They can be purchased through bookshops or directly from the
auction houses.

For more immediate information concerning auction house activities, it is advisable to subscribe to the newsletters which are published by
most of the auction rooms. The major rooms will send this free of charge
to established clients. The neophyte may be forced to spend a modest
annual subscription fee to receive these useful publications. Upcoming
sales for the worldwide market are listed together with price highlights
from immediate past sales. New developments in the services offered by
an auctioneer will naturally be included in this promotional material so
that if Sotheby's decide to open an office in Mexico City or if Christie's
wish you to learn that they are going to conduct a mammoth house sale
in Philadelphia, this is a likely source of such news.

Most houses also generate a wide variety of brochures, pamphlets
and departmental promotional material which may be easily procured.
It should be borne in mind that this type of material tends to be sensitive
to the ravages of time. Thus, changes in rates and personnel can lead to
inaccuracies. The brochures, therefore, reflect this tendency by addressing only the broadest aspects of the services offered. Specific enquiries
should usually accompany the use of such material, particularly with
regard to any rates quoted.

Institutional histories tend to be of interest primarily to members of
the institutions portrayed, but the body of literature on the auction business itself is growing steadily. The growth of the major rooms is a fasci-

nating study in and of itself. The quality of the literature on the subject varies considerably.

The willingness of the auction rooms to share their knowledge with the public and the educational opportunities thus afforded are directly related to the promotional value of such efforts. This should not, however, deter the seeker from taking advantage of an opportunity, because the auction house recognizes that the interested student of today may well become the committed client of tomorrow. Thus, the education may range from aggressive browsing in a saleroom exhibition to a nine-month course of instruction in London, replete with classroom lectures and diploma. These resources should not be ignored by any who would wish to further their knowledge of the art market.

PRICE RECORDS: AVAILABILITY OF THE FACTS

Auction records have been previously discussed as a vital resource to the appraiser, whether he is preparing a formal document for tax authorities or estimating the potential sale price of a work of art. Because auction records are the only published prices in the art market, they need to be carefully understood and interpreted, as was seen in the earlier discussion on criteria of value. With the development of computerization, "price guides" have begun to appear in some profusion and the collector no longer has to carry an entire market history in his head. The convenience of instant comparative analysis should not, however, allow the collector to overlook the need for more detailed study of prices recorded. The ever-present danger of false comparison must be stressed, as anyone who has had occasion to confer with the tax authorities on an evaluation issue will testify.

The tendency to assume that the world record work of art is not only identical to one's own but actually inferior in quality is yet another example of the collecting syndrome, known informally in the trade as "owneritis." The auction houses, in fact, can provide so much information on sales prices that the recipient may be placed in the position of being unable to see the wood for the trees. It is possible to acquire too much information and to be led to false conclusions by such a surfeit. In a sense, the records speak for themselves, provided they are intelligently analyzed. It is strongly recommended that those who make use of auction records develop the habit of seeking their interpretation from those who created the prices. There is no better authority, for instance, on the reason why Picasso's self-portrait, *Yo Picasso* (see illustration), sold in 1981 for $5.3 million (£2.5 million) than the expert who catalogued the work, who would be quick to point out that this price does not necessarily indicate that all Picasso's paintings have increased in value by the 800% which this work had registered in the previous six years.

There are a growing number of independent newsletters whose subscribers receive regular commentary on the vagaries of the art market, together with market analysis and, in some cases, a fair amount of unsubstantiated art world gossip. The more responsible of these publications provide serious and valuable information from a relatively objective point of view. The leader in this category is the magazine *Art and*

Pablo Picasso, SELF-PORTRAIT.

Auction, a relative newcomer to the market and a worthwhile addition to the field. Others vary in the degree of responsibility shown in their interpretation of the market. The better market newsletters spend much of their staff time acquiring information directly from the auction houses and passing it on to their subscribers. This useful service saves the individual collector a number of telephone calls to already hard-pressed information officers and the facts garnered can be instrumental to collecting decisions. The collector needing more immediate market information can contact the auction rooms directly and, in the major cities of London and New York, can consult the regular auction reports in the major newspapers. The monthly art magazines, such as *Apollo, Connoisseur, Art News, Antiques,* the *Burlington Magazine* and *Country Life* also contain regular commentaries on auction activity.

Various indexes of annual price levels are published in many of the fields covered by the auction houses. The danger of misinterpretation has been emphasized already. Nevertheless, the usefulness of such auction records far outweighs the concomitant risks.

OFF-PREMISES SALES
Selling on Site

The off-premises sale or "house sale" is one of the most popular forms of auction sale, from both the seller's and the buyers' points of view. For the seller, there is the enormous advantage that no material has to be packed or shipped. Additionally, prices for lesser items are traditionally higher at house sales. There are several reasons for this. Firstly, and not to be underestimated, the carnival atmosphere of a house sale, especially when it is held in a tent, leads buyers to spend more money than they would in the more staid atmosphere of the permanent auction room. Secondly, a house sale encourages buying by local souvenir hunters who have always wanted to gain entrance to the big house and are now afforded an opportunity to purchase some minor item by which to remember the former occupant. Needless to say, the more prestigious the name, the greater this effect will be. Mrs. Geraldine Rockefeller Dodge's bath towels will realize more than John Doe's. Local house sales tend to generate an inordinate amount of publicity relative to the importance of the property being sold. Thus, much to the auctioneer's satisfaction, the sale becomes a big local event, attracting large crowds, all of them potential bidders when they assume the carnival mood.

For the buyer, the reasons for higher prices at house sales contain salutary warnings. Because house sales are fun, there is no reason to abandon the traditional guidelines. One should continue to establish in advance the price level one is prepared to bid. One should not buy anything purely on the basis of its past ownership. It is also important to recognize the potential cost of shipment. The writer recalls the sale of a pipe organ in an off-premises sale. The sale price was under $5,000. The estimate for its removal and shipment was over $10,000. The buyer should remember that he is likely to be paying a premium on the lesser material. However, should there be a few isolated items of a specialized nature, the possibility arises that a collector may pay less at a house sale. Dealers and collectors from distant points may not feel that the journey is justified on the outside chance of acquiring one or two items. They come to specialist auctions knowing that there will be a wide variety of choice in their field. The house sale does not usually offer this inducement to the specialist. Thus, if a house sale contains mainly American furniture, every dealer and collector in that field will appear. Should that same house sale contain one good French commode and two fine Dutch seventeenth century paintings, there is an increased chance that these latter items will sell at least reasonably.

When dealing with vast quantities of material, the auction house will often advise the use of both an off-premises sale, the removal of a few specialized items to their permanent rooms and the sale of the lesser material by tag sale. This avoids the possibility, described above, of having a few good items sell at less than their full value. The tag sale on lesser items is simply a cheaper method of disposing of items which do not merit the full cataloguing process, let alone the time spent in the actual auction room. These items, usually modestly priced, sell out rapidly and cease to be a burden on the seller, in most cases a professional executor, who has little use for four hundred used tea-towels.

The seller who is considering a house sale should be guided by the auctioneer as to the suitability of his property to this method. Such matters as the location of the property geographically, the ease of erecting a tent, the availability of accommodation in hotels and motels, the ease and availability of parking space, the existence of a good local buying constituency and, most important, the nature of the property to be sold, together with the time of year and the weather patterns for the area, all have to be considered along with many other variables before taking the step of deciding on a house sale.

The increased price levels mean higher commissions for the auctioneer, but it should be acknowledged that the off-premises event involves the auction house in abnormal expenditures. Often a large crew and several specialists will be out of town for an extended period, This involves significant expenses. All the usual facilities, from an accounts department to a shipping department, have to be created on site, as well as the less usual demands of a house sale, such as catering and toilet facilities. These less obvious costs mount up and therefore it should not come as a surprise that a major auction room is unlikely to make a profit from an off-premises sale unless the property sold is worth in the region of a million dollars. This does not mean that they may not be willing to undertake the sale, either because they are removing a few highly important items that will make a handsome profit at their permanent facilities or because there is other business to be obtained from the same source on a future occasion.

The owner of a large collection of lesser material who cannot offer one of these two inducements can still consider the use of the house sale as a means of disposal, but should be prepared to make use of a local auctioneer, who will be well versed in the procedure, but whose costs will be less dramatic. In effect, there comes a point when it becomes futile to use a sledgehammer to crack a nut!

The seasoned auction *afficionado* will recognize the dangers of a house sale, run by a less than reputable organization. The property is likely to be "salted"; that is the auctioneer will add property from other sources to take advantage of the euphoric atmosphere. The application of common sense can often identify the presence of this phenomenon. If the house whose contents are up for sale has one dining room and if there are six sideboards in the sale, there is a distinct possibility that as many as five of them are recent arrivals on the premises. The salted property is likely to be material that has failed to sell on previous occasions and, as such, is less than desirable. A further risk at a house sale can be the presence of a dealer "ring" or syndicate, because a local auctioneer may not have the expertise to counteract this activity in the manner described earlier in this work. The buyer should ignore such combinations and exercise his bid to the level previously determined. Attempting to outbid a ring to teach them a lesson is not recommended.

The unscrupulous and dishonest auctioneer is offered a tantalizing opportunity in a house sale for the use of "shills," employees placed in the audience to increase the bidding. Often hard to detect, they will usually become apparent, however, by bidding on many different lots, whose connection defies logic. The auctioneer will tend to treat them differently and use them too quickly on consecutive lots. Without laboring the point, the cure for the bidder is the same as that for rings. He should bid only to the level he has decided upon before coming to the sale.

A similar, though slightly different, off-premises sale is sometimes promoted by the major auction rooms. This takes the form of what, for convenience, can be called the "hotel sale." Such sales consist of multiple properties, usually gathered in one geographical area, sold in temporary salesroom premises, usually in a hotel. These sales tend to occur in major cities which have an adequate supply of both material to be sold and interested buyers and which support a representative office of the large auction room which is promoting the sale. Thus, the auctioneer has an office, from which the cataloguers can work to bring in the property and from which the logistics of the sale procedure can be managed. The advantages of this type of sale for the auctioneer are similar to those described in the house sale, with the additional benefits that the exhibition and salesroom need only be hired for a week and that the catering and supply features are readily taken care of by the hotel staff. These sales are only as good as the reputation of the firm conducting them and the buyer should beware of the auction of rugs and carpets held in the motel nearest the airport. The overnight auctioneer may be near the airport for good reason—it affords a quick departure from the scene of the crime.

ESTATE SERVICES
The Special Needs of the Executor

Because a significant portion of an auction house's business tends to come from estates, it will come as no surprise that the major houses have departments specializing in the services provided to the professional executor. A large estate property may involve as many as a dozen different expert departments and the sales process may extend for at least a year. The executor will probably appreciate the advantages of specialized sales and the need to wait for the appropriate sale but, nevertheless, be anxious to control the disposition of the estate in a responsible manner. The estate services departments in auction houses have been created to allay his fears.

From the first contact through to the final settlement, the "account executive" in the estates department coordinates the processing of the estate, representing the executor in any activity that needs to be undertaken within the large auction house organization. Every detail, already described in the sale process, is monitored so that, at any moment, an account may be given to the estate of the current status of progress towards final disposition. The estates department representative thus acts as a channel of communication between the client and the relevant member of the auction house staff. Well-established relationships between these departments and both legal and financial fiduciaries lead to further business and the development of mutual confidence, so that the efficient auction house will tend to be offered a fair proportion of its estate business on the basis of previous business satisfactorily concluded and trust in an individual's ability to deliver the required product, an efficient coordination of the estates process, where every detail must be accurately administered. The wealth of experience these estate department representatives bring to their task make them an invaluable ally to the professional executor, who would be well-advised to establish a relationship with such a representative before the need for services actually arises.

MUSEUM SERVICES
The Auction House and the Institution

Because the needs of museums vary considerably from those of the private collector or dealer, the major rooms have found it advantageous to create offices specifically designed to respond to these needs. Museums not only buy at auction; they are, more often than is realized, a useful source of material for sale. "Deaccession" is an essential part of a museum's operation and it is in the sale of duplicates and inferior examples that a museum increases its purchasing power for the top quality example when it appears.

In their public position, trustees of museums need to be sure that any sales made are at fair market price. An auction protects such fiduciaries from any accusation of selling at less than full market price and provides a suitable means of bringing the museum's unwanted material to its appropriate buyer. A change in a museum's philosophy can bring about the sale of the very finest quality of works from museums. One is reminded of the sale of old master paintings from the Guggenheim Museum, an institution ill-adapted to the display of sixteenth century Flemish masterpieces.

Auction houses are also consulted by museums in the area of evaluation and their appraisal departments have on occasion been engaged to create total inventories of museum collections, a task for which they are well equipped. The natural relationship which builds between the museum curator and the auction house specialist leads to considerable communication in matters of expertise and research. The cross-fertilization of the academic and the pragmatic means that both parties have something to offer each other. The museum services department, as in the case of the estates services department, offers a coordinating function to the museum representative who may encounter some difficulty in tracking down the particular individual required within the auction house organization.

The "Heirloom Discovery Day," already described, is yet another example of the type of service offered by the auction house that can be of use to the museum and its members and visitors.

INSTITUTIONAL SERVICES
AND CORPORATE SALES
Corporations Collect

As the auction business becomes more competitive and interest in the art market expands, the auction houses continue to seek means of increasing their share of the art market by developing services to new constituencies. In this area, it is generally conceded that Sotheby's have taken a more aggressive stance than their competitors, who tend to be critical of such initiatives, at least until they have been seen to be successful.

It is easy to suggest that the commercialization of fine art is to be deplored and yet there are few artists who are unwilling to accept money for their efforts and no one can satisfactorily claim that institutional support of the art market is a new phenomenon. The Sistine Chapel ceiling and the role of the Medicis as patrons compare well with current corporate patronage of the arts; the Frick collection and the Chase Manhattan Bank collection have worthy predecessors in years gone by. It takes a Duveen to build a Tate Gallery.

Particularly in America, the entry of businesses as clients in the art market creates a new demand on the auction houses. Whether it be a major oil painting for the president's office or a print of quality for the typing pool, the decoration of corporate facilities with good works of art has obvious advantages. It raises the public image of a corporation, it gives the employees more pleasant surroundings in which to work and, if well selected, corporate art can appreciate in value, rather than lose all its value the day it is purchased, which must be the case of much of the so-called art which adorns the corridor of many an office building today. It is interesting to note that Chase Manhattan Bank lists the appreciation in value of its art collection as part of its corporate assets in its annual report.

As the needs of corporations vary considerably from those of the private collector, once again the established auction house will address those needs specifically. This does not prevent the corporate curator from dealing with individual departments, but should a more formalized relationship seem desirable, it can be developed through contact with those appointed to deal with institutions. It is unlikely that any auction house will turn away corporate business. The extent to which they will publicize this activity may vary, but Sotheby's have developed their department in recognition of the fact that they were already doing business with corporations and institutions on an individual basis, that there was a large untapped market to be developed, requiring the formalization of a departmental structure for the convenience of the potential client and that they would be the first to establish such a service. Such institutional services also tend to include much of the coordination of marketing and promotional activities with banks, law firms and other professional bodies.

As new initiatives are taken to develop the art market responsibly it seems likely that corporations will be playing an increasingly active role. The availability of a wide variety of works of art through the auction medium makes it logical to assume a continuing need for specialized handling of corporate needs on the auction house's part.

CHARITY SALES
Guidelines and the Most Frequent Myths

The increased popularity of auctions in general has led to a proliferation of charity auction sales. From the guest auctioneer's point of view, these can be the cause of considerable distress and some popular myths need to be exploded while, at the same time, some fundamental guidelines are enumerated.

The principal myth about the charity sale is that, because the sale is in aid of charity, the guests will pay more. In fact, the contrary is true and every participant comes convinced that a bargain is to be found because it is a charity sale. The second myth, whose consequences can be more fatal than the first, is that, provided everyone present has had sufficient quantities to drink, success is assured. The reverse is true. Beyond a certain point, the cocktail hour eliminates bidders at an alarming rate, rendering them either sleepy and inactive or noisy and unwilling to concentrate on the job at hand. Uncontrolled noise is the prime enemy of a good auctioneer. The third myth concerns the ability of the guest at a charity auction to eat, drink, talk and bid at one and the same time. Attempting to hold an auction during a meal is suicidal. Besides which, an auditorium arrangement of seating has a distinct advantage over arrangements of circular tables, each holding eight to twelve individuals of whom half must necessarily have a limited line of sight to the auctioneer. The fourth myth involves the erroneous belief that one can hold the guests' attention for four hours and persuade them to bid on any object or service offered because one is selling for charity. Even when selling major works of art, four hours is too long.

Having thus listed the principal myths, what are the guidelines? They follow in no fixed order of importance because circumstances will vary:

• Start collecting material one year before the event.

• Make sure that an active committee is prepared to work to find the material. It will not flow in of its own accord.

• If cocktails and / or a meal are involved, have them after the sale.

• Limit the number of lots to under one hundred, so that the sale will take less than three hours.

• Locate the auction in a separate room from the refreshments and arrange the room in auditorium style.

• Make certain that there is a superb speaker system which will function under any conditions.

• Distribute the most attractive lots evenly throughout the catalogue.

• Beware of overloading the sale with services. (Offers to act as amateur butler and maid in another's house are more entertaining than salable!).

• Be absolutely certain not to overprice any entrance fee, thereby eliminating potential bidders. It is better to have public access to the auction and to limit the subsequent wining and dining.

• Be sure to have a professional auctioneer. Amateur auctioneers can, on occasion, be amusing but they will almost invariably become diverted and fail to keep the sale moving at an appropriate pace. They cannot be expected to grasp the subtleties of the task. If a noteworthy guest auctioneer is mandatory, allow him or her to sell the first lot and then hand over to a professional, who may be persuaded to offer his services as an act of charity.

• Remember to provide a record-keeper, an accountant, several bid-spotters and a crew to show and move the various lots.

• It is essential to have the successful bidder sign a card of acknowledgement at the sale of each lot. Memory can be surprisingly weak come the cold light of dawn.

• Money spent on advertising and promotion is seldom wasted.

• Check to ensure that there are not already two or more charity auctions scheduled in the same area within the month. The public becomes bored by too much repetition of this style of fund-raising.

• Most importantly of all, consult a professional, who, if approached diplomatically and placed on the committee, will prevent the organization from turning an interesting event into a prescription for disaster.

As may have been insinuated, charity sales involve an enormous quantity of hard work, are best run in conjunction with a professional auctioneer and must be planned well ahead. If a local auctioneer can be persuaded to allow a charity to use his premises, facilities and staff, half the battle is won. Expenses may be greater in these circumstances, but the built-in organization is hard to reproduce in a rented ballroom.

Any attitude of negativism that might be detected in the foregoing remarks arises from the bitter experience of one who can, however, claim to have set the world record for a ton of cow manure at a charity auction—seven hundred and fifty dollars, with the provision that the buyer

was responsible for spreading his purchase himself. At least the seller
was generous enough to make delivery to the purchaser's property rather
than to the parking lot of the auction site!

A final warning needs to be given. It is sad but true that, the wealth-
ier the audience, the better the chances of success. It is vital that the
organizers of a charity auction ensure the participation of as many people as possible who cannot only afford the merchandise, but will be able
to buy substantially without a second thought. As professionals realize,
finding the material creates the auction but finding the buyers creates
the success.

BRANCH OPERATIONS
Regional Networks and Their Services

It has long been realized by the major rooms that it is impossible to
service their clients from only a few principal auction centers. Equally,
economic factors prevent these organizations from running full auction
facilities in every major city. Space and expertise are too expensive for
this purpose.

Thus, the principal houses are represented in various ways
throughout the world. The visitor to a branch office should not, however, expect an auction room in miniature. Indeed, many representatives work from their own homes.

In expanding their operations, the major rooms face several decisions. Should they buy out the local competition? Sotheby's bought Parke-
Bernet in New York. Should they set up their own operation? Christie's
opened their New York operation from scratch. Should they set up an
auction room or just a representative office? Should the representative
work from an office or from their home?

Representative offices, in whatever form they are constituted, have
three principal tasks. They are created to attract more property for sale
in the auction centers, to provide an avenue of communication for those
who wish to bid in one of the auction centers and to act as a link between
the client and the parent organization ensuring the efficient availability
of whatever service the client requires. In the selection of a branch representative, the auction house puts its reputation on the line, a reputation which can be enhanced or destroyed by the actions of that
representative.

Experience has shown that, by and large, the branch representative
offices of the major houses provide valuable assistance in nearly every
aspect of the auction process. They are supplied with information and
catalogues covering upcoming sales. They are knowledgeable about
packing, shipping and insurance. They can receive property for con-

signment anywhere in the world. They monitor that consignment throughout the process and are usually able to tell a consignor the exact status of property within twenty-four hours of an inquiry. They have the great advantage of knowing whom to call. They will send photographs and descriptions of property to the relevant experts for a free pre-sale estimate. They can arrange for appraisal and other services for a minimum of expense.

A visit to such a representative will thus put the potential client in contact with the total organization of a major auction house and reduce substantially the risks involved in conducting business at a great distance. The decision, for instance, on the most suitable location for the sale of a specific item can often be made in conjunction with a branch representative, thus ensuring the best possible chances of a successful sale.

The very proliferation of representative operations for the large auction concerns speaks to their success. Not a season passes without further expansion of these already vast networks. The international scope of the auction market demands the continued improvement of communications, which can only be brought about by systematic coverage of major population centers. An effective branch operation has to remain one of the keys to success for the international auction house, for it forms the basis of any future expansion.

SPECIAL CLIENT SERVICES

Branch representatives can meet most of the needs of the collector who resides some distance from a principal auction center. However, there are some clients and some needs which are sufficiently out of the ordinary and demand that the client have a particular agent at the auction center itself. For this reason, the major rooms have created what amount to account executives who act on behalf of those clients who deal with several different departments or who wish to have someone known to them execute bids for them because of their inability to be present at an auction and their need to allow their representative to apply some discretion in bidding.

These are the employees often to be found at the ends of telephone lines at major auctions, bidding against the room for absent bidders. These are the roving customer representatives to be found in the exhibition rooms during the pre-sale exhibition, assisting their clients in whatever way possible. Highly professional and experienced, they can be extremely useful in gaining information on particular lots from the experts, information not necessarily included in the printed catalogue. Working closely with the relevant expert, these representatives are able to give their clients advance notice when an item appears that may be of interest to them. The services of these customer representatives are available to all and are in no way limited to the client with the large bank account.

The notion that the major auction houses are only interested in the major client is inaccurate, because the bulk of auction business is conducted at a moderate price level. As a service industry, the importance of offering every possible aid to the client is well recognized and finds expression in such departments as special client services, a function whose title may vary from organization to organization.

CUSTOMER RELATIONS: COMPLAINTS AND HELP IN ADVERSITY

"Customer relations," an euphemism for complaints, is an inevitable department in any large organization. Any company that fails to recognize the need for such a department is probably ignoring the possibility of human error in a complex commercial operation. The nature of the complaints handled in an organization tends to point to its weaknesses.

In the auction business, the standard problems arise from the very nature of the process. Works of art, which have to be moved as often as twenty times during the auction process, are prone to damage. Insurance claims are complicated and lengthy. The auction process, as it has been described, is itself lengthy and subject to delay. Clients can, on occasion, become impatient. The settlement function following a number of sales for a multiple property is highly complicated and sometimes involves adjustment to the specific terms of an individualized contract. The vast quantity of items catalogued under restricted time conditions occasionally induces error of description in the catalogue. Auction houses like to correct these errors in an equitable fashion and reoffer the property, duly recatalogued. Where the error has been made by the auction house, it is frequently the auction house which absorbs the loss.

The fact that the auction business is a service industry forces the reputable house to do its utmost to maintain good customer relations. Adverse publicity arising from one bad experience can seriously damage a good image. As the auction houses become larger, the matter of quality control with respect to the treatment of clients becomes an increasingly vital issue. The dissatisfied client should not hesitate to approach the appropriate department or representative. Only by hearing of its shortcomings can a large business improve its services. Everyone prefers criticism to be constructive but, as new systems are installed and perfected to assist the collector, the auction house needs to be aware of any shortcomings that appear. Many of the standard procedures of today stem from problems that were encountered in the past.

The customer relations department places top priority on the solution of problems, works closely with the legal department and acts on the client's behalf. The personnel in such a department are selected and trained on the basis of their ability to handle clients who are less than happy with the organization. They, therefore, exhibit unusual patience and understanding in difficult circumstances and can be relied upon to provide a sympathetic ear.

TAX ADVISORY SERVICES:
LINKS TO THE PROFESSIONAL TAX ADVISOR

Both Christie's and Sotheby's in London offer tax advisory services to those clients who may need assistance in the complicated areas of capital gains and capital transfer taxes as they apply to works of art. While the service is not available formally in the United States, the major houses are able to refer clients to well-qualified outside specialists with particular knowledge of the problems in tax-planning for the collector.

The case law in this field is constantly changing and the ramifications of the U.S. Tax Reform Acts and subsequent regulations require current legal interpretation of a highly sophisticated nature. The potential seller is strongly urged to address the tax consequences of selling property as part of overall economic planning. The dramatic rise in values in many areas over the last decade has led to equally dramatic increases in capital gains liability. It is a pleasant problem to have, but it remains a problem which demands professional attention.

CHAPTER SIX

The Role of the Auction House in the Art Market

THE HISTORY of the various major auction rooms has been the subject of several books, notably *The Elegant Auctioneers* by Wesley Towner (New York: Hill & Wang, 1970) and *Sotheby's: Portrait of an Auction House* by Frank Hermann (New York: Norton, 1981). What will be learned by any who would read these works is that the development of the fine art auction market as it is known today is the result of the activities of many notable individuals who saw the possibilities that existed in what was a relatively somnambulant business until the last twenty years.

The large auction houses formerly did their work from a single headquarters in London or New York and consisted of small private partnerships, usually composed of gentlemen who could afford to carry the firms through rough economic passages and had chosen their task as auctioneers more as a hobby than a means of earning a living. The old world atmosphere was encouraged and the emphasis was on elegance of the low key variety and unstated, but evident, exclusivity. The writer remembers a senior partner walking through the caverns of Sotheby's some twenty years ago, dismayed to find the storage areas in immaculate condition and exclaiming: "Not enough dust, not enough dust!"

Until 1958, it was expected that the occasional big name sale would occur, such as the Rothschild sale in 1937, and the regular disposal of property of the English aristocracy, of which the lion's share traditionally went to Christie's. The contents of artist's studios also formed some of the more notable auction sales over the years. The emphasis was upon personal contact. Young men entered the business on the basis of whom rather than what they knew and the businesses were run like extended families.

The single event which changed this style of conducting an auction house was the sale of seven paintings by Cézanne, Monet, Renoir and Van Gogh, from the estate of Jakob Goldschmidt of New York, held at Sotheby's in London on Wednesday, October 15th, in 1958. Here was a major American property being sold in London for what appeared, at the time, to be astronomical prices. The sale took place in the evening, an innovation, and was over in twenty-one minutes. Sotheby's had announced to the world that there was a new method of selling art. The next twenty years would see the transition from family affair to big business. At the time of the Goldschmidt sale, Sotheby's had eight partners, one associate and some one hundred and fifty employees. At the time of this writing, Sotheby's has nearly eight times that number worldwide.

The auction houses can thus take some credit for bringing the art market to the people. Highly visible as their activities are at the center of the art market, they still must share the credit, however, with the dealers, whose marketing efforts have also done much for the market over the last twenty years. The old style of the exclusive private view for the special customer has in most cases given way to the "Saturday crawl around the galleries." This change is part of the transition in the art market that has been virtually completed.

Nevertheless, it must be emphasized that, as the art market has broadened and the methods of big business have been introduced, major auction rooms have seen the need to concentrate on the personal approach more than ever. The leader will remain the auction room which provides exceptional expertise and the best personal service.

What does the future hold? Having become major businesses, the auction houses will have to adopt the methods of big business to survive economically. Administrative control and efficiency will continue to be the chief prescriptions for success and profitability. The major rooms are already involved in extensive computerization. A brief glance at the masthead of any of the international auction firms will indicate that there are now more administrative and support staff than there are specialist experts. There is grave danger in allowing an auction room to be run by those who do not understand the business from the ground up, but there is equal danger in assuming that one who is a world expert in one facet of the art market is qualified to make strategic decisions in a multi-million dollar corporation. Thus, the experts have to become acclimatized to their new bedfellows from the business schools who control their costs, budgeting their departments where previously they would proceed on intuition. They have to understand what the computer technician can do for them, which begins with the need to learn a whole new language. The adoption of modern technical methods to cut costs and to further a full service concept lies at the heart of future profitability. Word processors have to replace the quill pen; audiovisual aids must be used to improve the efficiency of worldwide communication within the auction house organization. The accounting processes, hard pressed by the incredible growth of the last ten years, must win the current paper war. Fast and accurate settlement of sales becomes essential in this competitive business. The lessons learned by the banks and brokerage houses in the sixties and seventies must be adapted and adopted by the auction houses of the eighties. The increasing battle to achieve profitability in the face of rising costs will be won with the full application of modern, sophisticated methods in this complex business.

In the face of these technical challenges, one must be reminded of the vital role played by the auction house in the art market, a role which involves people and personal services, not machines. The saleroom is the only public part of the art market. Its very openness contributes to the health of the art market. In this visible marketplace, the buyer and the seller meet in open competition, thus encouraging fair trade. The auction house provides a forum for the serious collector in which he may garner highly qualified advice. This forum also gathers together interested parties from a diverse group of constituencies around a specific field. Collectors, dealers, scholars of art history, museum curators and auction house experts provide a pool of sophisticated information within this open marketplace. As major collections change hands through the auction rooms, the educational process continues.

Diversification may also become a key factor and Sotheby's venture into the real estate business has met with signal success. The development of services in areas that are naturally associated with the fine art auction business could well make an enormous difference to the auction market in the next ten years. The possibilities are only restricted to the limits of imagination.

Whatever direction the business takes, two prime factors will continue to obtain. The contact of the individual with the work of art is the key to expertise which cannot be replaced and the magic, the drama and the thrill of the auction event itself will continue to be the backbone of this fascinating business.

APPENDIX A
Useful Facts and Documents*

*Most of this material, dated spring, 1984, is from Sotheby's but other auction houses use the same or similar forms.

1. CONSIGNMENT AGREEMENT

Sotheby's

1334 York Avenue   New York 10021   (212) 472-3400

MASTER CONSIGNMENT AGREEMENT

This confirms our agreement under which all property which you consign to us from time to time and which we accept (the "property") will be offered by us as your agent at public auction on the following terms and subject to the Terms of Guarantee, if any, and the Conditions of Sale in effect at the time of the auction. The current Terms of Guarantee and Conditions of Sale are attached hereto solely for your information as Exhibits A and B, respectively.

1. <u>The Auction.</u> If we decide to include your property in an auction, we will inform you of our acceptance by a confirmation notice identifying the property and specifying the date of sale. We will have absolute discretion as to seeking the views of any expert regarding authenticity, value or condition of any property or otherwise, grouping the property into such lots, with such catalogue descriptions, as we deem appropriate, and the date of the auction and the manner in which it is conducted. We have no obligation to accept any property for sale.

2. <u>Commission.</u> You will pay us a commission of 10% of the successful bid price for each lot sold for more than $3000 and 15% of the successful bid price for each lot sold for $3000 or less, subject to a minimum commission of $80 on each lot sold. In either case, you also authorize us, as your agent, to collect from the purchaser and retain as our additional commission from you an amount equal to 10% of the successful bid price for each lot sold.

3. <u>Settlement.</u> 35 days after the last session of an auction (the "settlement date"), we will mail to you the net sales proceeds we receive and collect, less our commission and reimbursable expenses, if the purchaser has not given us notice of intention to rescind such sale (as provided in paragraph 10). Out of net proceeds remaining after deduction of our commission and expenses, we may deduct and retain any other amounts you owe us, whether arising out of the sale of the property or otherwise.

We have no obligation to enforce payment by, or collection from, any purchaser. If a purchaser does not pay, and you and we do not agree on another course of action, we reserve the right to cancel the sale and return the property to you. You authorize us, in our discretion, to impose on the purchaser and retain for our account a late charge if payment is not made in accordance with the Conditions of Sale.

4. <u>Reserves.</u> Each lot of the property will be offered subject to a reserve determined as follows:

Unless a different reserve has been agreed upon by us and confirmed by you in writing received by us before the auction, the reserve will be the following percentage of our latest announced or published low presale estimate: (i) 25% for any lot having a low estimate of less than $300, (ii) 40% for any lot having a low estimate of $300 or more up to and including $1000, or (iii) 60% for any lot having a low estimate of more than $1000. At our option, however, we may sell any property at a price below the reserve, provided that we pay you on the settlement date the net amount which you would have been entitled to receive had the property been sold at the reserve (that is, the reserve less our selling commission, reimbursable expenses and any other amount you owe us). In no case will the reserve exceed the range of our presale estimates.

You agree not to bid on the property; all bids to protect your reserves will be made by us as your agent. If, however, you violate your foregoing commitment and you or your agent or representative become the successful bidder on your property, you will pay us the commission set forth in paragraph 2 (including buyer's premium) on the sale price, we may sell the property without any reserve, and you will not be entitled to the benefit of any Terms of Guarantee. You will pay us a commission of 5% of the reserve for any property not reaching its reserve and bought-in by us for your account, subject to a minimum commission of $50 on each bought-in lot.

5. <u>Sotheby's Arcade Auctions.</u> If we deem it appropriate, we may, in our sole discretion, include in a Sotheby's Arcade Auction any property with a low presale estimate in our opinion of $5,000 or less. In such event, or if you and we mutually agree to include any property in a Sotheby's Arcade Auction, the confirmation notice referred to in paragraph 1 above will so specify, and we will offer the item subject to the Conditions of Sale for Sotheby's Arcade Auctions in effect at the time of the auction and the provisions of this agreement, except that the settlement date will be 12 business days after the sale and the minimum commission on each sold and bought-in lot will be $40. If you have previously signed a Sotheby's Arcade Auction Consignment Agreement, this agreement will supersede that agreement. Attached hereto solely for your information as Exhibit C are the current Conditions of Sale for Sotheby's Arcade Auctions.

6. <u>Representations and Warranties; Indemnity.</u> You represent and warrant that you have the right to consign the property for sale; that it is now and until its sale will be kept free of all liens, claims and encumbrances of others including, but

not limited to, claims of governments or governmental agencies; that good title and right to possession will pass to the purchaser free of all liens, claims and encumbrances; and that there are no restrictions on our right to reproduce photographs of it.

You agree to indemnify and hold us harmless from and against any and all claims, actions, damages, losses, liabilities and expenses (including reasonable attorneys' fees) relating to the breach or alleged breach of any of your obligations, representations or warranties herein.

Your representations, warranties and indemnity herein shall survive completion of the transactions contemplated by this agreement.

7. _Expenses._ You agree to bear the expenses of and pay us for: (i) our assumption of risk of loss of or damage to the property (unless you elect to bear such risk as provided in paragraph 8), (ii) our standard fees then in effect for catalogue illustration (you grant us the right to reproduce illustrations of your property, both before and after the sale, and agree that we retain all rights in blocks, prints, plates and the right of reproduction therefrom), (iii) agreed-upon special advertising, (iv) framing and restoration necessary to put the property in proper condition for sale, if you approve the estimated cost, (v) customs duties and shipping to our premises and (vi) a service charge of 10% of the total cost of any framing, restoration, customs duties, shipping and other services and charges paid by us on your behalf. In addition to other remedies available to us by law, we reserve the right to impose a late charge of 1-1/2% per month on any amount due us and remaining unpaid more than 15 days after we notify you.

8. _Risk of Loss._ If you elect to bear the risk of loss of or damage to the property while in transit to and on our premises, you must prior to the date of shipment (i) notify us in writing of your election, such notice to be signed by you and stating that we will not be responsible for, and that you release us from, all liability for loss of or damage to the property, regardless of the cause thereof, and (ii) provide us with a valid certificate of insurance acceptable to and naming us as an additional insured party under your insurance policy to the extent of our expenses and commissions.

If you do not elect to bear the risk of loss or damage as provided in the preceding paragraph, we will assume such risk while the property is on our premises and, subject to prior written notice to us of your shipment of the property and our written acknowledgement of receipt of such notice, while it is in transit to our premises. In consideration of our assumption of such risk, you will pay us the amount of one dollar per hundred dollars of the amount of our maximum liability described in the next succeeding paragraph.

The maximum amount of our liability, if any, under the preceding paragraph will be (i) the successful bid price if the property has been sold, (ii) the reserve (but not more than the mean of our latest presale estimates) if the property has been bought-in for your account, or (iii) the mean of our latest presale estimates if the property has not otherwise been sold at the time of loss or damage. In no event, however, will our liability include our expenses or commissions, nor will we have any liability for damage caused by (i) acts or omissions of restorers, framers or other independent contractors employed with your consent, (ii) changes in humidity or temperature, (iii) normal wear and tear, (iv) inherent conditions or defects in the property, or (v) acts of war, or damage to glass or frames, regardless of cause.

9. _Withdrawal._ You may not withdraw any property from sale after the date on which we issue a receipt for the property. Regardless of whether we have previously issued a receipt or a notice confirming that we have accepted property for sale, we may withdraw any property at any time before sale if we believe (i) there is doubt as to its authenticity of authorship or attribution or (ii) any of your representations or warranties concerning it are inaccurate or (iii) you have breached this agreement. In the event of any such withdrawal by us or you, you will pay us the commission set forth in paragraph 2 (including buyer's premium) on the mean of our presale estimates, reimburse us for all out-of-pocket costs incurred in connection with the proposed sale and pay us any other amount you owe us, and we will then return such property to you at your expense.

10. _Rescission._ You authorize us to rescind the sale of any property in accordance with the Terms of Guarantee, if any, or if we learn that the property is inaccurately described in the catalogue. If prior to the settlement date we receive from a purchaser a notice of intention to rescind and we determine that the property is subject to rescission, we will credit the purchaser with the purchase price rather than remitting the net proceeds to you, and we will return the property to you upon your reimbursing us for our expenses incurred in connection with the rescinded sale and paying us any other amounts you owe us. If we receive such notice after the settlement date and make such determination, we will refund the purchase price to the purchaser and the property will become ours, unless at the time of consignment you had reason to believe that the property would be subject to rescission, in which event you will pay us the amount refunded to the purchaser, our expenses incurred in the rescission and any other amounts you owe us, and we will then return the property to you.

11. _Private Sales._ If any lot fails to reach its reserve and is bought-in for your account, you authorize us, as your exclusive agent for a period of 60 days following the auction, to sell the lot privately for a price that will result in a payment to you of not less than the net amount (after our commissions and expenses) to which you would have been entitled had the lot been sold at a price equal to the agreed reserve. In such event, your obligations to us hereunder with respect to such lot are the same as if it had been sold at auction.

12. _Treatment of Unaccepted or Unsold Property._ If we determine not to accept for sale any property delivered to us, or to withdraw any property from sale, or if any accepted property remains unsold for any reason after the auction, we will notify you. If such property has not been sold privately pursuant to paragraph 11, and if it is not reconsigned to us for sale on mutually agreed-upon terms or picked up within 60 days after such mailing, we may sell it at public auction without reserve at a place and date determined by us. The proceeds of such sale will be applied to any amount you owe us, including but not limited to our commissions and expenses incurred hereunder, and any excess will be remitted to you. Unless and until we reoffer and sell such property, we will hold it without charge for a period of 30 days after the auction in which it is offered but not sold; thereafter a handling charge of 1% per month of the mean of our presale estimates will be payable by you to cover

our costs of insurance, storage and handling.

13. Inappropriate Property. If we do not deem any consigned property appropriate for public auction, we may sell it privately for a price agreed upon by you and us. You will pay us a commission of 25% of such selling price.

14. Estimates; Catalogue Descriptions. Presale estimates, if any, are intended as guides for prospective bidders; we make no representation or warranty of the anticipated selling price of any property and no estimate anywhere by us of the selling price of property may be relied upon by you as a prediction of the actual selling price. Estimates included in receipts, confirmation notices, catalogues or elsewhere are preliminary only and subject to revision by us from time to time in our sole determination.

We will not be liable for any errors or omissions in catalogue or other descriptions of property and make no guarantees, representations or warranties whatsoever to you with respect to the property, its authenticity, condition, value or otherwise.

15. Use of Name. We may use your name as owner of the property when we offer it for sale or advertise or otherwise promote the sale, both before or after the auction, unless you initial the box below. If we may use your name, but in a form other than that appearing on the first page of this agreement, please type or print it on the line below and place your initials in the box next to it.

You may not use my name: ☐ .
You may use my name as follows:

_____ ☐ .

16. Legal Status. If you are acting as a fiduciary in executing this agreement and in the transactions comtemplated hereunder, initial "Fiduciary" below and sign and return to us our standard "Fiduciary Agreement", together with any additional documents we may require. If you are acting as an agent for someone who is not signing this agreement, initial "Agent" below, which will constitute your agreement that you and your principal jointly and severally assume your obligations and liabilities hereunder. If you are a corporation or other entity, initial "Corporation or other entity" below, which will constitute your agreement to furnish to us any additional documents we may require.

Fiduciary ( )   Agent ( )   Corporation or other entity ( )

17. Applicable Laws; Successors. This agreement shall be governed by and construed and enforced in accordance with the laws of the State of New York. This agreement shall be binding upon your heirs, executors, beneficiaries, successors and assigns, but you may not assign this agreement without our prior written consent.

18. Notices; Paragraph Headings. Any notices given hereunder to you shall be in writing to your address indicated on the first page of this agreement (or to such other address as you may instruct us in writing received by us) and shall be deemed to have been given upon mailing to such address. Any notices given hereunder to us shall be in writing addressed to us at the address indicated on the first page of this agreement (or to such other address as we may instruct you in writing mailed to you) and shall be deemed to have been given when received by us.

The paragraph headings contained in this agreement are for convenience of reference only and shall not affect in any way the meaning or interpretation of this agreement.

19. Term of Agreement; Amendment. Either you or we may terminate this agreement at any time upon 30 days' prior written notice to the other. No such termination shall relieve either you or us of any obligations or liabilities incurred prior to the effective date of such notice.

Neither you nor we may amend, supplement or waive any provision of this agreement other than by means of a writing signed by both parties, except that if at any time we propose by written notice to you to amend or supplement any provision of this agreement, or provide additional terms or conditions as to your future consignments, you will be deemed to have agreed thereto with respect to any property consigned to and received by us at any time after such notice, unless you notify us in writing to the contrary before such property is received by us.

Please date, sign and forward to us the duplicate copy of this agreement.

Very truly yours,

ACCEPTED AND AGREED TO: SOTHEBY PARKE BERNET INC.

_____   By _____
            Consignor

Dated:_____   © 1982 Sotheby Parke Bernet Inc.

2. CONDITIONS OF SALE
("Exhibit B" to Sotheby's Consignment Agreement)

This catalogue, as amended by any posted notices or oral announcements during the sale, is Sotheby Parke Bernet Inc.'s and the Consignor's entire agreement with the purchaser relative to the property listed herein. The following Conditions of Sale, the Terms of Guarantee and any glossary contained herein are the complete and only terms and conditions on which all property is offered for sale. The property will be offered by us as agent for the Consignor, unless the catalogue indicates otherwise.

1. The authenticity of the Authorship of property listed in the catalogue is guaranteed as stated in the Terms of Guarantee; except as provided therein all property is sold "AS IS", and neither we nor the Consignor make any warranties or representations of the correctness of the catalogue or other description of the physical condition, size, quality, rarity, importance, provenance, exhibitions, literature or historical relevance of the property and no statement anywhere, whether oral or written, shall be deemed such a warranty or representation. Prospective bidders should inspect the property before bidding to determine its condition, size and whether or not it has been repaired or restored. We and the Consignor make no representation or warranty as to whether the purchaser acquires any reproduction rights in the property.

2. A premium of 10% of the successful bid price will be added thereto and is payable by the purchaser as part of the total purchase price.

3. We reserve the right to withdraw any property before sale.

4. Unless otherwise announced by the auctioneer, all bids are per lot as numbered in the catalogue.

5. We reserve the right to reject any bid. The highest bidder acknowledged by the auctioneer will be the purchaser. In the event of any dispute between bidders, or in the event of doubt on our part as to the validity of any bid, the auctioneer will have the final discretion either to determine the successful bidder or to reoffer and resell the article in dispute. If any dispute arises after the sale, our sale record is conclusive. Although in our discretion we will execute order bids or accept telephone bids as a convenience to clients who are not present at auctions, we are not responsible for any errors or omissions in connection therewith.

6. If the auctioneer decides that any opening bid is below the value of the article offered, he may reject the same and withdraw the article from sale, and if, having acknowledged an opening bid, he decides that any advance thereafter is insufficient, he may reject the advance.

7. On the fall of the auctioneer's hammer, title to the offered lot will pass to the highest bidder acknowledged by the auctioneer, subject to fulfillment by such bidder of all the conditions set forth herein, and such bidder thereupon (a) assumes full risk and responsibility therefor, (b) will sign a confirmation of purchase thereof, and (c) will pay the full purchase price therefor or such part as we may require. In addition to other remedies available to us by law, we reserve the right to impose a late charge of 1½% per month of the total purchase price if payment is not made in accordance with the conditions set forth herein. The late charge will be imposed pro rata for periods of less than one month. All property must be removed from our premises by the purchaser at his expense not later than 3 business days following its sale and, if it is not so removed, (i) a handling charge of 1% of the purchase price per month until its removal will be payable to us by the purchaser, with a minimum of 5% for any property not so removed within 60 days after the sale, and (ii) we may send the purchased property to a public warehouse for the account, risk and expense of the purchaser. If any applicable conditions herein are not complied with by the purchaser, in addition to other remedies available to us and the Consignor by law, including without limitation the right to hold the purchaser liable for

the total purchase price, we at our option may either (a) cancel the sale, retaining as liqui-
dated damages all payments made by the purchaser or (b) resell the property at public
auction without reserve, and the purchaser will be liable for any deficiency, costs, including
handling charges, the expenses of both sales, our commission on both sales at our regular
rates, all other charges due hereunder and incidental damages. In addition, a defaulting
purchaser will be deemed to have granted us a security interest in, and we may retain as
collateral security for such purchaser's obligations to us, any property in our possession
owned by such purchaser regardless of when we may acquire possession. We shall have all
of the rights afforded a secured party under the New York Uniform Commercial Code
with respect to such property and we may apply against such obligations all monies held
or received by us for the account of, or due from us to, such purchaser. At our option,
payment will not be deemed to have been made in full until we have collected funds represented by checks, or, in the case of bank or cashier's checks, we have confirmed their
authenticity.

8. Lots marked with ▪ immediately preceding the lot number are offered subject to a
reserve, which is the confidential minimum price below which such lot will not be sold. We
may implement such reserves by bidding on behalf of the Consignor. In certain instances,
the Consignor may pay us less than the standard commission rate where a lot is "bought-
in" to protect its reserve. Where the Consignor is indebted to or has a monetary guarantee
from us, and in certain other instances, where we or our affiliated companies may have an
interest in the offered lots and the other proceeds therefrom other than our commissions,
we may bid therefor to protect such interests.

9. Unless exempted by law, the purchaser will be required to pay the combined New
York State and Local sales tax applicable compensating use tax of another state on the total
purchase price. The rate of such combined tax is 8¼% in New York City and ranges from
4¼% to 8¼% elsewhere in New York State.

10. These Conditions of Sale as well as the purchaser's and our respective rights and
obligations hereunder shall be governed by and construed and enforced in accordance
with the laws of the State of New York. By bidding at an auction, whether present in
person or by agent, order bid, telephone or other means, the purchaser shall be deemed
to have consented to the jurisdiction of the state courts of, and the federal courts sitting
in, the State of New York.

11. We are not responsible for the acts or omissions of carriers or packers of purchased lots, whether or not recommended by us. Packing and handling of purchased lots
by us is at the entire risk of the purchaser. In no event will our liability to a purchaser
exceed the purchase price actually paid.

3. INFORMATION FOR PROSPECTIVE BIDDERS

Important Information for Prospective Bidders

Please note Paragraph 8 of the Conditions of Sale dealing with the subjects of "reserves" and our "interest in offered lots other than normal selling commissions." The following definitions of terms and explanations of policies on these subjects and the implementation thereof are provided for your information and guidance.

Reserve

Definition:
A "Reserve" is the confidential minimum price agreed between the seller and us, below which the lot will not ordinarily be sold. On unsold lots, less than full commission may be paid.

Policy:
All lots marked with ● immediately preceding the lot number are being offered subject to a reserve. Our standard advice to sellers is that reserves be set at a percentage of the mean of the estimates, generally somewhat below the low estimate shown in the estimate sheet provided with this catalogue. In no case do we permit a reserve to exceed the high estimate shown in the estimate sheet. Unsold lots, i.e., those which do not meet their reserve, are omitted from the price lists issued following sales.

Implementation:
We as agent for the seller protect reserves, that is, place bids during the auction if and when the highest outstanding bid at any time during the sale is below the reserve on the lot being offered.

Owned Property

Definition:
"Owned property" is property which, at the time it is offered for sale at auction, is owned solely or partially by us or an affiliate (and in the sale of which we are acting as a principal and not an agent).

Policy:
The purchase of property by us for sale at auction is an insignificant part of our overall business. Direct purchases are only made at the request of a client and, in these cases, only after standard commission sales or guaranteed minimum price sales have been rejected by the client. Reserve prices of property owned by us are set on the same or a lower basis than property sold for other consignors, that is, reserves usually will be set below the low pre-sale estimates provided with this catalogue and in no case will they be higher than the low estimates. Any owned property which is unsold at the auction will be omitted from the price lists following the sale. All property owned by us will be identified in the catalogue as "Property of Sotheby Parke Bernet Inc." or a similar recognizable designation. In some cases, the prior source of property will be identified, e.g., "Property from the Estate of John Doe sold by order of the present owner Sotheby Parke Bernet Inc."

Implementation:
Our representatives will make no bids on our behalf except to protect a reserve placed by us as owner. Bidding by us to protect reserves on property is effected in the same way as bidding to protect reserves on property consigned by an outside seller.

Buyer's Premium

A premium of 10% will be added to the successful bid price of all property sold by us, whether consigned to us or "owned property" as defined above, and whether picked up or delivered, and this premium is payable by all purchasers, whether dealers, institutions, private collectors, or others.

Exportation Permits

Certain property sold at auction by us may be subject to the provisions of the Endangered Species Act of 1973. In order to export these items, special licenses must be obtained from the Department of the Interior, U.S. Fish and Wildlife Service. There are no assurances that any such license can be obtained. Please contact the appropriate expert department if you have any questions.

Notice:

Due to a change in New York State Tax Law, all out-of-state dealers are now required to file with us a copy of an Out-Of-State Resale Permit issued by the New York State Department of Taxation & Finance. Otherwise, New York sales tax will be charged on any purchases picked up or delivered in New York. We will be pleased to provide you application forms for the Permit. All inquiries should be directed to the Customer Billing Department on the second floor.

4. ADVICE TO PROSPECTIVE BUYERS AND SELLERS

Advice to Prospective Buyers and Sellers

Standard Commission Rates

Our standard commission for selling fine art property at auction is 10% of the successful bid price of each lot sold for more than $3000 and 15% of the successful bid price of each lot sold for $3000 or less, in either case together with an amount equal to the 10% premium paid by the buyer as part of the total purchase price. A minimum commission of $80 will be charged on all lots sold.

Bidding

Successful bidders attending the auction are required to sign a bid confirmation card upon the fall of the hammer and will not be permitted to take delivery of purchases until their checks have cleared unless they have previously established credit or made payment arrangements. A premium equal to 10% of the successful bid price will be added thereto and is payable by the buyer as part of the total purchase price.

Catalogues, Price Lists and Newsletters

Catalogues, prepared by the expert departments involved, are published for all regularly scheduled auctions. These may be purchased singly or by annual subscription. (Catalogue subscribers receive post-sale price lists and *Sotheby's Newsletter* at no additional charge.) Detailed information on subscriptions and individual catalogues are available at the galleries or by mail. Please specify sale number when ordering individual catalogues.

Printed lists of the prices realized for all lots sold at an auction are available at our galleries and sent directly to catalogue purchasers.

Sotheby's Newsletter, published ten times a year, provides an advance calendar of sales scheduled in New York, London, Toronto, and elsewhere for $5 annually ($8 overseas). A complimentary copy is available upon request.

To order New York publications by mail or for more information, please write or call: Sotheby's Subscription Department, P.O. Box 4020, Woburn, MA 01801, (617) 229-2282.

Inspection of Property

You may bring your property (or photographs if the pieces are not portable) to 1334 York Avenue at 72nd Street for auction estimates and advice from our experts. There is no charge for this service, but it is requested that you telephone for an appointment. Hours of inspection are 9:30 a.m. to 5:00 p.m., Monday through Friday.

Visits to advise clients and evaluate property can be arranged.

The usual fees for such initial visits are:

Manhattan	$25 per hour
Other boroughs of N.Y.C.	$100 per ½ day
Elsewhere in North America	$250 per day

Travel expenses are additional.

The fee may be rebated upon consignment of the property for sale at Sotheby's.

Experts from our Los Angeles office are available to make inspection visits in the western United States. For information about these inspection fees, please call (213) 937-5130.

Appraisals

Appraisals may be done for insurance, estate tax, family division or other purposes *(excluding* gift tax).

Appraisal fees vary according to circumstances. Flat rates will be quoted based upon expert time involved, total appraisal value, and costs of processing. Travel expenses are additional. Appraisals can be delivered within three weeks from the date of the appraisal visit.

A partial rebate of our fee will be made on any property subsequently consigned to us for sale within a year of our appraisal. For further information please call (212) 472-3452.

To order International catalogues please write or call our International Office, (212) 472-3460.

Currency Conversion Display Board

A currency conversion display board will be operated at certain sales for the convenience of bidders. Foreign currency amounts displayed on the board are approximations determined by reference to New York foreign exchange market rates in effect at the close of business on the last business day prior to the sale. We assume no responsibility for any errors or omissions in foreign or U.S. currency amounts shown. The total purchase price and applicable taxes are payable by purchasers, in accordance with the conditions of sale, in U.S. dollars, at our offices in New York.

Removal of Property

Unless different arrangements have been agreed upon, all purchases must be removed by the buyer by 5 p.m. on the third business day following the sale. Purchases not so removed will be subject to a handling charge. See paragraph 7 of the "Conditions of Sale."

Clients are advised that packing and handling of purchased lots by our employees are undertaken solely as a courtesy for the convenience of clients; and in the case of fragile articles, will be undertaken at our sole discretion. In no event will we be liable for damage to glass or frames, regardless of the cause.

Although we recommend the use of professional packers, books and small articles which are not fragile can be packed on our premises, and, at our sole discretion, can be sent by mail or other carrier for a nominal charge. Prints and drawings in glazed frames cannot be handled in this manner. Charges for packing, insurance, and freight are payable by the purchaser. For further information:
Miss Kathleen Him, (212) 472-4853.

Sales Conducted by

John L. Marion, James J. Lally, John D. Block, David J. Nash, Robert C. Woolley, William W. Stahl, Jr., Eunice S. Carroll, Michael B. Grogan, Gerard J. Hill, Annette Kluss, David N. Redden, Marc E. Rosen, Pamela Brown Sherer, Jean H. Witmer, Howard A. Zar

Licensed Auctioneers Numbers: 524728, 718514, 733768, 764786, 760961, 678346, 738576, 767877, 761969, 793375, 736142, 690713, 767154, 778346, 769242.

5. TERMS OF GUARANTEE

We guarantee the authenticity of Authorship of each lot contained in this catalogue on the terms and conditions set forth below.

1. Definition of Authorship.

"Authorship" means the identity of the creator, the period, culture, source of origin of the property, as the case may be, as set forth in the BOLD TYPE HEADING of such catalogue entry.

2. Guarantee Coverage.

Subject to the exclusions of (i) attributions of paintings, drawings or sculpture executed prior to 1870, and (ii) periods or dates of execution of the property, as explained in Paragraph 5 below, if within five (5) years from the date of the sale of any lot, the original purchaser of record tenders to us a purchased lot in the same conditions as when sold through us and it is established that the identification of Authorship (as defined above) of such lot set forth in the BOLD TYPE HEADING of this catalogue description of such lot (as amended by any posted notices or oral announcements during the sale) is not substantially correct based on a fair reading of the catalogue including the terms of any Glossary contained herein, the sale of such lot will be rescinded and the original purchase price refunded.

3. Non-Assignability.

It is specifically understood that the benefits of this Guarantee are not assignable and shall be applicable only to the original purchaser of the lot from us and not to the subsequent owners or others who have or may acquire an interest therein.

4. Sole Remedy.

It is further specifically understood that the remedy set forth herein, namely the rescission of the sale and refund of the original purchase price paid for the lot, is exclusive and in lieu of any other remedy which might otherwise be available as a matter of law.

5. Exclusions.

The Guarantee covers only the correctness of description of Authorship (as defined in 1 above) as identified in the BOLD TYPE HEADING of the catalogue item but does *not* extend to (i) the identity of the creator of paintings, drawings, and sculpture executed before 1870 unless these works are determined to be counterfeits, as this is a matter of current scholarly opinion which can change, (ii) the identification of the periods or dates of execution of the property which may be proven inaccurate by means of scientific processes not generally accepted for use until after publication of the catalogue, or (iii) titles or other identification of offered lots or descriptions of physical condition and size, quality, rarity, importance, provenance, exhibitions and literature of historical relevance, which information normally appears in lower case type below the BOLD TYPE HEADING identifying the Authorship. Although our best judgment is used in attributing paintings, drawings and sculpture created prior to 1870 through the appropriate use of glossary terms, and due care is taken to insure the correctness of the supplemental material which appears below the BOLD TYPE HEADING of each entry in the catalogue, the Guarantee does not extend to any possible errors or omissions therein.

— From a Sotheby's catalogue

6. GLOSSARY OF TERMS
FOR PAINTINGS

Paintings Glossary

The following are examples of the terminology used in this catalogue. PLEASE NOTE THAT ALL STATEMENTS IN THIS CATALOGUE AS TO AUTHORSHIP, PERIOD, CULTURE, SOURCE OR ORIGIN ARE QUALIFIED STATEMENTS AND ARE MADE SUBJECT TO THE PROVISIONS OF THE CONDITIONS OF SALE AND THE "TERMS OF GUARANTEE".

a. "*GIOVANNI BELLINI"—Followed, under the heading "AUTHORSHIP", by the words "ascribed to the named artist". The work is ascribed to the named artist either by an outside expert or by our own staff and such ascription is accepted as reliable by the Galleries. While this is our highest category of authenticity in the present catalogue, and is assigned only upon exercise of our best judgment, no unqualified statement as to authorship is made or intended.

b. ATTRIBUTED TO GIOVANNI BELLINI—In our best judgment, the work can be ascribed to the artist on the basis of style, but less certainty as to authorship is expressed than in the preceding category.

c. CIRCLE OF GIOVANNI BELLINI—In our best judgment, a work by an unknown hand closely associated with the named artist.

d. STUDIO OF GIOVANNI BELLINI—In our best judgment, a work by an unknown hand executed in the style of the artist under his direct supervision.

e. SCHOOL OF . . .;FOLLOWER OF GIOVANNI BELLINI—In our best judgment, a work by a pupil or follower of the artist.

f. MANNER OF GIOVANNI BELLINI—In our best judgment, a work in the style of the artist, but not by him and probably of a later period.

g. AFTER GIOVANNI BELLINI—In our best judgment, a copy of a known work of the artist.

h. SIGNED—A work which has a signature which in our best judgment is a recognized signature of the artist.

i. DATED—A work which is so dated and in our best judgment was executed at that date.

7. BIDDING FORM

SOTHEBY'S

1334 York Avenue, New York, NY 10021
(212) 794-3019, 3022, 3020, 3021

Date: _____

I desire to place the following bids for sale # _____ to be held on _____. These bids are to be executed by Sotheby Parke Bernet up to but not exceeding the amount or amounts specified below. Each bid is *PER LOT*, as indicated, and all bids will be executed and are accepted subject to the *"Conditions of Sale"* and, if applicable, the "Terms of Guarantee," printed in the catalogue of this sale. Please see "Advice to Bidders" on reverse of this bid slip, and note that a premium of 10% is added to the hammer price as part of the total purchase price. Also, please note that tax must be collected, if applicable, on purchases delivered to the following states: New York — 4¼% to 8¼% (depending upon county), Massachusetts, Florida, Texas, Illinois, Pennsylvania, Washington, D.C.

SPB A C # _____

Please print or type:

Name (as it should appear on invoice) _____

Address _____
(Street)

_____
(City)   (State)   (Zip)

Telephone Number(s) _____ Check if address has changed since last Sotheby's purchase ☐

Shipping Address _____
(If Different)   (Street)   (Apt.)

_____
(City)   (State)   (Zip)

Bank Reference Contact _____
(If bidder is not known to Sotheby Parke Bernet Inc.)

Important: Furniture bidders, please see reverse side

Lot Number	Item	Top Limit of Bid, excluding 10% Premium. (Bid is per lot number as listed in the catalogue)

Signed _____

BID DEPT. COPY

8. ADVICE TO ORDER BIDDERS

If instructed, Sotheby Parke Bernet Inc. will execute bids and advise prospective purchasers. This service is free. Lots will always be bought as cheaply as is allowed by such other bids and reserves as are on our books or bids executed in competition from the audience. PLEASE NOTE: Sotheby Parke Bernet Inc. offers this service as a convenience to its clients who are unable to attend the sale and will not be held responsible for error or failure to execute bids.

Commission bids, when placed by telephone, are accepted only at the sender's risk, and must be confirmed by letter or telegram (Cable address: PARKGAL, NEW YORK)

Please use the bidding slips provided and be sure to carefully note lot numbers and descriptions.

Always quote the sale number of the catalogue to avoid any possible confusion.

Please bid as early as possible. In the event of identical bids, the earliest will take precedence. "Buy" bids are not accepted. The limit you leave should be the amount to which you would bid if you were to attend the sale.

Each bidding slip should contain bids for one sale only.

Alternative bids can be placed by using the word "OR" between lot numbers.

In order to avoid delay in clearing purchases, buyers unknown to us are advised to make arrangements *before the sale* for payment or for references to be supplied. If such arrangements are not made, checks will be cleared before purchases are delivered.

IMPORTANT NOTE: Successful bidders will be notified and invoiced within a few days of the sale.

Unsuccessful bidders will not be specifically notified, but will receive a price list indicating results of the sale if a stamped, self-addressed envelope is enclosed with the submitted bid.

Your bid is for the hammer price; a premium of 10% will be added to the hammer price of each lot sold and paid by the buyer.

All property must be removed from our premises by the purchaser at his expense not later than 3 business days following its sale.

Advice to Furniture Bidders

Due to Sotheby's very limited storage capacity, all furniture must be picked up within three business days after the sale to avoid a charge for storage. If your bid is successful, you must retrieve your purchase, or make other arrangements with Sotheby's, within three business days after the sale. Otherwise, your purchase will be sent, at your expense and risk, to our warehouse or to a public warehouse. Storage charges will be accrued from the third business day after the sale onward until pick-up.

9. BIDDING CONFIRMATION CARD

Sotheby Parke Bernet

Memorandum of successful Bid   Sale no._____

Lot no._____   Price_____   Signature_____

_____   _____   _____

_____   _____   _____

_____   _____   _____

Name_____

Agent_____ Agent for_____

Address_____

City_____ State_____

Zip_____ Telephone_____

If requested, may we release your name as buyer?

Yes_____No_____

The Buyer acknowledges familiarity with the "Conditions of Sale" governing purchase at Auction as published in the Catalogue. The Buyer understands that a premium of 10% will be added to the hammer price as part of the total purchase price.

10. APPRAISAL CONTRACT

Sotheby's Appraisal Company

1334 York Avenue at 72nd Street, New York, NY 10021
Tel. (212) 472-3452

Name of Owner _____ Bill to (if different) Name _____

Address _____ Address _____

_____ _____

Telephone (Home #) _____ Telephone (Business #) _____

Gentlemen:

This will confirm the request of the undersigned that you furnish your written appraisal of the insurance or fair market value of the property described in the right hand column or in an attached schedule. Please indicate the appraisal you wish by checking the appropriate box.

It is agreed that your appraisal:

(i) represents only your best judgment and opinion as to current fair market or insurance value and any other matters covered therein, and is not a statement or representation of fact;

(ii) is not to be deemed a representation or warranty with respect to the authenticity of authorship, period of creation, description, genuineness, attribution, provenance or condition of the property;

(iii) is not to be deemed a representation or warranty that the property will bring the appraised value if offered for sale at public auction or otherwise;

(iv) is not furnished and will not be used or relied upon in connection with any transaction involving the property, including but not limited to any purchase, sale, donation, exchange or loan; and

(v) is requested by the undersigned solely for estate tax, family division or insurance purposes.

The undersigned represents and warrants that he or she owns the property free and clear of any claims, liens, encumbrances or interests of others. The undersigned agrees that you may consult others in connection with your appraisal.

The undersigned releases Sotheby Parke Bernet Inc. and its officers, directors, employees, agents and affiliates (collectively, "Sotheby's") from any liability or damages whatsoever arising out of or related to the appraisal furnished pursuant to this agreement and agrees to indemnify and hold Sotheby's harmless from any claims, actions, liabilities, damages or expenses incurred as a result of claims by third parties based on or related to the appraisal.

Upon receipt of the appraisal, the undersigned agrees to pay you therefor a fee as follows:

[ ] A. For collections valued at up to $100,000, the fee is $1,000 or 1½% of the appraised value, whichever is less, for one appraiser to perform up to one day's work. For each additional appraiser, there will be a charge of $500. The minimum fee is $500.

   B. For collections exceeding $100,000 in valuation, the fee will be quoted on request, based on a preliminary survey. The amount of the fee depends on the nature of the collection and the number of appraisers required and will be confirmed in writing.

[ ] Fixed Fee of $ _____

[ ] Plus expenses for travel, lodging, and appraisal processing.

If the undersigned consigns any of the appraised property to Sotheby's within one year from the date of the appraisal, Sotheby's will refund at the time of settlement of the sale of the consigned property a pro rated portion of the appraisal fee based on the appraised value of the consigned property. For example, if the property is appraised at $100,000 and items appraised at $50,000 are consigned, one-half of the appraisal fee (excluding out-of-pocket expenses) will be credited to the selling commission.

_____
Signature of owner   Date

Please sign and return white copy to Sotheby's Appraisal Co. and retain yellow copy for your records.

Please check one of the following to indicate the purpose for which the appraisal is being requested.

☐ Fair Market (Estate Tax or Family Division) ☐ Insurance

Please fill out description and location of property below, sign both copies and return original to Sotheby's in enclosed envelope.

Descriptions of Property	Location of Property

11. I.R.S. REGULATIONS

INTERNAL REVENUE PROCEDURE 66-49 ON APPRAISALS OF DONATED PROPERTY*

SECTION 1. PURPOSE.

The purpose of this procedure is to provide information and guidelines for taxpayers, individuals appraisers, and valuation groups relative to appraisals of contributed property for Federal income tax purposes. The procedures outlined are applicable to all types of noncash property for which an appraisal is required such as real property, tangible or intangible personal property, and securities. These procedures are also appropriate for unique properties such as art objects, literary manuscripts, antiques, etc., with respect to which the determination of value often is more difficult.

SECTION 2. LAW AND REGULATIONS

.01 Numerous sections of the Internal Revenue Code of 1954, as amended, give rise to a determination of value for federal tax purposes; however, the significant section for purposes of this Revenue Procedure is section 170, Charitable, Etc., Contributions and Gifts.

.02 Value is defined in section 1.170-1 (c) of the Income Tax Regulations as follows:

... The Fair market value is the price at which the property would change hands between a willing buyer and a willing seller, neither being under any compulsion to buy or sell and both having reasonable knowledge of relevant facts ...

.03 This section further provides that:

.... If the contribution is made in property of a type which the taxpayer sells in the course of his business, the fair market value is the price which the taxpayer would have received if he had sold the contributed property in the lowest usual market in which he customarily sells, at the time and place of contribution (and in the case of a contribution of goods in quantity, in the quantity contributed). ...

.04 As to the measure of proof in determining the fair market value, all factors bearing on value are relevant including, where pertinent, the cost, or selling price of the item, sales of comparable properties, cost of reproduction, opinion evidence and appraisals. Fair market value depends upon value in the market and not on intrinsic worth.

.05 The cost of actual selling price of an item within a reasonable time before or after the valuation date may be the best evidence of its fair market value. Before such information is taken into account, it must be ascertained that the transaction was at arm's length and that the parties were fully informed as to all relevant facts. Absent such evidence, even the sales price of the item in question will not be persuasive.

.06 Sales of similar properties are often given probative weight by the courts in establishing fair market value. The weight to be given such evidence will be affected by the degree of similarity to the property under appraisal and the proximity of the date of sale to the valuation date.

.07 With respect to reproductive cost as a measure of fair market value, it must be shown that there is a probative correlation between the cost of reproduction and fair market value. Frequently, reproductive cost will be in excess of the fair market value.

.08 Generally, the weight to be given to opinion evidence depends on its origin and the thoroughness with which it is supported by experience and facts. It is only where expert opinion is supported by facts having strong probative value, that the opinion testimony will in itself be given appropriate weight. The underlying facts must corroborate the opinion; otherwise such opinion will be discounted or disregarded.

A procedure to be used as a guideline by all persons making appraisals of donated property for U.S. Federal income tax purposes.

.09 The weight to be accorded any appraisal made either at or after the valuation date will depend largely upon the competence and knowledge of the appraiser with respect to the property and the market for such property.

SECTION 3. APPRAISAL FORMAT

.01 When it becomes necessary to secure an appraisal in order to determine the values of items for Federal income tax purposes, such appraisals should be obtained from qualified and reputable sources, and the appraisal report should accompany the return when it is filed. The more complete the information filed with a tax return the more unlikely it will be that the Internal Revenue Service will find it necessary to question items on it. Thus, when reporting a deduction for charitable contributions on an income tax return, it will facilitate the review and acceptance of the returned values if any appraisals which have been secured are furnished. The abovementioned regulations prescribe that support of values claimed should be submitted and a properly prepared appraisal by a person qualified to make such an appraisal may well constitute the necessary substantiation. In this respect, it is not intended that all value determinations be supported by formal written appraisals as outlined in detail below. This is particularly applicable to minor items of property or where the value of the property is easily ascertainable by methods other than appraisal.

.02 In general, an appraisal report should contain at least the following:

(1) A summary of the appraiser's qualifications.

(2) A statement of the value and the appraiser's definition of the value he has obtained.

(3) The bases upon which the appraisal was made, including any restrictions, understandings, or convenants limiting the use or disposition of the property.

(4) The date as of which the property was valued.

(5) The signature of the appraiser and the date the appraisal was made.

.03 An example of the kind of date which should be contained in a typical appraisal is included below. This relates to the valuation of art objects, but a similar detailed breakdown can be outlined for any type of property. Appraisal of art objects, paintings in particular, should include.

(1) A complete description of the object, indicating the size, the subject matter, the medium, the name of the artist, approximate date created, the interest transferred, etc.

(2) The cost, date and manner of acquisition.

(3) A history of the item including proof of authenticity such as a certificate of authentication if such exists.

(4) A photograph of a size and quality fully identifying the subject matter, preferably a 10″ × 12″ or larger print.

(5) A statement of the factors upon which the appraisal was based, such as:

(a) Sales of other works by the same artist particularly on or around the valuation date

(b) Quoted prices in dealers' catalogs of the artists' works or other artists or comparable stature.

(c) The economic state of the art market at or around the time of valuation, particularly with respect to the specific property.

(d) A record of any exhibitions at which the particular art object had been displayed.

(e) A statement as to the standing of the artist in his profession and in the particular school or time period.

.04 Although an appraisal report meets these requirements, the Internal Revenue Service is not relieved of the responsibility of reviewing appraisals to the extent deemed necessary.

SEC. 4. REVIEW OF VALUATION APPRAISALS

.01 While the Service is responsible for reviewing appraisals, it is not responsible for making appraisals; the burden of supporting the fair market value listed on a return is the taxpayer's. The Internal Revenue Service cannot accord recognition to any appraiser or group of appraisers from the standpoint of unquestioned acceptance of their appraisal. Furthermore, the Service cannot approve valuations or appraisal prior to the actual filing of the tax return to which the appraisal pertains and cannot issue advance rulings approving or disapproving such appraisals.

.02 In determining the acceptability of the claimed value of the donated property, the Service may either accept the value claimed based on information or appraisals submitted with the return or make its own determination as to the fair market value. In either instance, the Service may find it necessary to:

(1) contact the taxpayer and ask for additional information,

(2) refer the valuation problem to a Service appraiser or valuation specialist,

(3) recommend that an independent appraiser be employed by the Service to appraise the asset in question. (This latter course is frequently used by the Service when objects requiring appraisers of highly specialized experience and knowledge are involved.)

12. PROPERTY RECEIPT FORM

SOTHEBY'S CONSIGNMENT RECEIPT YORK AVENUE GALLERIES 1334 YORK AVENUE NEW YORK, NY 10021	PAGE: DATE: RECEIPT #: ACCOUNT #:

CONSIGNOR
(NAME)
(ADDRESS)

COMMENTS

TELEPHONE 1: (000) 000–0000
TELEPHONE 2:

DEPARTMENT:
SHIPPED VIA:
RECEIPTED BY:

ITEM DESCRIIPTION	PRELIMINARY LOW EST. HIGH EST.	PRELIMINARY RESERVE

SAMPLE

THIS RECEIPT IS SUBJECT TO THE CONDITIONS OF RECEIPT PRINTED ON THE REVERSE SIDE. SOTHEBY'S WILL HAVE NO LIABILITY FOR LOSS OF, OR DAMAGE TO, PROPERTY, WHETHER CAUSED BY SOTHEBY'S NEGLIGENCE OR OTHERWISE, UNLESS ESTIMATES OF VALUE HAVE BEEN WRITTEN BY SOTHEBY'S IN THE "PRELIMINARY ESTIMATES" COLUMN NEXT TO THE ITEM. SEE PARAGRAPHS 6 AND 7 ON THE REVERSE.

PAY TO ACCOUNT #:	RECEIVED BY . . . .
(NAME) (ADDRESS)	RECEIVED FROM . . . . DATE . . . .

[continued on next page]

CONDITIONS OF RECEIPT

The following are the terms under which your property is received by Sotheby Parke Bernet Inc.

1. Catalogue presale estimates are intended as guides for prospective bidders; we make no representation of the anticipated selling price of any property and no estimate anywhere by us of the selling price of property may be relied upon by you as a prediction of the actual selling price. We will not be responsible for any errors or omissions in presale estimates and catalogue descriptions and make no guarantees, representations or warranties whatsoever to you with respect to the property or its estimated selling price. The estimates and reserves included herein are preliminary only. The estimates are subject to revision by us from time to time, including upon subsequent inspection of the property and changes in market conditions.

2. If it is necessary for the proper evaluation of jewelry, you authorize us to test any pieces received, and you will reimburse us for any reasonable expenses for such tests.

3. You agree that any restoration, framing, special advertising, research, illustration, shipping, customs and other expenses which have been agreed upon will be borne by you.

4. Unless you notify us to the contrary, we may use your name as owner of the property when we offer it for sale or advertise or otherwise promote the sale.

5. You agree not to withdraw any of the property after the date of this receipt. In the event of any withdrawal by you in breach of your foregoing commitment, you will pay us an amount equal to our commissions (including buyers premium) on the mean of our most recent presale estimates and reimburse us for all out-of-pocket costs incurred in connection with your property.

6. If you elect to bear the risk of loss of or damage to the property while in transit to and on our premises, you must prior to the date of shipment (i) notify us in writing of your election, such notice to be signed by you and stating that we will not be responsible for, and that you release us from, all liability for loss of or damage to the property, regardless of the cause thereof, and (ii) provide us with a valid certificate of insurance naming us as an additional insured party under your insurance policy to the extent of our expenses and commissions.

If you do not elect to bear the risk of loss or damage as provided in the preceding paragraph, we will assume such risk while the property is on our premises and, subject to prior written notice to us of your shipment of the property and our written acknowledgment of receipt of such notice, while in transit to our premises. In consideration of our assumption of such risk, you will pay us the amount of one dollar per hundred dollars of (i) the successful bid price if the property has been sold, (ii) the reserve (but not more than the mean of our latest presale estimates) if the property has been bought-in for your account, or (iii) the mean of our latest presale estimates at the time of loss or damage in all other cases.

In no event however, will we have any liability for damage caused by changes in humidity or temperature, inherent conditions or defects in the property, or damage to glass or frames, regardless of cause.

Subject to paragraph 7 below, you agree that the value of the property for all purposes under this paragraph will be (i) the successful bid price if the property has been sold, (ii) the reserve (but not more than the mean of our latest presale estimates) if the property has been bought-in for your account, or (iii) the mean of our latest presale estimates at the time of loss or damage in all other cases, less in any case our expenses and commissions.

7. SOTHEBY'S WILL HAVE NO LIABILITY FOR LOSS OF, OR DAMAGE TO, PROPERTY, WHETHER CAUSED BY SOTHEBY'S NEGLIGENCE OR OTHERWISE, UNLESS ESTIMATES OF VALUE HAVE BEEN WRITTEN BY SOTHEBY'S IN THE "PRELIMINARY ESTIMATES" COLUMN NEXT TO THE ITEM.

8. If any of the terms of the consignment agreement between you and us conflict with any of the terms herein, the terms of the consignment agreement shall prevail.

13. FIDUCIARY AGREEMENT

FIDUCIARY AGREEMENT

This Agreement must be signed and all documents requested herein must be delivered to us by you if you are acting in a fiduciary capacity, and the same must be accepted by us, before the Consignment Agreement between us becomes binding on us. A person "acting in a fiduciary capacity" includes an executor, administrator, trustee under a will, a trustee under an inter vivos trust instrument, a guardian of the property of a minor, and the committee of an incompetent. If you are acting as a co-fiduciary, then at our request all other co-fiduciaries must countersign the Consignment Agreement and this Agreement. The following documents are to be delivered to us within thirty days after you execute the Consignment Agreement:

(i)   A court certificate evidencing the appointment of a fiduciary dated within sixty days before the date of the Consignment Agreement, and indicating no restrictions on the powers of the fiduciary to sell the property to which the Consignment Agreement relates.

(ii) If the fiduciary is an executor or a trustee under a will, or a trustee under an inter vivos instrument, a copy of the will or trust instrument certified as a true copy by your attorney. If, in our opinion, the will or trust instrument indicates that any person or persons other than the fiduciary have or may have an interest in or power of disposition or control of the subject property, you agree to deliver all documents or instruments necessary to satisfy us that good title will pass to the purchaser.

(iii) If you are acting as an executor or administrator, a tax waiver or equivalent document where required by us. You warrant that all debts, funeral and administration expenses, taxes and other liabilities of the estate have been paid or are adequately provided for.

SOTHEBY PARKE BERNET INC.

By _____

ACCEPTED AND AGREED:

_____
Signature and Title of Fiduciary

APPENDIX B
London Facts and Documents*

Most of this material is from Sotheby's but other auction houses use the same or similar forms.

1. LONDON RECEIPT AND
AUTHORIZATION TO SELL

Sotheby Parke Bernet & Co.

34-35 New Bond Street, London W1A 2AA
Telephone: 01-493 8080 Telex: 24454 SPBLON-G VAT No. 238 7788 06

PROPERTY RECEIPT:– Please complete in Block Capitals Clearly
Name Title *(Owner, Agent, Executor Trustee)*

3	Account No.	8	9	Sort Name	14	15	Property No.	20

427673

1		**4** Trade	YES/NO ²¹
Address		Registered for VAT	YES/NO ²²
2		Selling in Sp'l Scheme	YES/NO ²³
		²⁴ VAT No :	³²
3		Insurance Required	YES/NO ³³
Re:		Country Code ³⁴	³⁵

Telephone Number	Carrier	May designate YES/NO	May Illustrate YES/NO	Import Docs. YES/NO	Country of origin if not as in address

Qty.	Description/Block Capitals	Dept.	Estimate	Reserve	Illust. & Cost	ITEMS FOR FAST SALE SERVICE	Enter Yes or No

I request you to sell the above property as indicated above in accordance with your conditions of business available on request.

Signature *(Owner, Agent, Executor, Trustee)*	Previously sold at Sotheby's YES/NO	Accepted on behalf of Sotheby Parke Bernet & Co. by: BLOCK CAPITALS	Date

2. LONDON CONDITIONS OF BUSINESS

CONDITIONS OF BUSINESS
(EXCEPT THOSE CONCERNING THE FAST SALE SERVICE REFER PAGE ix)

Sotheby's carries on business (whether with actual or prospective buyers and sellers or consignors requiring inspection, appraisal or valuation of property or persons reading catalogues, or otherwise) on the following terms and conditions and on such other terms, conditions and notices as may be set out in all relevant catalogues. The definition of words and phrases with special meanings appear in Condition 38.

Conditions mainly concerning buyers

1   The Buyer.
The highest bidder shall be the buyer at the "hammer price" and any dispute shall be settled at the auctioneer's absolute discretion. Every bidder shall be deemed to act as principal unless there is in force a written acknowledgement by Sotheby's that he acts as agent on behalf of a named principal.

2   Minimum Increment.
The auctioneer shall have the right to refuse any bid which does not exceed the previous bid by at least 5 per cent or by such other proportion as the auctioneer shall in his absolute discretion direct.

3   The Premium.
Except in respect of "special category items", the buyer shall pay to Sotheby's a premium of 10% on the "hammer price" together with Value Added Tax at the standard rate on the premium, and agrees that Sotheby's, when acting as agent for the seller, may also receive commission from the seller in accordance with Condition 19.

4   Value Added Tax (VAT).
Lots on which Value Added Tax is payable by the buyer on the "hammer price" are indicated in the catalogue with the sign † (where the tax is payable at the standard rate) and with the sign ‡ (where the tax is payable at a different rate). Value Added Tax, the rates of which are subject to alteration by law, is payable at the rates prevailing on the day of the auction.

5   Currency Converter.
A currency converter will be operated at some auctions but only for the guidance of bidders. Sotheby's will not accept any responsibility in the event of error on the currency converter whether in the foreign currency equivalent of bids in pounds sterling or otherwise.

6   Payment.
Immediately a lot is sold the buyer shall :–
(a) give to Sotheby's his name and address and, if so requested, proof of identity; and
(b) pay to Sotheby's the "total amount due" (unless credit terms have been agreed with Sotheby's before the auction).
7   Sotheby's may, at its absolute discretion, agree credit terms with the buyer before an auction under which the buyer will be entitled to take possession of lots purchased up to an agreed amount in value in advance of payment by a determined future date of the "total amount due".
8   Any payments by a buyer to Sotheby's may be applied by Sotheby's towards any sums owing from that buyer to Sotheby's on any account whatever without regard to any directions of the buyer or his agent, whether express or implied.

9   Collection of Purchases.
The ownership of the lot purchased shall not pass to the buyer until he has made payment in full to Sotheby's of the "total amount due".
10   (a) The buyer shall at his own expense take away the lot purchased not later than 5 working days after the day of the auction but (unless credit terms have been agreed in accordance with Condition 7) not before payment to Sotheby's of the "total amount due".

(b) The buyer shall be responsible for any removal, storage and insurance charges on any lot not taken away within 5 working days after the day of the auction.
11   For wines, spirits and cigars not available for collection from Sotheby's premises, the supply of a release order authorising the release of the lot to the buyer will constitute delivery by Sotheby's.

12   Buyers Responsibilities for Lots Purchased.
The buyer will be responsible for loss or damage to lots purchased from the time of collection or the expiry of 5 working days after the day of the auction, whichever is the sooner, and neither Sotheby's nor its servants or agents shall thereafter be responsible for any loss or damage of any kind, whether caused by negligence or otherwise, while any lot is in its custody or under its control.
13   The buyer of a "motor vehicle" is responsible for complying with the provisions of the Road Traffic Act 1972 and all relevant regulations made under section 40 thereof (including the Motor Vehicles (Construction and Use) Regulations 1973) and any statutory modification thereof.
14   The buyer of a firearm is responsible for obtaining a valid firearm certificate, shot gun certificate or certificate of registration as a firearms dealer and for conforming with the regulations in force in Great Britain relating to firearms, notice of which is published in catalogues of firearms. Sotheby's will not deliver lots to buyers without production of evidence of compliance with this condition.

15   Remedies for Non-Payment or Failure to Collect Purchases.
If any lot is not paid for in full and taken away in accordance with Conditions 6 and 10, or if there is any other breach of either of those Conditions, Sotheby's as agent of the seller shall at its absolute discretion and without prejudice to any other rights it may have, be entitled to exercise one or more of the following rights and remedies:–
(a) to proceed against the buyer for damages for breach of contract;
(b) to rescind the sale of that or any other lots sold to the defaulting buyer at the same or any other auction;
(c) to re-sell the lot or cause it to be re-sold by public auction or private sale and the defaulting buyer shall pay to Sotheby's any resulting deficiency in the "total amount due" (after deduction of any part payment and addition of re-sale costs) and any surplus shall belong to the seller;
(d) to remove, store and insure the lot at the expense of the defaulting buyer and, in the case of storage, either at Sotheby's premises or elsewhere;
(e) to charge interest at a rate not exceeding 1.5% per month on the "total amount due" to the extent it remains unpaid for more than 5 working days after the day of the auction;
(f) to retain that or any other lot sold to the same buyer at the same or any other auction and release it only after payment of the "total amount due";
(g) to reject or ignore any bids made by or on behalf of the defaulting buyer at any future auctions or obtain a deposit before accepting any bids in future;
(h) to apply any proceeds of sale then due or at any time thereafter becoming due to the defaulting buyer towards

settlement of the "total amount due" and to exercise a lien on any property of the defaulting buyer which is in Sotheby's possession for any purpose.

16 Liability of Sotheby's and Sellers.
(a) Goods auctioned are usually of some age. All goods are sold with all faults and imperfections and errors of description. Illustrations in catalogues are for identification only. Buyers should satisfy themselves prior to sale as to the condition of each lot and should exercise and rely on their own judgment as to whether the lot accords with its description. Subject to the obligations accepted by Sotheby's under this Condition, none of the seller, Sotheby's, its servants or agents is responsible for errors of description or for the genuineness or authenticity of any lot, no warranty whatever is given by Sotheby's, its servants or agents, or any seller to any buyer in respect of any lot and any express or implied conditions or warranties are hereby excluded.
(b) Any lot which proves to be a "deliberate forgery" may be returned by the buyer to Sotheby's within 5 years of the date of the auction in the same condition in which it was at the time of the auction, accompanied by a statement of defects, the number of the lot, and the date of the auction at which it was purchased. If Sotheby's is satisfied that the item is a "deliberate forgery" and that the buyer has and is

able to transfer a good and marketable title to the lot free from any third party claims, the sale will be set aside and any amount paid in respect of the lot will be refunded: Provided that the buyer shall have no rights under this Condition if:

(i) the description in the catalogue at the date of the sale was in accordance with the then generally accepted opinion of scholars and experts or fairly indicated that there was a conflict of such opinion; or

(ii) the only method of establishing at the date of publication of the catalogue that the lot was a "deliberate forgery" was by means of scientific processes not generally accepted for use until after publication of the catalogue or a process which was unreasonably expensive or impractical; or

(c) A buyer's claim under this Condition shall be limited to any amount paid in respect of the lot and shall not extend to any loss or damage suffered or expense incurred by him.

(d) The benefit of this Condition shall not be assignable and shall rest solely and exclusively in the buyer who, for the purpose of this Condition, shall be and only be the person to whom the original invoice is made out by Sotheby's in respect of the lot sold.

Conditions mainly concerning sellers and consignors

17 Warranty of title and availability.
(a) The seller warrants to Sotheby's and to the buyer that he is the true owner of the property or is properly authorised to sell the property by the true owner and is able to transfer good and marketable title to the property free from any third party claims.
(b) The seller of property not held by Sotheby's on its premises or under its control, warrants and undertakes to Sotheby's and the buyer that the property will be available and in a deliverable state on demand by the buyer.
(c) The seller will indemnify Sotheby's, its servants and agents and the buyer against any loss or damage suffered by either in consequence of any breach of (a) or (b) above on the part of the seller.

18 Reserves.
The seller shall be entitled to place prior to the auction a reserve on any lot, being the minimum "hammer price" at which that lot may be treated as sold. A reserve once placed by the seller shall not be changed without the consent of Sotheby's. Sotheby's may at their option sell at a "hammer price" below the reserve but in any such cases the sale proceeds to which the seller is entitled shall be the same as they would have been had the sale been at the reserve. Where a reserve has been placed, only the auctioneer may bid on behalf of the seller. Where no reserve has been placed, the seller may bid, either personally or through the agency of any one person.

19 Authority to Deduct Commission and Expenses.
The seller authorises Sotheby's to deduct commission at the "stated rates" and "expenses" from the "hammer price" and acknowledges Sotheby's right to retain the premium payable by the buyer in accordance with Condition 3.

20 Insurance.
Unless otherwise instructed, Sotheby's will insure property (other than "motor vehicles") consigned to it or put under its control for sale and may, at its discretion, insure property put under its control for any other purpose. In all cases save where Sotheby's is required to insure, the property shall remain at all times at the risk of the seller or consignor and neither Sotheby's nor its servants or agents will be responsible for any loss or damage whether caused by negligence or otherwise. Such insurance will be at the expense of the seller or consignor, will be for the amount estimated by Sotheby's to be, from time to time, the current

value of the property at auction and will subsist until whichever is the earlier of the ownership of the property passing from the seller or the seller or consignor becoming bound to collect the property.

21 Electrical and Mechanical Goods.
The seller or consignor of electrical or mechanical goods warrants and undertakes to Sotheby's that at the date on which the same are consigned to Sotheby's or put under Sotheby's control and except as previously disclosed to Sotheby's the same are safe if reasonably used for the purpose for which they were designed and free from any defect not obvious on external inspection which could prove dangerous to human life or health, and will indemnify Sotheby's its servants and agents against any loss or damage suffered by any of them in consequence of any breach of the above warranty and undertaking.

22 Rescission of the Sale.
If before Sotheby's remit the "sale proceeds" to the seller, the buyer makes a claim to rescind the sale under Condition 16 if appropriate and Sotheby's is of the opinion that the claim is justified, Sotheby's is authorised to rescind the sale and refund to the buyer any amount paid to Sotheby's in respect of the lot.

23 Payment of Sale Proceeds.
Sotheby's shall remit the "sale proceeds" to the seller not later than one month (or, in the case of numismatic items, 14 days) after the auction, but if by that date Sotheby's has not received the "total amount due" from the buyer then Sotheby's will remit the "sale proceeds" within five working days after the day on which the "total amount due" is received from the buyer. If credit terms have been agreed between Sotheby's and the buyer, Sotheby's shall remit to the seller the sale proceeds not later than one month (or, in the case of numismatic items, 14 days) after the auction unless otherwise agreed by the seller: Provided that where in the case of postage stamps Sotheby's has granted an extension it shall remit the "sale proceeds" when a certificate of genuineness is received by Sotheby's or sixty-five days after the auction, whichever is the sooner, but if by then Sotheby's has not received the "total amount due" from the buyer then Sotheby's will remit the "sale proceeds" within five working days after the day on which the "total amount due" is received from the buyer.

24 If the buyer fails to pay to Sotheby's the "total amount due" within 3 weeks after the auction, Sotheby's will endeavour to notify the seller and take the seller's instructions as to the appropriate course of action and, so far as in Sotheby's opinion is practicable, will assist the seller to recover the "total amount due" from the buyer. If circumstances do not permit Sotheby's to take instructions from the seller, the seller authorises Sotheby's at the seller's expense to agree special terms for payment of the "total amount due", to remove, store and insure the lot sold, to settle claims made by or against the buyer on such terms as Sotheby's shall in its absolute discretion think fit, to take such steps as are necessary to collect moneys due by the buyer to the seller and if necessary to rescind the sale and refund money to the buyer.

25 If, notwithstanding that the buyer fails to pay to Sotheby's the "total amount due" within three weeks after the auction, Sotheby's remits the "sale proceeds" to the seller, the ownership of the lot shall pass to Sotheby's.

26 *Charges for Withdrawn Lots.*
Where a seller cancels instructions for sale, Sotheby's reserves the right to charge a fee of 10% of Sotheby's then latest estimate or middle estimate of the auction price of the property withdrawn, together with Value Added Tax thereon and "expenses" incurred in relation to the property.

27 *Rights to Photographs and Illustrations.*
The seller gives Sotheby's full and absolute right to photograph and illustrate any lot placed in its hands for sale and to use such photographs and illustrations and any photographs and illustrations provided by the seller at any time at its absolute discretion (whether or not in connection with the auction).

28. *Unsold Lots*
Where any lot fails to sell, Sotheby's shall notify the seller accordingly. The seller shall make arrangements either to re-offer the lot for sale or to collect the lot and to pay the reduced commission under Condition 29 and "expenses". If such arrangements are not made:–
(a) within 7 days of notification, the seller shall be responsible for any removal, storage and insurance expenses;
(b) within 3 months of notification, Sotheby's shall have the right to sell the lot at public auction without reserve and to deduct from the "hammer price" any sum owing to Sotheby's including (without limitation) removal, storage and insurance expenses, the "expenses" of both auctions, reduced commission under Condition 29 in respect of the first auction as well as commission at the "stated rates" on the sale and all other reasonable expenses before remitting the balance to the seller or, if he cannot be traced, placing it in a bank account in the name of Sotheby's for the seller.

29 Sotheby's reserves the right to charge commission up to one-half of the "stated rates" calculated on the "bought-in price" and in addition "expenses" in respect of any unsold lots.

General conditions and definitions

30 Sotheby's sells as agent for the seller (except where it is stated wholly or partly to own any lot as principal) and as such is not responsible for any default by seller or buyer.
31 Any representation or statement by Sotheby's, in any catalogue as to authorship, attribution, genuineness, origin, date, age, provenance, condition or estimated selling price is a statement of opinion only. Every person interested should exercise and rely on his own judgment as to such matters and neither Sotheby's nor its servants or agents are responsible for the correctness of such opinions.
32 Whilst the interests of prospective buyers are best served by attendance at the auction, Sotheby's will if so instructed execute bids on their behalf, neither Sotheby's nor its servants or agents being responsible for any neglect or default in doing so or for failing to do so.
33 Sotheby's shall have the right, at its discretion, to refuse admission to its premises or attendance at its auctions by any person.
34 Sotheby's has absolute discretion without giving any reason to refuse any bid, to divide any lot, to combine any two or more lots, to withdraw any lot from the auction and in case of dispute to put up any lot for auction again.
35 (a) Any indemnity under these Conditions shall extend to all actions proceedings costs expenses claims and demands whatever incurred or suffered by the person entitled to the benefit of the indemnity.
(b) Sotheby's declares itself to be a trustee for its relevant servants and agents of the benefit of every indemnity under these Conditions to the extent that such indemnity is expressed to be for the benefit of its servants and agents.
36 Any notice by Sotheby's to a seller, consignor, prospective bidder or buyer may be given by first class mail or airmail and if so given shall be deemed to have been duly received by the addressee 48 hours after posting.
37 These Conditions shall be governed by and construed in accordance with English law. All transactions to which these Conditions apply and all matters connected therewith shall also be governed by English law. Sotheby's hereby submits to the exclusive jurisdiction of the English courts and all other parties concerned hereby submit to the non-exclusive jurisdiction of the English courts.
38 In these Conditions:–

(a) "Sotheby's" means Sotheby Parke Bernet & Co.;
(b) "catalogue" includes any advertisement, brochure, estimate, price list and other publication;
(c) "hammer price" means the price at which a lot is knocked down by the auctioneer to the buyer;
(d) "total amount due" means the "hammer price" in respect of the lot sold together with any premium, Value Added Tax chargeable and additional charges and expenses due from a defaulting buyer under Condition 15, in pounds sterling;
(e) "special category items" means numismatic items, wines, spirits and cigars;
(f) "book" means any item included or proposed to be included in a sale of books and includes a manuscript or print;
(g) "deliberate forgery" means an imitation made with the intention of deceiving as to authorship, origin, date, age, period, culture or source which is not shown to be such in the description in the catalogue and which at the date of the sale had a value materially less than it would have had if it had been in accordance with that description;
(h) "sale proceeds" means the net amount due to the seller being the "hammer price" of the lot sold less commission at the "stated rates" and "expenses" and any other amounts due to Sotheby's by the seller in whatever capacity and howsoever arising;
(i) "stated rates" means Sotheby's published rates of commission for the time being and Value Added Tax thereon;
(j) "expenses" in relation to the sale of any lot means Sotheby's charges and expenses for insurance, illustrations, special advertising, packing and freight of that lot and any Value Added Tax thereon;
(k) "motor vehicle" means any item included or proposed to be included in a sale of motor vehicles;
(l) "bought-in price" means 5 per cent more than the highest bid received below the reserve.
39 Special terms may be used in catalogues in the description of a lot. Where terms are not self-explanatory and have special meanings ascribed to them, a glossary will appear before Lot 1 in the catalogue of the auction.
40 The headings in these Conditions do not form part of the Conditions but are for convenience only.

(i)
Alternative Condition 16 for Catalogues for sales of Impressionist, Modern and Contemporary Art.

16.   Liability of Sotheby's and Sellers
(a) Goods auctioned are usually of some age. All goods are sold with all faults and imperfections and errors of description. Illustrations in catalogues are for identification only. Buyers should satisfy themselves prior to sale as to the condition of each lot and should exercise and rely on their own judgment as to whether the lot accords with its description. Subject to the obligations accepted by Sotheby's under this Condition, none of the seller, Sotheby's, its servants or agents is responsible for errors of description or for the genuineness or authenticity of any lot, no warranty whatever is given by Sotheby's, its servants or agents, or any seller to any buyer in respect of any lot and any express or implied conditions or warranties are hereby excluded.
(b) Any lot which was executed by someone other than the person described in the catalogue as the artist may be returned by the buyer to Sotheby's within five years of the date of the auction, in the same condition in which it was at the time of the auction, accompanied by a statement of defects, the number of the lot and the date of the auction at which it was purchased. If Sotheby's is satisfied that the lot was so executed and that the buyer has and is able to transfer a good and marketable title to the lot free from any third party claims the sale will be set aside and any amount paid in respect of the lot will be refunded.
(c) A buyer's claim under this Condition shall be limited to any amount paid in respect of the lot and shall not extend to any loss or damage suffered or expense incurred by him.
(d) The benefit of this Condition shall not be assignable and shall rest solely and exclusively in the buyer who, for the purpose of this Condition, shall be and only be the person to whom the original invoice is made out by Sotheby's in respect of the lot sold.

(ii)
Alternative Condition 16 for Catalogues for sales of "Books".

16.   Liability of Sotheby's and Sellers
(a) Goods auctioned are usually of some age. All goods are sold with all faults and imperfections and errors of description. Illustrations in catalogues are for identification only. Buyers should satisfy themselves prior to sale as to the condition of each lot and should exercise and rely on their own judgment as to whether the lot accords with its description. Subject to the obligations accepted by Sotheby's under this Condition, none of the seller, Sotheby's, its servants or agents is responsible for errors of description or for the genuineness or authenticity of any lot, no warranty whatever is given by Sotheby's, its servants or agents, or any seller to any buyer in respect of any lot and any express or implied conditions or warranties are hereby excluded.
(b) If within 21 days of the auction, the buyer gives notice to Sotheby's in writing that an item is defective in text or illustration and returns the lot to Sotheby's in the same condition in which it was at the time of the auction indicating the number of the lot and the date of the auction at which it was purchased, and it is established that the lot is defective, Sotheby's will rescind the sale and refund any amount paid in respect of the lot: Provided that such an item may not be returned nor will its sale be set aside or refund made if:-
(i) it is described in the catalogue as sold not subject to return; or
(ii) it is sold un-named in a lot; or
(iii) it comprises an atlas, an extra-illustrated book, a volume with fore-edge paintings, a periodical publication or a print or drawing; or

(iv) in the case of a manuscript, it was not described in the catalogue as complete; or
(v) the defect in question was mentioned in the catalogue; or
(vi) the defect complained of is other than in text or illustration. For example (but without limitation) an item may not be returned nor will its sale be set aside on account of damage to bindings, stains, foxing, marginal wormholes, lack of blank leaves, or other conditions not affecting the completeness of the text or illustration, lack of list of plates, inserted advertisements, cancels or any subsequently published volume, supplement, appendix or plates or error in the enumeration of the plates.
(c) A buyer's claim under this Condition shall be limited to any amount paid in respect of the lot and shall not extend to any loss or damage suffered or expense incurred by him.
(d) The benefit of this Condition shall not be assignable and shall rest solely and exclusively in the buyer who, for the purpose of this Condition, shall be and only be the person to whom the original invoice is made out by Sotheby's in respect of the lot sold.

(iii)
Alternative Condition 16 for Catalogues for sales of Gemstones and Pearls.

16.   Liability of Sotheby's and Sellers
(a) Goods auctioned are usually of some age. All goods are sold with all faults and imperfections and errors of description. Illustrations in catalogues are for identification only. Buyers should satisfy themselves prior to sale as to the condition of each lot and should exercise and rely on their own judgment as to whether the lot accords with its description. Subject to the obligations accepted by Sotheby's under this Condition, none of the seller, Sótheby's, its servants or agents is responsible for errors of description or for the genuineness or authenticity of any lot, no warranty whatever is given by Sotheby's, its servants or agents, or any seller to any buyer in respect of any lot and any express or implied conditions or warranties are hereby excluded.
(b) Gemstones, and pearls are sold as genuine, untreated and of natural origin, unless stated to be otherwise in the catalogue or by the auctioneer at the sale. If within 21 days of an auction the buyer of a gemstone or pearl gives notice in writing to Sotheby's that an item purchased is not genuine, untreated, or of natural origin, and returns the lot to Sotheby's in the same condition as it was at the date of the sale, and it is established by a test carried out by a competent authority that the defect complained of is justified, Sotheby's will rescind the sale and refund any amount paid in respect of the lot, together with the testing fee, if paid by the buyer:
(c) A buyer's claim under this Condition shall be limited to any amount paid in respect of the lot and shall not extend to any loss or damage suffered or expense incurred by him.
(d) The benefit of this Condition shall not be assignable and shall rest solely and exclusively in the buyer who, for the purpose of this Condition, shall be and only be the person to whom the original invoice is made out by Sotheby's in respect of the lot sold.

(iv)
Alternative Condition 16 for Catalogues for sales of Numismatic items.

16.   Liability of Sotheby's and Sellers
(a) Goods auctioned are usually of some age. All goods are sold with all faults and imperfections and errors of description. Illustrations in catalogues are for identification only. Buyers should satisfy themselves prior to sale as to the condition of each lot and should exercise and rely on their own judgment as to whether the lot accords with its

description. Subject to the obligations accepted by Sotheby's under this Condition, none of the seller, Sotheby's, its servants or agents is responsible for errors of description or for the genuineness or authenticity of any lot, no warranty whatever is given by Sotheby's, its servants or agents, or any seller to any buyer in respect of any lot and any express or implied conditions or warranties are hereby excluded.

(b) If within eight days of the auction the buyer gives notice in writing to Sotheby's that an item purchased is a "deliberate forgery" and returns the lot to Sotheby's in the same condition as it was at the date of the sale and it is established that the item is a "deliberate forgery", Sotheby's will rescind the sale and refund any amount paid in respect of the lot.

(c) A buyer's claim under this Condition shall be limited to any amount paid in respect of the lot and shall not extend to any loss or damage suffered or expense incurred by him.

(d) The benefit of this Condition shall not be assignable and shall rest solely and exclusively in the buyer who, for the purpose of this Condition, shall be and only be the person to whom the original invoice is made out by Sotheby's in respect of the lot sold.

(v)
Alternative Condition 16 for Catalogues for sales of Postage Stamps.

16. Liability of Sotheby's and Sellers
(a) Subject to the obligations accepted by Sotheby's under this Condition, none of the seller, Sotheby's, its servants or agents is responsible for errors of description or for the genuineness or authenticity of any lot, no warranty whatever is given by Sotheby's, its servants or agents, or any seller to any buyer in respect of any lot and any express or implied conditions or warranties are hereby excluded.

(b) If within 21 days of the auction Sotheby's receives notice in writing from the buyer of a postage stamp lot claiming that an item is not genuine or does not correspond with the description in the catalogue and the lot is returned to Sotheby's by a date agreed by Sotheby's in the same condition as it was at the time of sale and on the original lot folder and Sotheby's agrees that the buyer's claim is justified, Sotheby's will rescind the sale and refund any amount paid to Sotheby's in respect of the lot: Provided that no return will be accepted nor sale rescinded nor refund made if:–
(i) the lot is described in the catalogue or is announced by the auctioneer at the sale as being not subject to return or as being defective; or
(ii) the lot is a collection or mixed lot containing more than four items, in which case the lot is purchased by the buyer with all (if any) faults, lack of genuineness and errors of description including the number of stamps in the lot; or
(iii) the lot has been illustrated and the defect complained of is apparent in the illustrations; or

(iv) there is a conflict of opinion between the Royal Philatelic Society London and B.P.A. Expertising Limited or either is unable to express a conclusive opinion.
(c) Where an extension has been granted under (d) below on an item which is proved not to be genuine then Sotheby's will rescind the sale and refund any amount paid to Sotheby's in respect of that item: Provided that:–
(i) within the extension period of 60 days Sotheby's receives back the item together with the certificate stating that it is not genuine; and
(ii) the buyer has paid for the lot in accordance with Conditions 6 or 7.
(d).If Sotheby's receives a written application for an extension on a lot not later than 24 hours before an auction from an intending buyer, Sotheby's may grant an extension for a maximum of 60 days from the date of the auction during which the buyer may obtain a certificate of genuineness or non-genuineness from the Royal Philatelic Society of London or B.P.A. Expertising Limited: Provided that no extension will be granted on:–
(i) a collection or mixed lot containing more than four items or a single item contained in such a lot; or
(ii) an item which is described as accompanied by a specified certificate of opinion dated within ten years of the sale.
(e) Sotheby's reserves the right on behalf of the seller to withdraw a lot on which an extension has been requested under (d) above.
(f) (i) The certificate of either the Royal Philatelic Society London or B.P.A. Expertising Limited obtained under (d) above is conclusive;
(ii) All costs in connection with obtaining such certificate are the responsibility of the buyer regardless of the opinion received.
(g) A buyer's claim under this Condition shall be limited to any amount paid in respect of the lot and shall not extend to any loss or damage suffered or expense incurred by him.
(h) The benefit of this Condition shall not be assignable and shall rest solely and exclusively in the buyer who, for the purpose of this Condition, shall be and only be the person to whom the original invoice is made out by Sotheby's in respect of the lot sold.

(vi)
Alternative Condition 16 for Sales of Wines, Spirits and Cigars, and for Sales of Motor Vehicles.

16. Liability of Sotheby's and Sellers
Goods auctioned are usually of some age. All goods are sold with all faults and imperfections and errors of description. Illustrations in catalogues are for identification only. Buyers should satisfy themselves prior to sale as to the condition of each lot and should exercise and rely on their own judgment as to whether the lot accords with its description. None of the seller, Sotheby's, its servants or agents is responsible for errors of description or for the genuineness or authenticity of any lot, no warranty whatever is given by Sotheby's, its servants or agents, or any seller to any buyer in respect of any lot and any express or implied conditions or warranties are hereby excluded.

[continued on next page]

(vii)
***Alternative Condition 16 for Sales of Musical
Instruments***

16. *Liability of Sotheby's and Sellers.*
(a) Goods auctioned are usually of some age. All goods are
sold with all faults and imperfections and errors of description. Illustrations in catalogues are for identification only.
Buyers should satisfy themselves prior to sale as to the
condition of each lot and should exercise and rely on their
own judgment as to whether the lot accords with its
description. Subject to the obligations accepted by Sotheby's
under this Condition, none of the seller, Sotheby's, its
servants or agents is responsible for errors of description or
for the genuineness or authenticity of any lot, no warranty
whatever is given by Sotheby's, its servants or agents, or any
seller to any buyer in respect of any lot and any express or
implied conditions or warranties are hereby excluded.
(b) Any lot which proves to be a "deliberate forgery" may
be returned by the buyer to Sotheby's within 5 years of the
date of the auction in the same condition in which it was at
the time of the auction, accompanied by a statement of
defects, the number of the lot, and the date of the auction at
which it was purchased. If Sotheby's is satisfied that the
item is a "deliberate forgery" and that the buyer has and is
able to transfer a good and marketable title to the lot free
from any third party claims, the sale will be set aside and
any amount paid in respect of the lot will be refunded:
Provided that the buyer shall have no rights under this
Condition if:

(i) the description in the catalogue at the date of the sale
was in accordance with the then generally accepted opinion
of scholars and experts or fairly indicated that there was a
conflict of such opinion; or

(ii) the only method of establishing at the date of publication
of the catalogue that the lot was a "deliberate forgery" was
by means of scientific processes not generally accepted for
use until after publication of the catalogue or a process
which was unreasonably expensive or impractical; or

(iii) in the case of musical instrument bows, where it is
established on removal of the lapping that the bow is a
composite piece.

(c) In the case of musical instrument bows if within 21 days
of the auction the buyer gives notice to Sotheby's in writing
that at the time of the auction the bow was broken in a
place other than underneath the lapping and returns the
bow to Sotheby's in the same condition in which it was at
the time of the auction and it is established that such a
claim is justified, Sotheby's will rescind the sale and refund
any amount paid in respect of such bow: Provided that such
a bow may not be returned nor will its sale be set aside or

refund made if: (i) it is described in the catalogue as having
been repaired; (ii) the lot also contains items other than
musical instrument bows.
(d) A buyer's claim under this Condition shall be limited
to any amount paid in respect of the lot and shall not extend
to any loss or damage suffered or expense incurred by him.
(e) The benefit of this Condition shall not be assignable
and shall rest solely and exclusively in the buyer who, for the
purpose of this Condition, shall be and only be the person
to whom the original invoice is made out by Sotheby's in
respect of the lot sold.

***Alternative Condition 20 for Motor Vehicle
Catalogues.***

20. *(a) Insurance*
Unless otherwise instructed, Sotheby's will insure property
(other than "motor vehicles") consigned to it or put under
its control for sale and may at its discretion insure property
put under its control for any other purpose. In all cases save
where Sotheby's is required to insure, the property shall
remain at all times at the risk of the seller or consignor and
neither Sotheby's nor its servants or agents will be responsible for any loss or damage whether caused by negligence or
otherwise. Such insurance will be at the expense of the seller
or consignor, will be for the amount estimated by Sotheby's
to be, from time to time, the current value of the property
at auction and will subsist until whichever is the earlier of
the ownership of the property passing from the seller or the
seller or consignor becoming bound to collect the property.

(b) "Motor Vehicles"
The seller or consignor of a "motor vehicle" warrants and
undertakes to Sotheby's that at the date on which it is
consigned to Sotheby's or put under Sotheby's control and
except as previously disclosed to Sotheby's:–
(i) such vehicle is in roadworthy condition and complies
with the provisions of all relevant regulations made under
section 40 of the Road Traffic Act 1972 (including the
Motor Vehicles (Construction and Use) Regulations 1973)
and any statutory modification thereof; and
(ii) there is, and will whilst the vehicle remains in Sotheby's
custody be in force in respect of the vehicle such test
certificate and insurance complying with the provisions of
the said Act and any statutory modification thereof as will
enable it to be driven lawfully by servants and agents of
Sotheby's on any highway, and will indemnify Sotheby's,
its servants and agents against any loss or damage suffered
by any of them in consequence of any breach of the above
warranty and undertaking.

[continued on next page]

CONDITIONS OF BUSINESS
RELATING TO THE FAST SALE SERVICE

Conditions mainly concerning buyers

1   *The Buyer.*
The highest bidder shall be the buyer at the "hammer price" and any dispute shall be settled at the auctioneer's absolute discretion. Every bidder shall be deemed to act as principal unless there is in force a written acknowledgement by Sotheby's that he acts as agent on behalf of a named principal.

2   *Minimum Increment*
The auctioneer shall have the right to refuse any bid which does not exceed the previous bid by at least 5% or by such other proportion as the auctioneer shall in his absolute discretion direct.

3   *The Premium*
The buyer shall pay to Sotheby's a premium of 10% on the "hammer price" together with Value Added Tax at the standard rate on the premium, and agrees that Sotheby's, when acting as agent for the seller, may also receive commission from the seller in accordance with Condition 15.

4   *Value Added Tax (VAT)*
Lots on which Value Added Tax is payable by the buyer on the "hammer price" are indicated in the catalogue with the sign † (where the tax is payable at the standard rate) and with the sign ‡ (where the tax is payable at a different rate). Value Added Tax, the rates of which are subject to alteration by law, is payable at the rates prevailing on the day of the auction.

5   *Currency Converter*
A currency converter will be operated at some auctions but only for the guidance of bidders. Sotheby's will not accept any responsibility in the event of error on the currency converter whether in the foreign currency equivalent of bids in pounds sterling or otherwise.

6   *Payment and Rescission of Sale*
(a) Immediately a lot is sold the buyer shall give to Sotheby's his name and address and, if so requested, proof of identity.
(b) The buyer shall pay to Sotheby's the "total amount due" (unless credit terms have been agreed with Sotheby's before the auction), not later than two working days after the auction, failing which the sale shall ipso facto be rescinded, time being of the essence of this Condition.

7   Sotheby's may, at its absolute discretion, agree credit terms with the buyer before an auction under which the buyer will be entitled to take possession of lots purchased up to an agreed amount in value in advance of payment by a determined future date of the "total amount due".

8   Any payments by a buyer to Sotheby's may be applied by Sotheby's towards any sums owing from that buyer to Sotheby's on any account whatever without regard to any directions of the buyer or his agent, whether express or implied.

9   *Collection of Purchases*
The ownership of the lot purchased shall not pass to the buyer until he has made payment in full to Sotheby's of the "total amount due", and any lot not paid for within two working days after the day of the auction shall be treated as unsold.

10   (a) The buyer shall at his own expense take away the lot purchased not later than two working days after the day of the auction but (unless credit terms have been agreed in accordance with Condition 7) not before payment to Sotheby's of the "total amount due".
(b) The buyer shall be responsible for any removal, storage and insurance charges on any lot not taken away within two working days after the day of the auction.

11   *Buyers Responsibilities for Lots Purchased*
The buyer will be responsible for loss or damage to lots purchased from the time of collection or the expiry of two working days after the day of the auction, whichever is the sooner, and neither Sotheby's nor its servants or agents shall thereafter be responsible for any loss or damage of any kind, whether caused by negligence or otherwise, while any lot is in its custody or under its control.

12   *Liability of Sotheby's and Sellers*
(a) Goods auctioned are usually of some age. All goods are sold with all faults and imperfections and errors of description. Illustrations in catalogues are for identification only. Buyers should satisfy themselves prior to sale as to the condition of each lot and should exercise and rely on their own judgement as to whether the lot accords with its description, and all lots are sold as viewed and not subject to return.
(b) Any lot which proves to be an imitation made with the intention of deceiving as to authorship, origin, date, age, culture or nature which is not shown to be such in the description in the catalogue, and which at the date of the sale had a value materially less than it would have had if it had been in accordance with that description, may be returned by the buyer to Sotheby's within five years of the date of the auction, accompanied by a statement of defects, the number of the lot and the date of the auction at which it was purchased. If Sotheby's is satisfied that the lot is in the same condition in which it was at the time of the auction, that the statement of defects is justified and that the buyer has and is able to transfer a good and marketable title to the lot, free from any third party claims, Sotheby's will set the sale aside and refund any amount paid to Sotheby's for the lot.
(c) A buyer's claim under this condition shall be limited to any amount paid to Sotheby's for the lot and for the purpose of this condition the buyer shall be the person to whom the original invoice was made out by Sotheby's.
(d) Subject to these Conditions any express or implied conditions or warranties on the part of Sotheby's, its servants or agents or any seller, are hereby excluded.

Conditions mainly concerning sellers and consignors

13   *Warranty of Title and Availability*
(a) The seller warrants to Sotheby's and to the buyer that he is the true owner of the property or is properly authorised to sell the property by the true owner and is able to transfer good and marketable title to the property free from any third party claims.

(b) The seller of property not held by Sotheby's on its premises or under its control, warrants and undertakes to Sotheby's and the buyer that the property will be available and in a deliverable state on demand by the buyer.
(c) The seller will indemnify Sotheby's, its servants and agents and the buyer against any loss or damage suffered by

either in consequence of any breach of (a) or (b) above on the part of the seller.

14   Reserves
The seller shall be entitled to place prior to the auction a reserve on any lot, being the minimum "hammer price" at which that lot may be treated as sold, such reserve not to exceed 75% of the lower estimate published by Sotheby's in the catalogue. *A reserve once placed by the seller shall not be increased without the consent of Sotheby's.* Where a reserve has been placed, only the auctioneer may bid on behalf of the seller. Where no reserve has been placed, the seller may bid, either personally or through the agency of any one person.

15   Authority to Deduct Commission and Expenses
The seller authorises Sotheby's to deduct commission at the "stated rates" from the "hammer price" and acknowledges Sotheby's right to retain the premium payable by the buyer in accordance with Condition 3.

16   Insurance
Sotheby's will insure property consigned to it or put under its control for sale. Such insurance will be for the amount estimated by Sotheby's to be, from time to time, the current value of the property at auction and will subsist until whichever is the earlier of the ownership of the property passing from the seller or the seller or consignor becoming bound to collect the property.

17   Electrical and Mechanical Goods
The seller or consignor of electrical or mechanical goods warrants and undertakes to Sotheby's that at the date on which the same are consigned to Sotheby's or put under Sotheby's control and except as previously disclosed to Sotheby's the same are safe if reasonably used for the

purpose for which they were designed and free from any defect not obvious on external inspection which could prove dangerous to human life or health, and will indemnify Sotheby's its servants and agents against any loss or damage suffered by any of them in consequence of any breach of the above warranty and undertaking.

18   Payments of Sale Proceeds
Sotheby's shall remit the "sale proceeds" to the seller within one week after the auction provided that the same is received from the buyer and except to the extent that these are applied to pay amounts owing from the seller to Sotheby's on any other account.

19   Charges for Withdrawn Lots
Where a seller cancels instructions for sale, Sotheby's reserves the right to charge a fee of 10% together with VAT thereon of the middle of Sotheby's estimate published in the catalogue.

20   Rights to Photographs and Illustrations
The seller give Sotheby's full and absolute right to photograph and illustrate any lot placed in its hands for sale and to use such photographs and illustrations and any photographs and illustrations provided by the seller at any time at its absolute discretion (whether or not in connection with the auction).

21   Unsold Lots
(a) Where any lot fails to sell or (b) the sale lapses under Condition 6, Sotheby's shall notify the seller accordingly. The seller shall make arrangements either to re-offer the lot for sale or to collect the lot.
If such arrangements are not made within ten working days of notification, Sotheby's shall have the right to sell the lot at public auction without reserve and to deduct from the "hammer price" commission at the stated rates.

General conditions and definitions

22   Sotheby's sells as agent for the seller (except where it is stated wholly or partly to own any lot as principal) and as such is not responsible for any default by seller or buyer.
23   Any representation or statement by Sotheby's in any catalogue as to authorship, attribution, genuineness, origin, date, age, provenance, condition or estimated selling price is a statement of opinion only. Every person interested should exercise and rely on his own judgement as to such matters and neither Sotheby's nor its servants or agents are responsible for the correctness of such opinion.
24   Whilst the interest of prospective buyers are best served by attendance at the auction, Sotheby's will if so instructed execute bids on their behalf, neither Sotheby's nor its servants or agents being responsible for any neglect or default in doing so or for failing to do so.
25   Sotheby's shall have the right, at its discretion, to refuse admission to its premises or attendance at its auctions by any person.
26   Sotheby's has absolute discretion without giving any reason to refuse any bid, to divide any lot, to combine any two or more lots, to withdraw any lot from the auction and in case of dispute to put up any lot for auction again.
27   (a) Any indemnity under these Conditions shall extend to all actions proceedings costs expenses claims and demands whatever incurred or suffered by the person entitled to the benefit of the indemnity.
(b) Sotheby's declares itself to be a trustee for its relevant servants and agents of the benefit of every indemnity under these Conditions to the extent that such indemnity is expressed to be for the benefit of its servants and agents.
28   Any notice by Sotheby's to a seller, consignor, pro-

spective bidder or buyer may be given by first class mail or airmail and if so given shall be deemed to have been duly received by the addressee 48 hours after posting.
29   These Conditions shall be governed by and construed in accordance with English law. All transactions to which these Conditions apply and all matters connected therewith shall also be governed by English law. Sotheby's hereby submits to the exclusive jurisdiction of the English courts and all other parties concerned hereby submit to the non-exclusive jurisdiction of the English courts.
30   In these Conditions:
(a) "Sotheby's" means Sotheby Parke Bernet & Co.;
(b) "catalogue" includes any advertisement, brochure, estimate, price list and other publication;
(c) "hammer price" means the price at which a lot is knocked down by the auctioneer to the buyer;
(d) "total amount due" means the "hammer price" in respect of the lot sold together with any premium and Value Added Tax chargeable in pounds sterling;
(e) "sale proceeds" means the net amount due to the seller being the "hammer price" of the lot sold less commission at the "stated rates" and any other amounts due to Sotheby's by the seller in whatever capacity and howsoever arising;
(f) "stated rates" means Sotheby's published rates of commission for the time being together with Value Added Tax thereon;
31   Special terms may be used in catalogues in the description of a lot. Where terms are not self-explanatory and have special meanings ascribed to them, a glossary will appear before Lot 1 in the catalogue of the auction.
32   The headings in these Conditions do not form part of the Conditions but are for convenience only.

3. LONDON ADVICE TO BIDDERS

ADVICE TO BIDDERS

If instructed we will execute bids and advise intending Purchasers. The service is free. Lots will always be bought as cheaply as is allowed by other bids and reserves. Commission bids, when placed by telephone, are accepted only at the sender's risk, and must be confirmed by letter or telegram.

Please use the bidding slips provided and check Lot numbers and descriptions.

Always quote the code name of the Sale Catalogue.

Please bid as early as possible

'Buy' bids are not accepted. The limit you leave should be the amount to which you would bid if you were to attend the Sale.

Each bidding slip should contain bids for one sale only.

Alternative bids can be placed by using the word 'OR' between Lot Numbers.

Should you be a successful bidder you will receive an invoice detailing your purchases and giving instructions for payment and clearance of goods.

Unsuccessful commission bidders will be advised. PLEASE CHECK YOUR BID

FURNITURE BIDDERS BY POST AND TELEPHONE are advised to check on the afternoon of sale whether they have been successful.

SUCCESSFUL FURNITURE BUYERS are earnestly requested to arrange early clearance of their goods (see NOTICE TO FURNITURE BUYERS for details).

SHIPPING INSTRUCTIONS

Please complete this section and we shall arrange for the despatch of all successful bids without delay.

I have/do not have a credit arrangement with Sotheby Parke Bernet & Co.

Account Number: ☐ ☐ ☐ ☐ ☐ ☐

Please tick (✓) as required   ☐ I will arrange collection

☐ Please instruct Shippers/Carriers on my behalf

METHOD OF DESPATCH Please tick (✓) as required

Air Freight	Sea Freight	Air Post	Surface Post	Road	Other (please specify)
☐	☐	☐	☐	☐	☐

LOTS TO BE PACKED AND SHIPPED TO: CHARGES TO BE FORWARDED TO:

....

....

....

....

....

....

Please arrange/do not arrange transit insurance

If insurance is requested, all lots will be insured at Aggregate Price, unless an alternative value is indicated.

Should any of my purchases require Export Licences prior to exportation I hereby authorise you to submit the application on my behalf, and when granted, despatch the goods via your nominated shipper.

Signed .... **Date**......................................

4. LONDON IMPORTANT INFORMATION

Important Information for Prospective Buyers and Sellers

Catalogues and Price Lists

Catalogues and Price Lists can be obtained on Annual Subscription. For details of terms please apply for our subscription list to Catalogue Subscription Department, 34-35 New Bond Street, London W1A 2AA. Telephone: (01) 493 8080. Requests for sundry catalogues and price lists should be accompanied by remittance.

Terms of Sale by Auction

The commission payable by the vendor (except for sales of Wines and Coins & Medals) is 10% of the hammer price (although in the case of book auctions in the Grosvenor saleroom there is a minimum commission of £10.00 per lot). For sales of Wine and Coins & Medals the commission payable by the vendor is 15% (although in the case of Coins & Medals there is a minimum commission of £7.50 per lot).

A buyer's premium of 10% of the hammer price is payable by the buyers of all lots, together with VAT on such premium, with the exception of Wine and Coins & Medals, in which case no buyer's premium is payable. Where indicated by a dagger' in the catalogue VAT is payable on the hammer price.

Overseas Property*

For vendors planning to send property to Sotheby Parke Bernet & Co. in London we are happy to quote both reserves and make payments in the currency of their choice. Also, if requested, we will buy currency forward at the rate of exchange prevailing on the day immediately following the sale.

*i.e. outside the United Kindom, Channel Islands, Gibraltar, Isle of Man and the Republic of Ireland.

Commission Bids

If instructed we will execute bids and advise intending purchasers. This service is free. Lots will always be bought as cheaply as is allowed by such other bids and reserves as are on our books. Commissions, when placed by telephone, are accepted only at the sender's risk and must be confirmed before the sale by letter or telegram.

Valuations

We undertake valuations for Probate and Insurance for which our fees are:—

$1\frac{1}{2}$% up to £10,000

1% from £10,001 to £100,000

$\frac{1}{2}$% thereafter

Written valuations for other purposes are undertaken in acccordance with fees previously negotiated with clients. If items are subsequently consigned for sale within a year of our visit, the fee (on a pro-rata basis if only part of the property is sold) will be refunded.

Inspections

We will inspect properties and advise owners who wish to sell at auction without charge. In certain instances however it may be necessary to charge out of pocket and travelling expenses.

Export Licences

A licence from the Department of Trade will be required before items of certain kinds may be exported from the United Kingdom. A further licence will also be required for any items made of or incorporting animal material (eg ivory, whalebone, tortoiseshell). Applications for both licences can be made by our Shipping Department upon request.

5. LONDON PAYMENT AND DESPATCH

PAYMENT AND DESPATCH OF PURCHASES

Payment for purchases should be by cheque, made payable to Sotheby Parke Bernet & Co., if you are residing in the United Kingdom. Should you be an overseas resident we recommend that you make payment by Sterling Bankers Draft, payable to Sotheby Parke Bernet & Co., stipulating the relevant sale titles and dates.

Purchases cannot be despatched until we are in receipt of your despatch instructions, full payment for the lots you have bought and any export licences that may be required.

Upon receipt of despatch instructions an acknowledgement will be sent to you. This will be followed by a despatch advice from the Shipper, once the consignment has been despatched. Please quote the consignment reference number on all subsequent enquiries.

Estimates and advice on all methods of despatch can be provided upon request, enquiries should be marked for the; attention of the Shipping Manager.

METHODS OF DESPATCH

Airfreight *This method must not be confused with airport. Airfreight consignments are usually packed and despatched within 5-7 days from the receipt of payment and instructions.*

Seafreight *This method must not be confused with surface post. Seafreight consignments are usually packed within 5-7 days and despatched within 18-20 days depending on the availability of vessels and sailing dates.*

Air Post/Surface Post *Parcels which do not exceed the limits of size and weight stipulated by the postal authorities may be despatched via this method. Postal despatches are usually packed and despatched within 5-7 days from the receipt of payment and instructions. Purchasers of books are advised to obtain estimates prior to the despatch of lots containing numerous or extremely large volumes in order to ascertain the most economical method of despatch.*

Road *United Kingdom consignments can usually be delivered within 3-16 days from the receipt of payment and instructions. Small items are 'cartonised' and all other items are 'blanket wrapped'. Please note that United Kingdom road consignments are not case packed unless specific instructions are given.*

Continental road consignments can usually be delivered within 18-28 days from receipt of payment and instructions and our Shippers ensure that all items are adequately packed.

Professional Courier Service *Small consignments can usually be delivered to the client within 24-48 hours of the receipt of payment, instructions and any necessary export licences, depending on destination.*

Export Licensing Regulations for Works of Art and Antiques

1 Any item valued at £8,000 or over, and manufactured or produced 50 years prior to the date of exportation requires a specific export licence. Therefore any item in this category which is 50 years old but of a value less than £8,000 will not require an export licence unless the item in question falls into categories 2, 3, 4 and 5.

2 Archaeological items (with the exception of coins) which are 50 years old and have been recovered at any time from the soil of the United Kingdom (including the bed of the sea within the United Kingdom Territorial Waters) require a specific export licence, irrespective of value.

3 Manuscipts, documents and archives which are 50 years old or over, irrespective of value require a specific export licence.

4 Photographic positives and negatives which are 60 years old or over and valued at £200 or more, each require specific export licences.

5 Illuminated manuscripts in Arabic, Persian, Turkish, Urdu and other oriental languages, miniature paintings with text by Persian, Indian and other Eastern artists, whether in or extracted from books or albums and manuscript books of hours, missals, psalters, antiphoners and graduals of an age exceeding 50 years irrespective of value require a specific export licence.

Firearms

Modern rifles, pistols and sporting guns require a specific export licence irrespective of value. Shotguns may be exported without an export licence if collected by the purchaser on condition that he has not been in the United Kingdom for more than a total of 30 days during the previous 12 month period.

A passport or similar documentary evidence must also be produced if collected by the purchaser or his authorised agent.

Endangered Species

Any item made of or incorporating animal material such as ivory, whale bone, tortoiseshell etc. irrespective of value will require a specific licence from the Department of the Environment, prior to exportation. Sotheby's do however, hold a Bulk Licence for African elephant and walrus ivory and therefore items made of or incorporating these materials will not be subject to application delays.

Applications for Export Licences

Sotheby's will submit the relevant export licence applications upon request, on condition that the licenced items are then exported by Sotheby Parke Bernet & Co., via our nominated shipper.

Export licences can usually be obtained within 3-4 weeks, but it can take much longer, being dependent on factors outside the control of Sotheby's.

6. LONDON GLOSSARY OF TERMS FOR OLD MASTER PAINTINGS

The forename(s) and surname of the artist	In our opinion a work by the artist
The initials of the forename(s) and the surname of the artist	In our opinion a work of the period of the artist which may be wholly or in part his work
The surname only of the artist	In our opinion a work of the school or by one of the followers of the artist or in his style and of uncertain date
Ascribed to	A traditional attribution
Attributed to	Tentative attribution of recent date based on style
"Italian School", "Spanish School", etc. (without date)	In our opinion a work executed at a later date than the style might suggest
"Signed"	Has a signature which in our opinion is a recognised signature of the artist
"Dated"	Is so dated and in our opinion was executed at that date

All references to signatures, inscriptions and dates refer to the present state of the work.

When an artist's forename is not known the appropriate conventional term in this glossary cannot be used. A series of asterisks, followed by the surname of the artist, whether preceded by an initial or not, indicates that in our opinion the work is by the artist named.

When in the Catalogue a reference to literature or a certificate is given the opinion is that of the author(s) or the authority(ies) referred to unless otherwise shown.

All other terms are self-explanatory.

7. LONDON BIDDING FORM

Sotheby Parke Bernet & Co.

34-35 New Bond Street, London W1A 2AA
Tel: 01-493 8080 Registered No. 874867

Date _____ Please bid on my behalf at the Sale of _____

_____

On (date) _____

for the following Lots up to the price mentioned below. These bids are to
be executed as cheaply as is permitted by other bids or reserves, if any,
and subject to the Conditions of Sale printed in the Catalogue. I
understand that in the case of a successful bid a premium of 10% will be
payable by me on the hammer price and VAT on the premium and, where
indicated by a dagger † in the catalogue, VAT on the hammer price.

LOT NO	TITLE OR DESCRIPTION	£ Bid price (excluding premium)

**In order to avoid delay in clearing purchases buyers unknown to
us are advised to make arrangements before the sale for payment
or for satisfactory references to be supplied. If such
arrangements are not made cheques will be cleared before
purchases are delivered.**

Full Name _____
(Please use block letters)
Address _____

_____

Telephone Number _____

Client's Signature _____

SPB USE ONLY:

Bid received by: _____

Method by which bid received: _____

8. LONDON BIDDING
CONFIRMATION FORM

Sotheby Parke Bernet & Co.

34-35 New Bond Street, London W1A 2AA
Registered at the above address No. 874867

Lot No. _____

Name _____

Permanent Address _____
(BLOCK LETTERS)

_____

_____

I acknowledge that my purchase(s) have been made in accordance with the Standard Conditions
of Sale. I understand that I may be required to provide proof of identity.

Signed _____ Sale Date _____

9. U.K. CAPITAL GAINS
TAX INFORMATION

General Guidance on the Liability to Tax on Capital Gains Arising on the Sale of works of art

---

There are many special cases and, if you are in doubt, you should consult your accountant or tax adviser, who may wish to contact our specialist taxation advisory service.

I The Main Principles

1. Foreign residents are not normally liable to United Kingdom taxation on capital gains.

2. The tax is levied on the 'profit' made (not on the 'sale proceeds') in any tax year.

3. If the sale proceeds of a separate article or set of articles (see point 4) do not exceed £2,000 (as from 6th April, 1978) there is no liability regardless of the number of sales in a tax year. Where the sale proceeds exceed £2,000 but are less than £5,000 marginal relief may be applicable (see Section V below).

4. But the proceeds of sale of separate articles have to be totalled to determine whether the £2,000 is exceeded if the circumstances are that the articles form a "set", and have been sold to the same person, or to persons associated. What makes a "set" is not defined. Plainly, articles that are made to be a unity—a suite of chairs, a pair of candlesticks—are a "set"; and this view of the matter would also see as a "set" a suite of chairs made up of any of the chairs from identical suites of chairs. The probability seems to be that articles that are only associated in another way are not "sets".

5. Where an article was acquired by gift or legacy, the cost of acquisition is, in general, deemed to be the market value at the time the gift was made. If it was acquired by gift between

husband and wife, the cost of acquisition is the cost of the article to whichever of them made the gift.

II   Definition of 'Sale Proceeds' and 'Cost'

The proceeds are the amount realised on sale, less allowable expenses of sale.

Example : Amount realised   £3,400
            Sale Commission   £340
            Transport and Advertising Expenses   £160
            _____
            Sale Proceeds   £2,900
            _____

The cost includes all expenses incurred in acquiring the object and enhancing its value while owned. For example, the cost of cleaning would be an allowed addition to cost but not the cost of insurance.

III   Calculation of Chargeable Gain

Articles acquired SINCE 6th April, 1965

The whole of the 'profit' is taxable :

Example : Sale Proceeds 25th November, 1970   £2,900
            Cost   12th May, 1966   £2,400
            _____
            Profit   £500
            _____
            Chargeable Gain   £500
            _____

Articles acquired BEFORE 6th April, 1965

A. *Normal Method—Time Apportionment*

The profit is split, on a time basis, into two parts :

i) from date of acquisition or 6th April, 1945 whichever is the later date, to 5th April, 1965;

ii) from 6th April, 1965 to date of sale.

Tax is payable on part (ii) only.

Examples of the Time Apportionment Method

(A) Purchase before 1945
    Sale Proceeds 5th April, 1977   £8,000
    Cost   25th March, 1941   £800
    _____
    Profit   £7,200
    _____

Proportion of profit from 6th April, 1945 (being later than 25th March, 1941) to 5th April, 1965 (20 years)	£4,500
Proportion of profit from 6th April, 1965 to date of sale (12 years)	£2,700
Profit, as above	£7,200
Chargeable Gain	£2,700

(B) Purchase after 6th April, 1945

Sale Proceeds 5th April, 1977		£8,000
Cost	5th April, 1957	£2,000
Profit		£6,000
Proportion of profit from date purchased to 5th April, 1965 (8 years)		£2,400
Proportion of profit from 6th April, 1965 to date of sale (12 years)		£3,600
Profit, as above		£6,000
Chargeable Gain		£3,600

B. *Alternative Method—Valuation*

The taxpayer may elect to be taxed by an alternative method by which the profit is the difference between the sale proceeds and the value of the article at 6th April, 1965 (as determined by professional valuation).

Example : Using the figures in example (B) above and a valuation of the article at 6th April, 1965 of £5,600

Sale Proceeds	£8,000
Value 6th April, 1965	£5,600
Difference	£2,400
Chargeable Gain	£2,400

In this case the taxpayer would choose the valuation method because less tax would be payable.

Important—Caution :

An election for the 'Alternative Method—Valuation' should not be made until it is certain that it is of benefit. However, the Inspector will not even discuss the valuation figure until an election has been made and he may not accept the professional valuation put forward. Once an election has been made the taxpayer cannot revert to the other 'normal' method.

IV   Calculation of Tax Liability

The rate of tax is 30 per cent. If the taxpayer is a company, the tax is corporation tax, not capital gains tax.

An individual is not chargeable to capital gains tax in respect of so much of his taxable amount for any year of assessment (beginning with the year of assessment 1980-81) as does not exceed £3,000. A person's taxable amount is what is left of the chargeable gains from all disposals (of chattels, stocks and shares, etc.) after the deduction of allowable losses. If the individual is married, then this exemption is shared between the spouses.

Taxable amounts of individuals in the years of assessment 1977/78, 1978/79, and 1979/80 that were less than £9,500 are assessable at rates lower than 30 per cent.

N.B.   Chargeable gains arising during a tax year will normally be offset by agreed losses incurred in the same tax year or losses carried forward from previous years. These are all losses, of course, not just losses resulting from the disposal of chattels.

V   Marginal Relief: Proceeds in excess of £2,000 but less than £5,000

In these circumstances the chargeable gain as calculated per Section III above may be reduced because the chargeable gain will be restricted to a maximum of 5/3rds of the excess over £2,000.

Example :	Sale Proceeds	£2,300
	Cost	£800
	Profit	£1,500

But the chargeable gain will be restricted as follows :—

Sale Proceeds	£2,300
Less	£2,000
	£300
Chargeable Gain 5/3rds thereof	£500

CAPITAL GAINS TAX CHANGES *

The Chattel exemption

Item I : 3 & 4.

Transactions that realise £3,000 or less
are exempt if they occur after the 5th
April 1982.

Item V Proceeds in excess of £3,000 but less than £7,500.

For transactions after the 5th April 1982, the
gain is limited to 5/3 rds of the amount that
the consideration on sale exceeds £3,000.

The Annual Exemption

Item IV

Year of assessment 6th April 1982/ 5th April 1983
: £5,000 of gains.

6th April 1983/ 5th April 1984
: £5,300 of gains.

It is provided that the exempt amount shall be
adjusted annually by reference to the retail prices
index.

Indexation

Item III

A capital gain that accrues in connection with
a sale after the 5th April 1982 may be reduced
by an indexation allowance. It will be if the object
has been owned for more than 12 months, and
the retail prices index for the month of the sale
is greater than that for the month which is
twelve months after the month in which it was
acquired. There is no allowance for the first

twelve months of ownership, nor for ownership
before March 1982.

The amount of the increase in the index between
the two months is expressed as a fraction of the
index for the earlier of them. The product of
this fraction and the cost of acquisition gives
the allowance.

* As of December 1983.

INDEX